SpringerWienNewYork

edition: ˈʌngewʌndtə

Book Series of the
University of Applied Arts Vienna
Edited by Gerald Bast, Rector

www.i-o-a.at

Wolf D. Prix
Dean, Institute of Architecture

FLUIDITY

TOTAL

Studio Zaha Hadid
Projects 2000 – 2010
University of Applied Arts Vienna

Edited by Institute of Architecture
Zaha Hadid and Patrik Schumacher

Springer Wien New York

TOTAL_FLUIDITY
Studio Zaha Hadid
Projects 2000 – 2010
University of Applied Arts Vienna

© 2011 Springer-Verlag/Wien
Printed in Austria
SpringerWienNewYork is a part of
Springer Science + Business Media
www.springer.at

EDITORS
Institute of Architecture
Zaha Hadid and Patrik Schumacher

EDITORIAL COORDINATOR / VISUAL CONCEPT
Mascha Veech-Kosmatschof

EDITORIAL ASSISTANCE
Susanne John

EDITING TEAM
Michael Budig, Mario Gasser, Christian Kronaus,
Jens Mehlan, Robert R. Neumayr, Johann Traupmann

DESIGN / LAYOUT
Dan Neiss Graphic Design

TRANSLATIONS / COPY-EDITING
Camilla R. Nielsen

PHOTO CREDITS
Peter Kainz (diploma models), Marcelo Slama (p.102,111)
and the authors

Cover image: "Phenomenal Similarity" Mario Gasser, Philipp Weisz

Printed by: Holzhausen Druck GmbH
1140 Vienna, Austria
Printed on acid-free and chlorine-free bleached paper

SPIN: 86083732
Library of Congress Control Number: 2011923332

With 955 color figures

ISSN 1866-248X
ISBN 978-3-7091-0486-6
SpringerWienNewYork

WITH THE SUPPORT OF

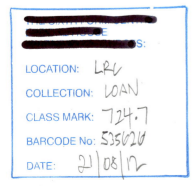

CONTENTS
Studio Zaha Hadid Projects 2000 – 2010
University of Applied Arts Vienna

CONCEPT FORM MEDIA

WHAT'S NEXT

FORMS OF METROPOLITAN LIVING

BIOMIMETIC

NEW URBAN GEOMETRIES

COMPRESSED COMPLEXITY

SIMULTANEITY & LATENCY

PARAMETRIC URBANISM

INTERIORITIES

4(X + Y) = WORLD

DIPLOMAS

ARCHITECTURE AS A DEVELOPMENT LABORATORY

Gerald Bast
Rector, University of Applied Arts Vienna

At the Vienna University of Applied Arts architecture is taught as an integrative discipline with a clearly international orientation, combining artistic, technical and organizational aspects with a social background and a humanities approach. This ambitious teaching style is made possible by a system of three classes with international professors of architecture (Zaha Hadid, Greg Lynn, Wolf D. Prix) within an internationally networked institute.

Architecture at the University of Applied Arts also means addressing all realms of life. It is the current three-dimensional reflection of all facets of our culture and is thus not a product but rather the result of a design process that is tantamount to a process of thinking. The implementation of a design that transcends the boundaries of the status quo also requires social strategies – thus strategic training is promoted in the development of the Institute of Architecture at the University of Applied Arts.

The mission that the Studio Zaha Hadid has pursued in the ten years of its activity at our school has been to critically examine the fundamental concepts of architecture, to develop a consummate formal idiom and to work with the suitable design media with the goal of expanding the repertory of the discipline to attain a new level of complexity and dynamic. Hadid's architectural creed is to create new habitats that reflect the beauty of life and enhance life – as she herself once put it: "It is the attempt to go to the limits of what is feasible and to also cross these boundary lines." But where does this act take us? Which visions should be formulated? These questions are constantly being probed anew in Zaha Hadid's class and reflected upon. When looking at the works published here, one can see that this exciting but difficult mission is being fulfilled with great virtuosity.

FOREWORD

Wolf D. Prix
Dean, Institute of Architecture

It's not enough to change the world,
it must also be interpreted. *- Günther Anders*

Apart from the necessary technical, functional and especially political
and social strategies for implementing ideas, the field of design
theories is one of the most important areas of training at our Institute
for Architecture at the University of Applied Arts.

The creative study of the aesthetic aspects of design as well as
everything that goes beyond them plays a crucial role in this studio's
report that we have titled "Total Fluidity".

The introduction of the term "fluid" in the definition of architecture,
which still seems to be helplessly clinging to an old-fashioned notion of
tectonics both in functional and economic terms, is new and innovative.

In this sense Zaha Hadid's design studio is one of the most exciting
studios in the field of architectural training. Today it resembles more
a field of research than a workshop in which one is simply trying to
solve problems with obsolete methods.

Problem solutions: How they should be dealt with and how is this
actually done in Zaha Hadid's training shows that a building today
can no longer be viewed as being merely the visible three-dimensional
result of a simple linear solution-seeking process. In our increasingly
complex society complex solutions – as difficult they are to find – are
what we should aim at. And this of course applies for architecture.

We are all able to recognize the difference between simple and
complex solutions. Simple solutions are easy to understand but they
are never new. By contrast, complex solutions that can be seen as
reflecting the saying "for every advantage there's also a disadvantage"
are always new. It is in this spirit that one should view the students'
projects at Zaha Hadid's Studio.

Only at first glance are they a study of surfaces. The resemblance
with a "Lady Gaga aesthetics" is perhaps pursued in a provocative
sense, but the buildings or cities that are created at the studio under
the guidance of Zaha Hadid und Patrik Schumacher are the sum
total of multi-functional patterns of thought.

The shift of focus from statics to a dynamics rooted in the personalities
and approaches of the teachers Zaha Hadid and Patrik Schumacher
plays a decisive role. This shift enables the students to substitute the
old grid notations with fields and to lend a more differentiated shape
to their ideas. All of this can be read up on in this book.

FOREWORD

Zaha Hadid

This book brings together 10 years of student work from the master class I have been teaching with my collaborator Patrik Schumacher at the University of Applied Arts in Vienna.

Total Fluidity is the slogan that most succinctly describes the objectives and the character of the work of Zaha Hadid Architects.

I have often used this slogan as a title for my lectures. The slogan is even more pertinent as a title for the creative work presented here, the work being from my master class at the University of Applied Arts in Vienna. The fluidity that I am aspiring to has truly become total here. Goals can be pursued more consistently within academia. In the context of working with students, we can be more experimental and go deeper and farther in probing the consequences of radical design hypotheses. Here we can afford to be more principled without making any pragmatic compromises. This space of unconstrained speculation is both refreshing and necessary for accelerating innovation within the discipline.

The master class has an organizational structure that is unique within architectural education. The class is about 70 students strong, with 7 assistant teachers of varying seniority. The students learn and work within the same class for the entire duration of their studies. (There are two more classes operating in parallel within the school – the Wolf Prix class and the Greg Lynn class.) The class is vertically integrated across years. Everybody works on the same design brief. All work takes place in small teams, often mixing younger and older students. Each year about 8 to 12 students graduate and about 12 to 16 new students join the class. The new students pick up the shared skills and are quickly acculturated into the design culture of the class. Project agendas extend over two semesters and these agendas build up each other. All these features together allow for an unusual degree of continuity. This continuity of tenure and agenda is a necessary precondition for cumulative design research.

Thanks to these mechanisms the master class has been able to contribute to the rapid evolution of contemporary architecture by further advancing the new architectural language that we and others have been pursuing in recent years. Here all elements of architecture become fluid, ready to engage with each other, and with diverse contexts, leading to an increase in complexity and an overall intensification of relations. The radicality and consistency with which this new language is being pursued, across all scales and programs, has resulted in an impressive body of work. I would like to thank all the students and assistants that have committed their time, energy and creative talent to the pursuit of this work.

Zaha Hadid, December 2010

ZAHA HADID Zaha Hadid, founder of Zaha Hadid Architects, was awarded the Pritzker Architecture Prize in 2004 and is internationally known for both her theoretical and academic work.

Zaha Hadid's work of the past 30 years was the subject of critically-acclaimed retrospective exhibitions at New York's Solomon R. Guggenheim Museum in 2006, London's Design Museum in 2007 and the Palazzo della Ragione, Padua, Italy in 2009.

Hadid's outstanding contribution to the architectural profession continues to be acknowledged by the most world's most respected institutions. She received the prestigious 'Praemium Imperiale' from the Japan Art Association in 2009, and in 2010, the Stirling Prize – one of architecture's highest accolades – from the Royal Institute of British Architects. Other recent awards include UNESCO naming Hadid as an 'Artist for Peace' at a ceremony in their Paris headquarters last year. Also in 2010, the Republic of France named Hadid as 'Commandeur de l'Ordre des Arts et des Lettres' in recognition of her services to architecture, and TIME magazine included her in their 2010 list of the '100 Most Influential People in the World' with Hadid ranking top of the "Thinkers" category.

Working with senior office partner Patrik Schumacher, Hadid's interest lies in the rigorous interface between architecture, landscape, and geology as her practice integrates natural topography and human-made systems, leading to experimentation with cutting-edge technologies. Such a process often results in unexpected and dynamic architectural forms. The MAXXI: National Museum of 21st Century Arts in Rome, Italy; the BMW Central Building in Leipzig, Germany and the Phaeno Science Center in Wolfsburg, Germany are demonstrations of Hadid's quest for complex, fluid space.

Zaha Hadid Architects continues to be a global leader in pioneering research and design investigation. Collaborations with corporations that lead their industries have advanced the practice's diversity and knowledge, whilst the implementation of state-of-the-art technologies have aided the realization of complex architectural structures.

Currently Hadid is working on a multitude of projects worldwide including: the London Aquatics Centre for the 2012 Olympic Games; High-Speed Train Stations in Naples and Durango; the CMA CGM Headquarters tower in Marseille; the Fiera di Milano masterplan and tower as well as major master-planning projects in Beijing, Bilbao, Istanbul and Singapore. Throughout the Middle East, Hadid's portfolio includes national cultural and research centres and in Jordan, Morocco, Azerbaijan, Abu Dhabi, Saudi Arabia, and the new Central Bank of Iraq.

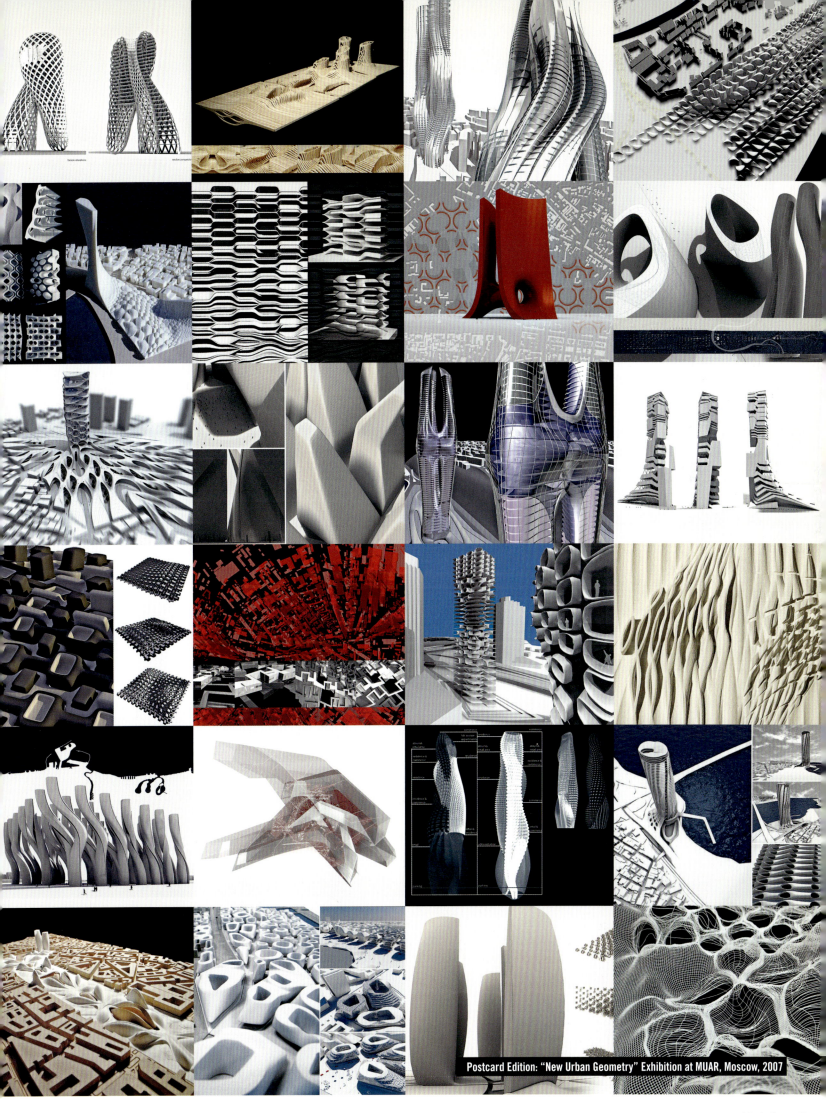

Postcard Edition: "New Urban Geometry" Exhibition at MUAR, Moscow, 2007

ARCHITECTURE SCHOOLS AS DESIGN RESEARCH LABORATORIES

Patrik Schumacher

The University of Applied Arts in Vienna is of one those rare schools where teaching gives rise to original design research in the form of a systematic, theory-led exploration of new architectural possibilities.

The University of Applied Arts in Vienna is of one those rare schools where teaching gives rise to original design research in the form of a systematic, theory-based exploration of new architectural possibilities. In the absence of dedicated research institutes it is certain schools, as well as certain professional firms, that have taken up the task of experimental design research and innovation. Together they form the avant-garde segment of the discipline responsible for the discipline's permanent innovation. Design research within a professional practice is limited in a serious way. It must construct its research agenda on the basis of chance commissions. Academic design research can be more systematic. The creative work of the Zaha Hadid Vienna master class testifies to this.

In the absence of explicitly dedicated research organizations architecture schools offer the closest approximation to a coherently structured research effort. Thus some schools become laboratories in distinct but equally important ways, performing two different tasks. 1. One task is to scan society to find architectural problems and define briefs, even if no client has yet articulated them. This updates the agenda of architecture and thus helps architecture to anticipate challenges rather than waiting to be prompted to do so by a client. The anticipation of challenges and the considered elaboration of sustainable responses are important to avoid a crisis of competency with myopic, ad-hoc reactions.

2. A second task is the proliferation of new formal repertoires in conjunction with the exploration of the new design media and modeling techniques. Such research leads to the expansion of the general solution space available to any architectural design effort. Initially such research should be independent of any stringent brief or strict criteria of instrumentalization. The task is to chart potentials that might inspire the search for problems on the basis of discovered «solutions». This latter reversal of the usual means-to-ends logic is impossible within mainstream professional practice – and highly constrained within avant-garde practice. The freedom to post-rationalize is greatest where no specific problem is posed from the outside – the only requirement being that a form–function relationship is established at the end. This is only possible within academia. The function of this academic laboratory research is thus not primarily to criticize professional practice and to directly lead the mainstream, but to irritate and inspire avant-garde practice and thus, indirectly, mainstream professional practice. The idea that academia itself could establish models of best practice is utterly misguided. This needs to be remembered in the calibration of the project's realism.

Innovation always emerges between the two tasks listed above: the investigation of a domain of problems and the expansion of the domain of potential solutions. Within the discipline of architecture this polarity of innovation has often been an occasion for a productive division of labour between the analysis of new societal/programmatic demands on the one hand and the proliferation of new spatial repertoires on the other hand. The independent elaboration of the two domains makes sense as a division of labour allowing for specialization. However, this divergence of orientation has led to two equally one-sided, opposing ideologies: the insistence on the priority of program versus to the insistence on the priority of form. This opposition poses the question of synthesis. Significant architectural innovations must involve both dimensions. The synthesis of new programs with new forms requires the oscillation between the two domains and is itself an act of creative intelligence. There are no one-to-one correspondences between "problems" and "solutions". Solutions can go in search of problems as well as problems in search of solutions.

It is the goal of the Hadid master class to establish design research agendas that allow the «solutions» that were evolving within an ongoing formal proliferation effort to find appropriately circumscribed programmatic problematic to demonstrate their performative potential. The master class sets a new research agenda every year – each framing the formal research within a broad programmatic frame. Agendas have included new mixed use high-rise typologies, parametric urbanism for new large-scale city extensions, public interiors. Within those broad programmatic frames the projects initially pursued a formal strategy. Some of the agendas were formulated without any programmatic given, e.g., the perception of space and orientation in complex urban scenes, or form-finding on the basis of environmental parameters. In all projects the specific programmatic articulation emerged later, driven by the potential of the evolving formal strategy rather than by a preconceived brief. This kind of form-to-program approach is only possible within the academic context. It means that each project has sufficient freedom to allow the formal logic to flourish. The overarching programmatic agenda acts as a guiding horizon. Formal strategies

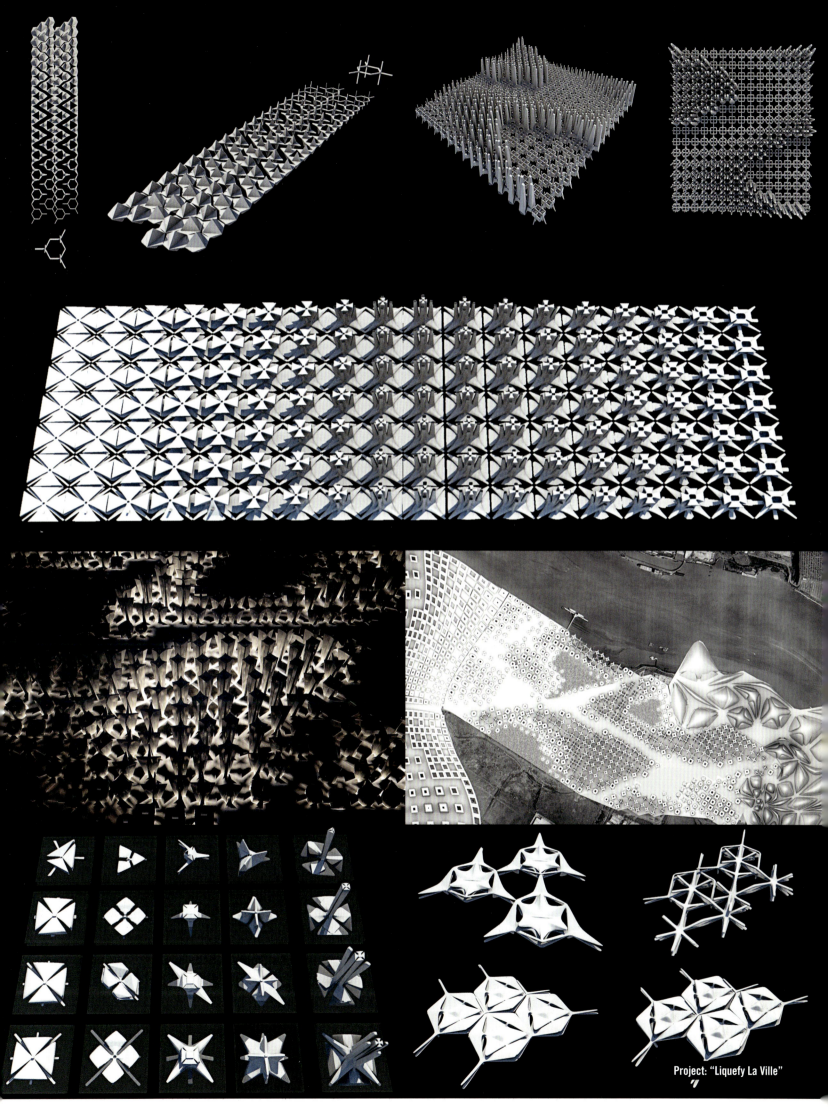

Project: "Liquefy La Ville"

are given the opportunity to specify programmatic particulars that suit them in their pursuit to discover convincing form-function alignments. The endgame of design research remains the establishment of new form-function relations.

Our method involves a consistent form-to-program heuristics, i.e., form-selects-function instead of function-selects-form. Project development thus extensively relies on post-rationalization, and programmatic adjustment to the initial briefs. But this procedural reversal is not a deficiency. Within contexts striving for a high level of innovation, such reversals of the normal course of ends-means rationality is acknowledged as a powerful form of rationality. However, less-stricter (premature) demands for precise purposes are certainly not intended to be a carte blanche. While our methodology and concept of rationality is in many important ways quite different from the linear and determinist conceptions of the early functionalists, functional requirements are only expelled at the very beginning of the design work. The projects oscillate between play and analysis throughout and aim at elaborating new form-function relations. "Function" is here understood as capacity or affordance that opens itself up for an evolutionary formation of new purposes rather than fulfilling a fully predetermined purpose.

While the master class works collectively on loosely set agendas with the focus on formal principles and computational processes, the students' final diploma projects are thesis projects that start with a specific, individually selected design task, for instance, the brief of a recent design competition. Here, in the final project, the student has to demonstrate his/her maturity by addressing a task that is much more like the tasks professional architects face. Now the student has to demonstrate that five years of design research have led up to a versatile formal repertoire and analytical intelligence capable of (innovatively and convincingly) addressing and solving real-world design tasks.

ARCHITECTURE'S RESPONSE TO 21ST CENTURY NETWORK SOCIETY

The prevalent institutions and communication patterns of society have undergone momentous changes during the last 30 years. Social communication has become dynamic, differentiated and intensified. The static organizing principles of Fordist mass society – separation, specialization, and mass repetition – have been replaced by the dynamic principles of self-organization of an emerging post-Fordist network society: variation, flexible specialization, and networking. Accordingly, modernist urbanism (zoning) and modernist architecture (serial monotony) have experienced a fatal crisis. The inherent limitations of the linear models of expansion that characterized Fordism became apparent both in terms of the ecological, the socio-economic, as well as the urban crises of the 1970s. The emerging network society implies that the intensity and complexity of social

interaction has increased exponentially. Even while the use of the Internet and mobile devices has increased, the demand for face-to-face communication – mediated by architectural and urban spaces – has increased as well.[1] Post-Fordism requires new, more variegated, complex, and densely integrated patterns of spatial ordering that are inherently multivalent and adaptive. Architecture has finally found the pertinent theoretical inspiration to answer this challenge in complexity theory analyzing and simulating self-regulating systems ranging from simple, homeostatic feedback mechanisms via organisms to evolving eco-systems. A second, related source of conceptual inspiration comes from the philosophy of Deleuze and Guattari. On the basis of this a new approach was developed to meet the societal challenges of our time. In retrospect Postmodernism (1980s) and Deconstructivism (1990s) might be understood as first tentative steps in this direction. They have since been superseded – their partial insights and discoveries having been preserved and elaborated – by a new powerful paradigm and style that promises to guide a new long wave of design research and innovation: Parametricism. The author first enunciated "parametricism" at the 11th Venice Architecture Biennale, arguing that an important new style has been maturing within the avant-garde segment of architecture during the past ten years, and that this style deserves recognition and explicit endorsement. In retrospect all the work done in the Hadid master class can be described in terms of parametricism.[2] By now the style encompasses a large part of the world's architectural avant-garde. There is no other movement of similar vitality and coherency. Parametricism is gathering momentum to become the first new global, unified style that can and must replace Modernism as a credible epochal style. Parametricism confronts both the remaining vestiges of Modernism's monotony and the cacophony of the urban chaos that has sprung up in the wake of Modernism's demise, with a complex, variegated order inspired by the self-organizing processes of nature.

The premise of Parametricism is that all urban and architectural elements must be parametrically malleable. Instead of assembling rigid and hermetic geometric figures – like all previous architectural styles – Parametricism brings malleable components into a dynamical play of mutual responsiveness as well as contextual adaptation. Key design processes are variation and correlation. Computationally, any property – positional, geometric, material – of any architectural element can be associated with – made the "cause" or "effect" of – any other property of any other element of the design. The designer invents and formulates correlations or rules akin to the laws of nature. Thus everything is potentially made to network and resonate with everything else. This should result in an overall intensification of relations that gives the urban field a performative density, informational richness, and cognitive coherence that makes for good legibility, easy navigation and thus quick, effective participation in a complex social arena where everybody's ability to scan an ever-increasing simultaneity of events and to move through a rapid successions of communicative encounters constitutes the essential, contemporary form of the cultural advancement.

Recently the Hadid master class has started taking on the ecological agenda. That the ecological challenge is among the defining moments of our epoch has been evident for a long time. Its impact on contemporary architecture and urbanism is second only to the challenge posed by the dynamic and complexity of post-Fordist Network Society. The same design concepts, techniques and tools of Parametricism that allow contemporary architects to ramp up the communicative complexity of the built environment are also congenial to the agenda of optimizing architectural forms with respect to ecological performance criteria.[3] Morphological output variables can be programmed to respond to environmental input parameters. For instance, a data set like a sun exposure map that maps the radiation-intensities a facade is exposed to during a given time period can serve as data input for the adaptive modulation of a sun-shading system. As the system of shading elements wraps around the facade the spacing, shape and orientation of the individual elements gradually transform and adapt to the specific exposure conditions of their respective location on the facade. The result is a gradient, continuously changing facade pattern that optimizes sun protection relative to light intake for each point on the facade. At the same time, this adaptive modulation gives the building an organic aesthetic that also makes the orientation of the building in the environment legible and thus facilitates the comprehension and navigation of the urban environment. The differentiated articulation of the facade contains and transmits information about its position rather than remaining indifferent and blind. The same principle of conspicuous, adaptive variation and correlation is applied to the activity and event parameters of the urban life process. The disorientating, generic neutrality and monotony of Modernism gives way to the ecologically adaptive eloquence of Parametricism.

Patrik Schumacher, London, December 2010

---

[1] *That is why the solution to the ecological crisis cannot involve the shutting down of the urban porosity and urban flow.*

[2] *For a full statement concerning the meaning and merits of Parametricism see: Patrik Schumacher, Parametricism: A new global style for architecture and urban design, in Neil Leach (ed), AD Digital Cities, Architectural Design, vol. 79, No 4, July/August 2009.*

[3] *The same theoretical resources and computational techniques that allow meteorologists to reconstruct and predict the global weather system and scientists*

to speculate about the earth's evolving climate are available to contemporary urbanists and architects in their effort to meet the challenges posed by the ongoing post-Fordist socio-economic restructuring. The task is to project the growth and transformation of cities as a rule-based, multi-variable morphogenetic process. Ecological parameters are but one subset of the potentially relevant parameter sets.

PATRIK SCHUMACHER is co-leading the Zaha Hadid Master-class since its inception in 2000.

He joined Zaha Hadid in 1988 and is partner at Zaha Hadid Architects, as well as co-author of many key projects, e.g. MAXXI – the National Italian Museum for Art and Architecture of the 21st century in Rome. In 1996 he founded the Design Research Lab (AADRL) with Brett Steele at the Architectural Association School of Architecture in London, and continues to serve as one of its co-directors. Since 2004 Patrik Schumacher is also tenured Professor at the Institute for Experimental Architecture, Innsbruck University. The aim and agenda of all of Patrik Schumacher's teaching arenas is to promote advanced computational design processes in the pursuit of a new language of architecture that is able to organize and articulate the increasing complexity of post-fordist network society.

Patrik Schumacher studied philosophy in Bonn (1980-1982) and London (1987-1990). His philosophical studies initially focused on logic, epistemology and the philosophy of language. His theoretical interests then expanded to social philosophy and political economy. From 1983 he studied architecture in Stuttgart University and at the Southbank University in London. He received his Diploma in architecture from Stuttgart University in 1990. He continued his studies in architectural history and theory at the Bartlett School of Architecture. In 1999 he completed his PHD on *The Function of Art and Design* in the Economic Process at the Institute for Cultural Science, Klagenfurt University.

In 2008 Patrik Schumacher launched a series of manifestos and essays promoting *Parametricism* as new epochal style for the 21st century. The style is based on the strategic application of generative computational processes, implying that all elements of architecture become parametrically malleable, allowing for a general intensification of relations, both internally within the project as well as externally between the project and its context. In 2010 Patrik Schumacher published the first volume of his theoretical opus magnum The *Autopoiesis of Architecture – A New Framework for Architecture*, a comprehensive, unified theory of architecture that analyses architecture an autonomous system of communications and great function systems of society. The second volume, *The Autopoiesis of Architecture – A New Agenda for Architecture* follows in 2011. This work moves from a comprehensive discourse analysis and rational reconstruction of the discipline to an agenda for architecture's strategic upgrading and forward projection.

Patrik Schumacher's further theoretical writings are available at **www.patrikschumacher.com**

This semester's task is to systematically probe into the design resources that enable and limit any specific design effort. The agenda here is to critically reflect the discipline of architecture as it is condensed in its most fundamental concepts, its most generic forms and approaches. The aim is to consciously appropriate the various extensions of the architectural repertoire witnessed in the 20th century and in particular to build on the momentous expansion of conceptual, formal and medial repertoires achieved over the last two decades.

We want to explore the new repertoires in terms of three dimensions: concept, form, medium. These terms indicate three semi-autonomous registers, which the discipline has build up to address any design task. At the same time these terms indicate three levels of abstraction with respect to any given design proposal or project. The interdependencies and relations between these levels – e.g., how media suggest concepts or can become formal catalysts, how conceptual restrictions can lead to formal proliferations, etc. – will be explored within the studio.

CONCEPTUAL DIMENSION

Architectural concepts are abstract and general principles of ordering space. Architecture might be explicitly *defined* as the organization and articulation of space. Its repertoire – on its most general and abstract level – consists in the various ways architecture might structure space. These might be referred to as concepts of space or *spatialities*.

Although all architecture might be classified with respect to general principles of spatial order, it was only in the 20th century that space became explicitly the most fundamental category of architecture. As, on the one hand, the emerging global communication at the end of the 19th century revealed the full diversity of world architecture across the ages and as, on the other hand, both functional requirements and structural possibilities proliferated far beyond the limits of the classical tradition, this new, abstract level of generalization – space – emerged as unifying dimension of the multitude of concepts devised to classify the proliferating phenomena.

Before architecture came to be understood as structuring space, the discipline was confined to the reproduction of different building types. Modern architecture broke this spell and gave itself the freedom to devise new types and – more significantly – new *concepts* thus radically reinventing its repertoire on the basis of abstraction.

Some examples of concepts (of space): territory, boundary, blurred boundary, axis, open versus bound space, isotropic versus differentiated space, smooth vs. striated space, space-time, figure-ground relation, solitaires vs. clustering, phenomenal transparency, juxtaposition, fragmentation, superposition, matrix, multiple affiliation, particle space, field space, vector of transformation, deformation, iteration versus repetition, single surface, bigness, intensive coherence. These concepts – collected from various sources – should not be expected to form a system.

A subcategory of principles concerns the constitution of (inhabitable) objects or artifacts within space rather than the structuring of space itself: cellular aggregation, carved object, modular constitution, articulated organism, loose assemblage, hybrid, swarm, tangle, weave, collage.

These concepts offer principle options with regard to spatially configuring the programmatic elements of any specific design task. The a priori set of conceptual options intervenes even on the level of the conception of the institutional program, i.e., the formulation of design task itself. Concepts are always already operating. Mostly they are discovered retrospectively. Whenever an operating principle is made explicit as a conscious concept a measure of freedom is gained. What was habitually taken for granted can now be chosen or rejected.

FORMAL DIMENSION

Architectural forms are specific ways of instantiating concepts. A solitaire can take the form of a cube, a cylinder or a sphere. Such simple geometric figures are the most obvious and most familiar (architectural) forms.

Each concept allows for many formal instantiations. But forms are not simply subcategories of concepts. They operate across concepts. A cube might be a solitaire, a cell, or a carved space. A point grid might realize either a striated or a smooth space.

Some more examples of forms are cone, paraboloid or blob. Forms might be "found" by means of analogy: amoeba, sponge or moraine. "Form" also includes formal systems: orthogonal structure, parallel striation or undulation. It is possible to extract forms from concepts: fields can be established through various types of grids or lattices, by various fractal patterns, or by specific series of morphological transformation; hybrids might be constructed by the interpenetration of specific geometric figures or by means of a specific morphing algorithm. Vectors of transformation might be linear, curved or radial.

MEDIUM

We will try to work with an unusually broad notion of the notion of a design *medium*. Each medium opens up or limits a universe of possibility: types of objects, their constitution, modes of manipulation and rules of association.

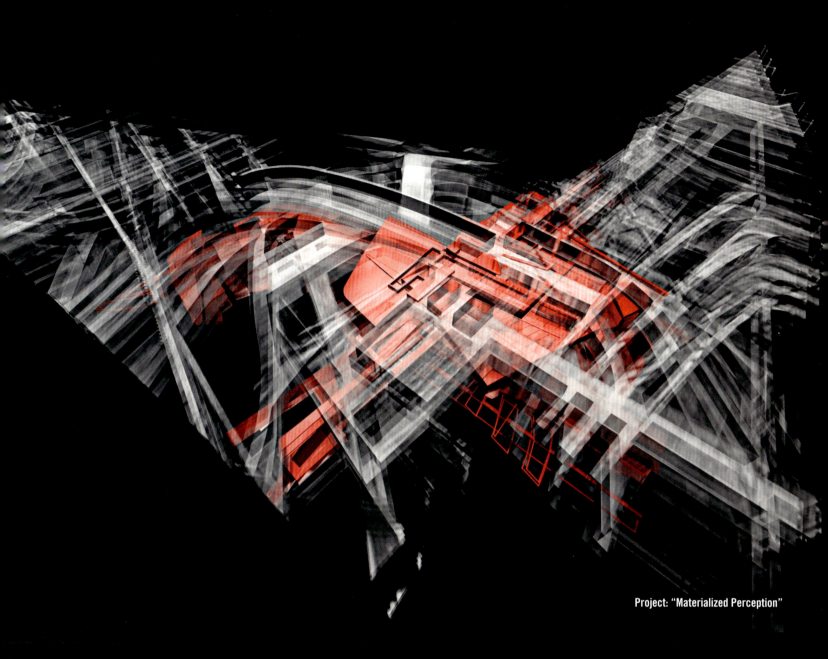

The most obvious and familiar medium can be found in pen and paper or various other graphic media. One of the premises of our studio is that already this level of material medium is pregnant with a certain formal, even conceptual thrust.

Material media include various physical modeling materials, even the final construction material on site within this notion of (material) medium. Modeling material has a strong bias with respect to tectonic operations like subtractive formation versus assembly, cutting and bending versus molding and plastic deformation. These operations – which we classify within the dimension of *medium* – limit the formal universe of possibility to such a degree that they have conceptual importance.

A radically new modeling material/technique requires and leads to radically new architectural concepts. Historically this was the role of the available construction material/technique. Quatremere de Quincy traces all (traditional) architectural articulation to three fundamental material/technological lineages: the tent leading to skin/skeleton structure (Chinese architecture), the cavern leading to mud and brick architecture (Egyptian architecture), the wooden hut leading to carpentry then also translated into other materials (Greek architecture). Such alignments of medium and form have been referred to as tectonic systems. But these alignments are not fixed. The forms and concepts derived from one material might well migrate into other materials (being transformed in the process).

The revolution of modern architecture and the emergence of space as the most fundamental concept of architecture is related to the introduction of steel and concrete as new construction materials.

The notion of media is not restricted to material media. The use of pen and paper is governed by well-established conventions, by determinate types of drawings: Orthogonal projections, oblique projections (axonometry, isometry), or perspective projections. The lines drawn on paper are all about the strict partitioning of space. This medium thus limits architectural thought to such partitioning. This need not be taken for granted. One might proliferate lines to blur boundaries to create textures of gradient density etc. One might interpenetrate perspectival vistas, work with sliding viewpoints, abuse perspectival projection as a technique of formation rather than representation.

A whole new set of tools has been introduced with the digital media, which had a huge impact on the development of the recent formal repertoire of the discipline. While CAD systems like Auto-Cad continue the world of pen and paper other software opens up a new universe of speculation. The critical reflection and inventive exploration of various design media will be an ongoing focus of the studio.

A repertoire will be built up through the analysis of paradigmatic projects. The analysis will proceed along all three dimensions, i.e., as conceptual analysis, formal analysis and analysis in terms of the media in which the project is presented and executed.

The projects are grouped according to three (assumed) levels of difficulty to account for the various levels of advancement of the students within the studio. Not just by chance the degree of difficulty distributes more or less chronologically. The later the project, the more is presupposed.

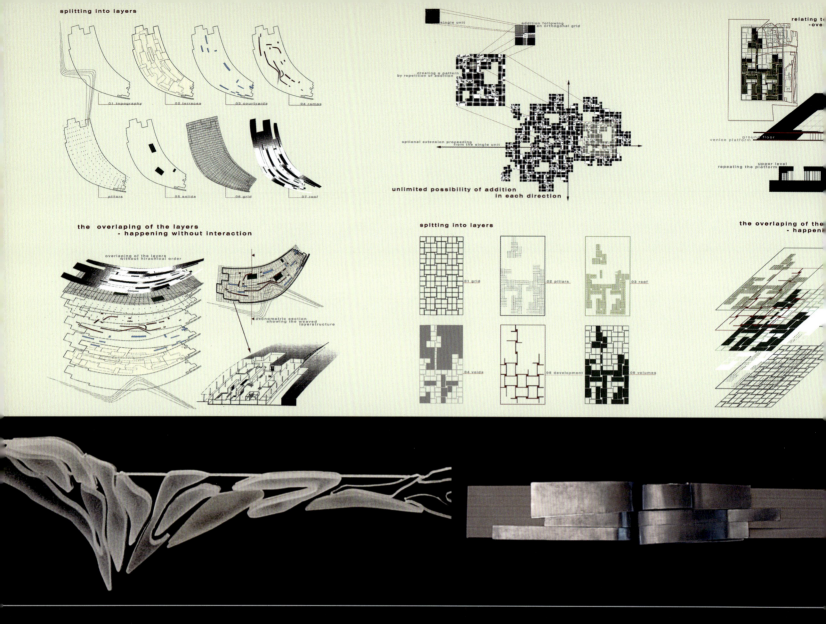

District Zero

Thomas Ausweger, Nina Gorfer, Anne Graupner, Jörg Hugo,
Andrea Kessler, Natalie Rosenberg, Nepomuk Wagner

Historically, Vienna is a monocentric city, an open-air museum focused solely on its very center. 'District Zero' aims at establishing a new city context by superimposing an additional linearly organized district. It seeks to trigger unanticipated connections between the currently unrelated parts of the urban fabric.

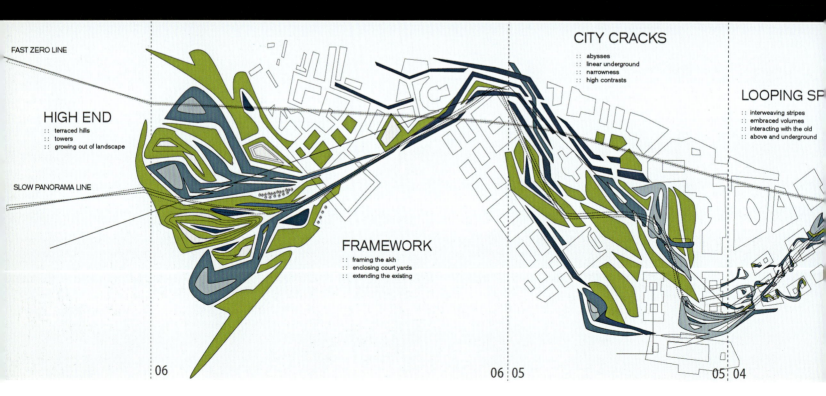

FAST ZERO LINE

CITY CRACKS

:: abysses
:: linear underground
:: narrowness
:: high contrasts

HIGH END

:: terraced hills
:: towers
:: growing out of landscape

LOOPING SP

:: interweaving stripes
:: embraced volumes
:: interacting with the old
:: above and underground

SLOW PANORAMA LINE

FRAMEWORK

:: framing the akh
:: enclosing court yards
:: extending the existing

06

06 05

05 04

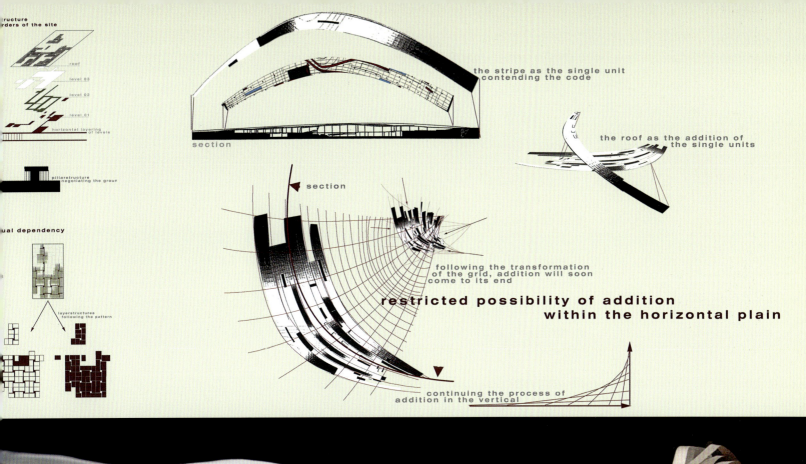

structure
orders of the site

roof
level 03
level 02
level 01
horizontal layering
of levels

pillarstructure
negotiating the ground

ual dependency

layerstructures
following the pattern

the stripe as the single unit
contending the code

section

the roof as the addition of
the single units

section

following the transformation
of the grid, addition will soon
come to its end

**restricted possibility of addition
within the horizontal plain**

continuing the process of
addition in the vertical

DISTRICT ZERO :: masterplan

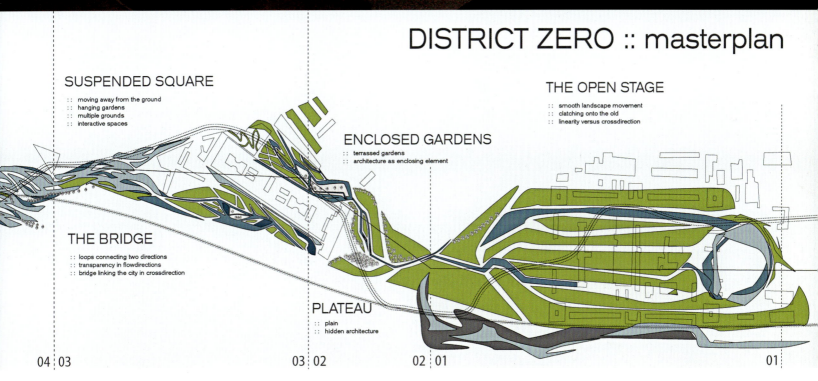

SUSPENDED SQUARE

:: moving away from the ground
:: hanging gardens
:: multiple grounds
:: interactive spaces

THE OPEN STAGE

:: smooth landscape movement
:: clatching onto the old
:: linearity versus crossdirection

ENCLOSED GARDENS

:: terrassed gardens
:: architecture as enclosing element

THE BRIDGE

:: loops connecting two directions
:: transparency in flowdirections
:: bridge linking the city in crossdirection

PLATEAU

:: plain
:: hidden architecture

04 : 03   03 : 02   02 : 01   01

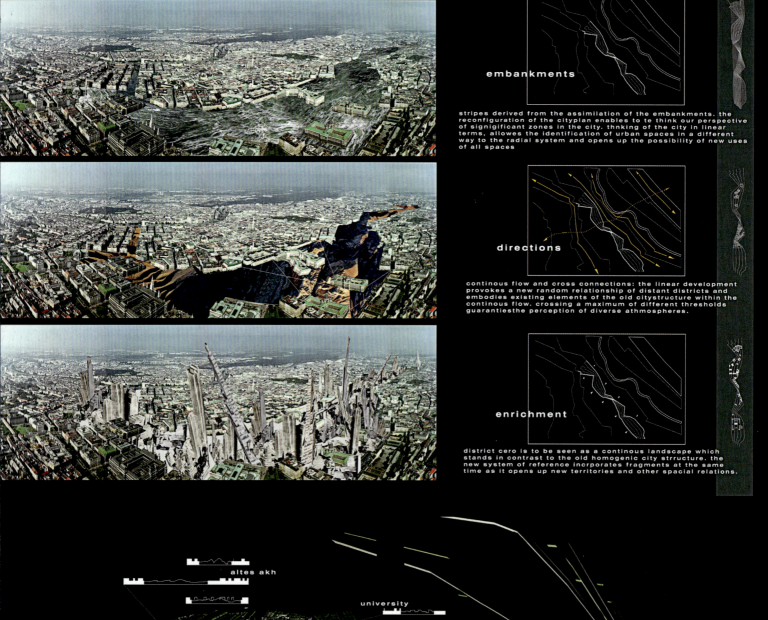

embankments

stripes derived from the assimilation of the embankments. the reconfiguration of the cityplan enables to te think our perspective of signigficant zones in the city. thnking of the city in linear terms, allows the identification of urban spaces in a different way to the radial system and opens up the possibility of new uses of all spaces

directions

continous flow and cross connections: the linear development provokes a new random relationship of distant districts and embodies existing elements of the old citystructure within the continous flow. crossing a maximum of different thresholds guarantiesthe perception of diverse athmospheres.

enrichment

district cero is to be seen as a continous landscape which stands in contrast to the old homogenic city strructure. the new system of reference incrporates fragments at the same time as it opens up new territories and other spacial relations.

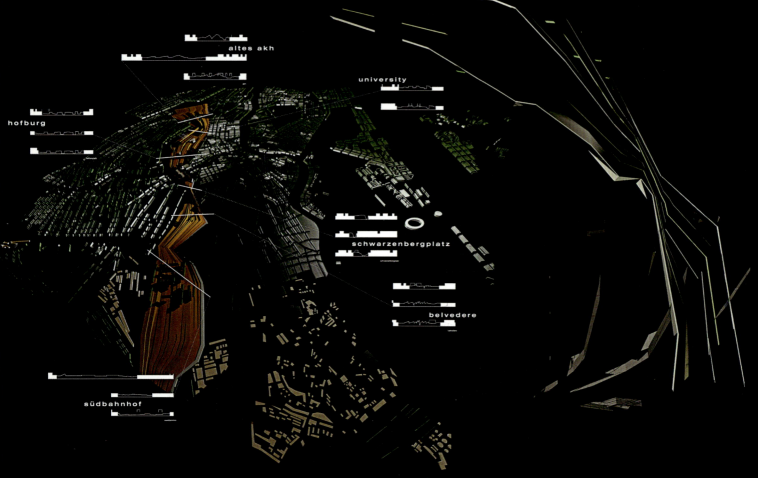

altes akh

university

hofburg

schwarzenbergplatz

belvedere

südbahnhof

district zero

district zero

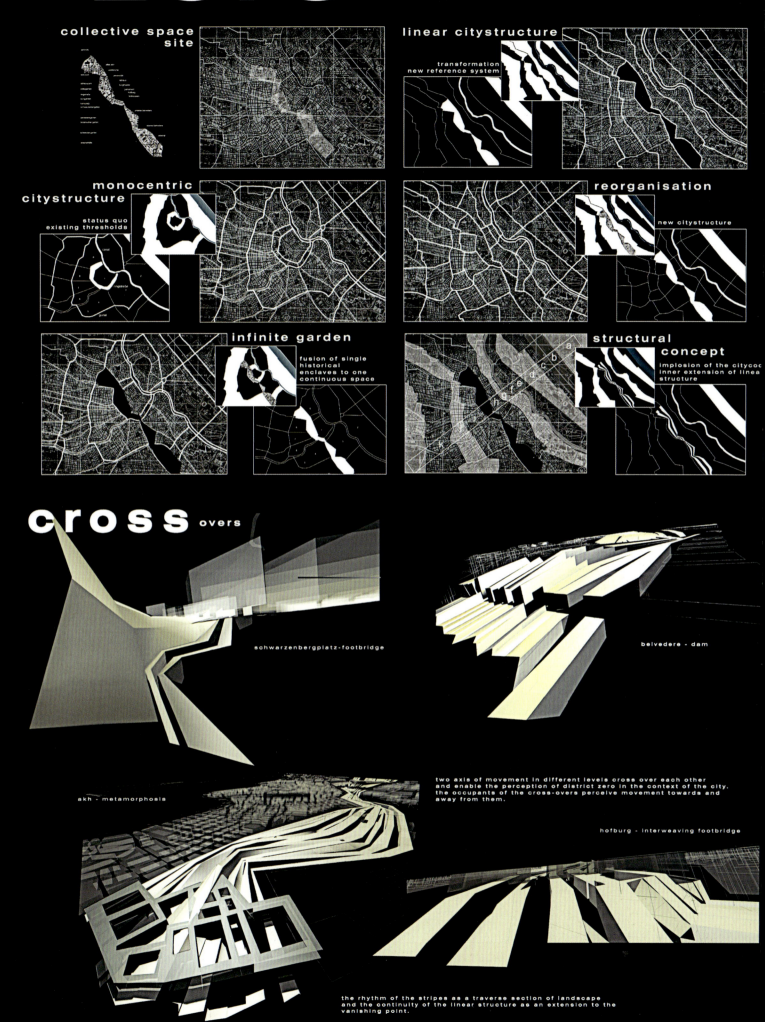

collective space site

linear citystructure

transformation
new reference system

monocentric citystructure

status quo
existing thresholds

reorganisation

new citystructure

infinite garden

fusion of single
historical
enclaves to one
continuous space

structural concept

implosion of the citycoo
inner extension of linea
structure

cross overs

schwarzenbergplatz-footbridge

belvedere - dam

akh - metamorphosis

two axis of movement in different levels cross over each other
and enable the perception of district zero in the context of the city.
the occupants of the cross-overs perceive movement towards and
away from them.

hofburg - interweaving footbridge

the rhythm of the stripes as a traverse section of landscape
and the continuity of the linear structure as an extension to the
vanishing point.

Fast_Foreward
Florian Pucher, Paul Peyrer-Heimstätt

The analysis of traffic flow at the Schwarzenbergplatz in Vienna is the first step in generating a field of forces that reorganizes the entire site. The new geometric pattern is derived from diagrams that refer to the speed of cars, trams and pedestrians. The project deals with the existing urban substance and deforms building masses according to a different "speed-geometry".

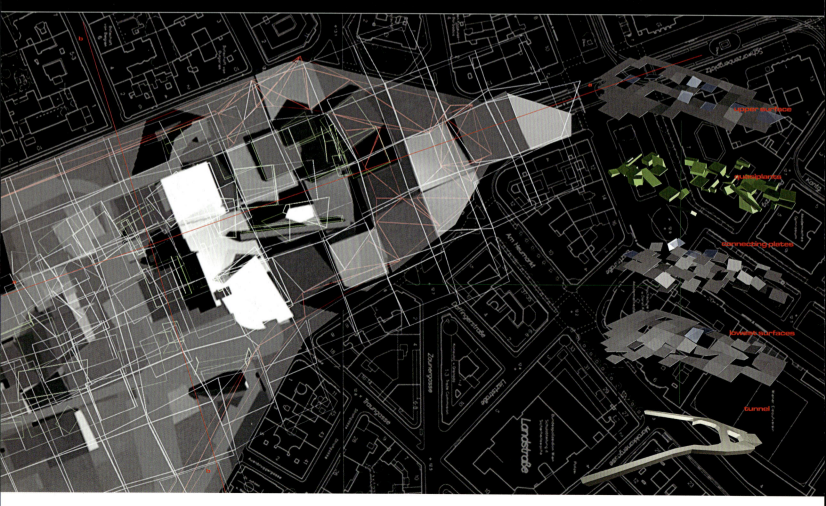

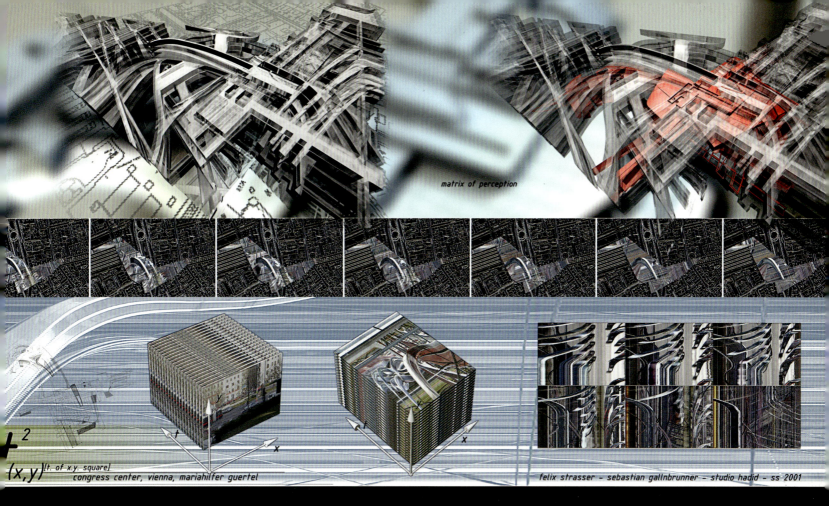

matrix of perception

$$\frac{2}{(x,y)}^{[t.\ of\ x.y.\ square]}$$

congress center, vienna, mariahilfer guertel

felix strasser - sebastian gallnbrunner - studio hadid - ss 2001

Materialized Perception

Sebastian Gallnbrunner, Felix Strasser

The project started with films of crowded scenes of weekend shoppers on Mariahilfer Strasse near Vienna's Westbahnhof. The traces of sequential movements of people within sequential film stills establish a complex motion diagram that is later scripted as a design tool. Thus the whole environment is developed as an extracted as well an eroded mass derived from the figurative pattern of the initial analysis.

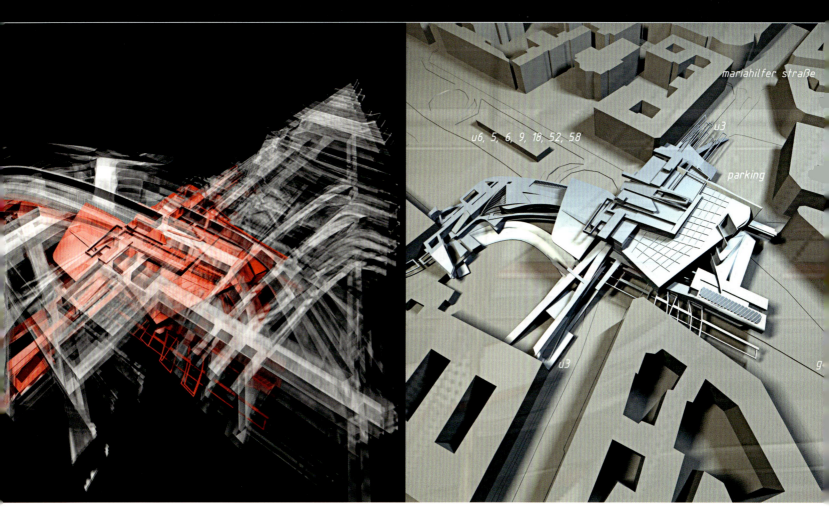

mariahilfer straße

u6, 5, 6, 9, 18, 52, 58

u3

parking

u3

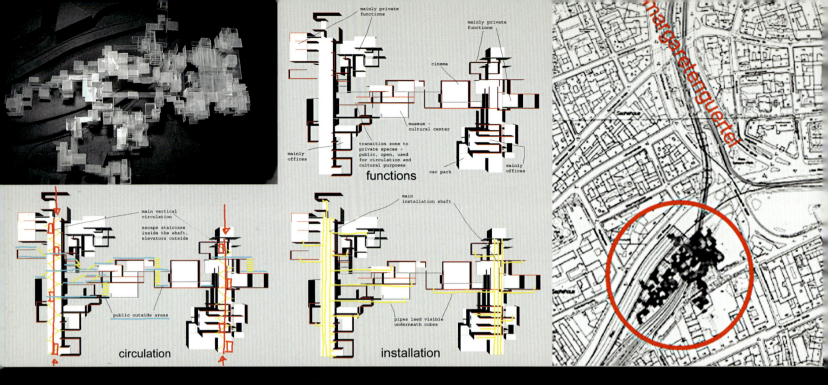

Malign

Caren Ohrhallinger, Daniela Overbeck, Peter Schamberger, Georg Wizany

Loos' "Raumplan", F. L. Wright's "Fallingwater" and Rietveld-Schröder House serve as the backdrop for the development of an open module, which is both indeterminate and flexible. The arrangement of these elements as a bridge-like megastructure on the Margaretengürtel site in Vienna provides adequate spatial qualities on an urban scale.

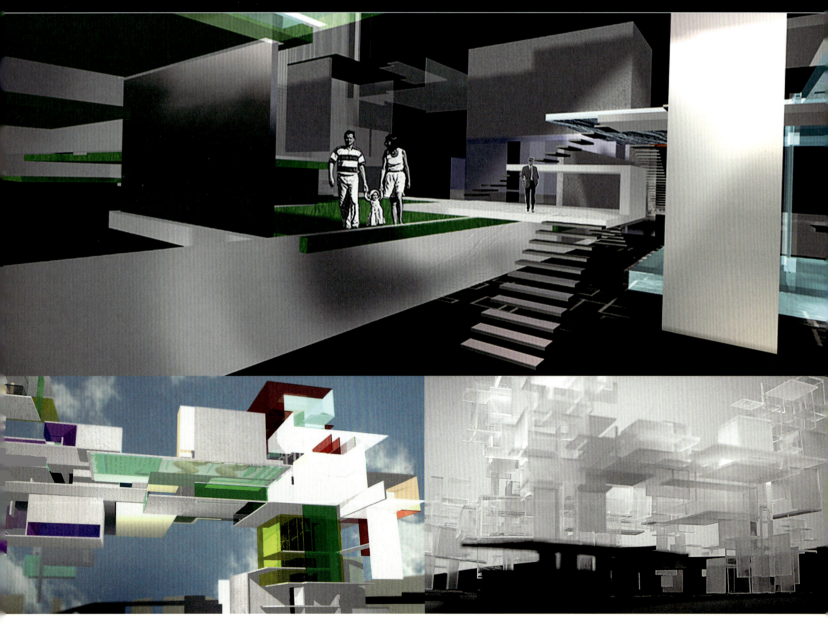

reorganizing
open space
function
circulation

open space

function A
function B
function C

technique

technique.

developing a spatial order of layers
using horizontal, vertical and twisted
combining them to a complex system

surrounding infrastructure

university
culture
shopping

site

national assembly louis i. kahn
analysis

national assembly louis i. kahn
analysis

horizontal

vertical

combination

technique
element

technique
project

Interventions

Andrea Kessler, Sandra Riess, Barbara Ziegerhofer

The analysis of three projects (Hanselmann-House / M. Graves, Dhaka-Project / L. Kahn, Bibliothèque de France / OMA) addressed the discourse of phenomenal transparency and the method of subtraction to be applied as a tool for a separate design. A system of multilayered depth was created with self-referential cutouts along all coordinate axes through various vertical and horizontal planes in the space.

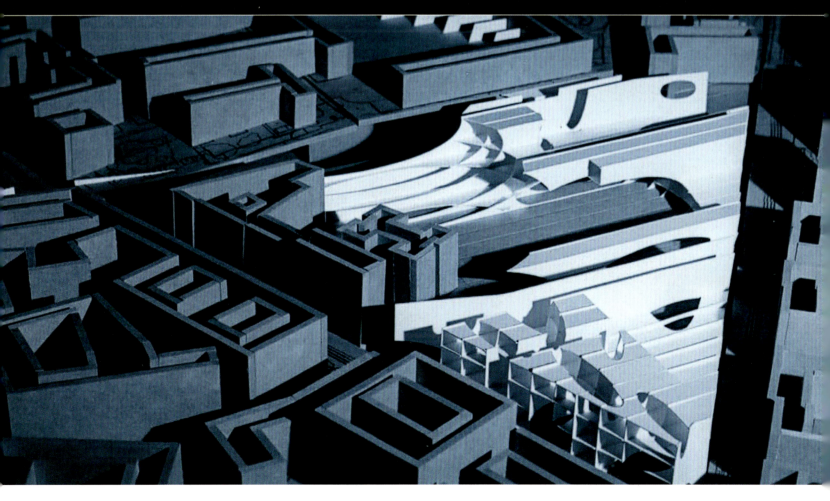

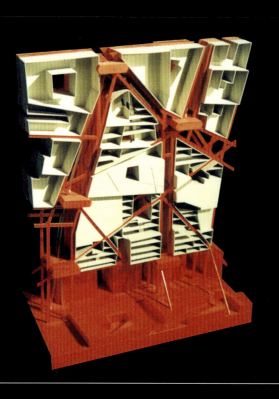

Vertical City
Florian Medicus, Katharina Tanzberger

Based on an analysis of MVRDV's 'Berlin Void' and Le Corbusiers 'Plan Obus' project for Algiers these compound 'Vertical City-Slabs' describe a synthesis method for both: a large-scale intervention with a maximum of formal and contextual references to an existing urban ('ready-made') fabric.

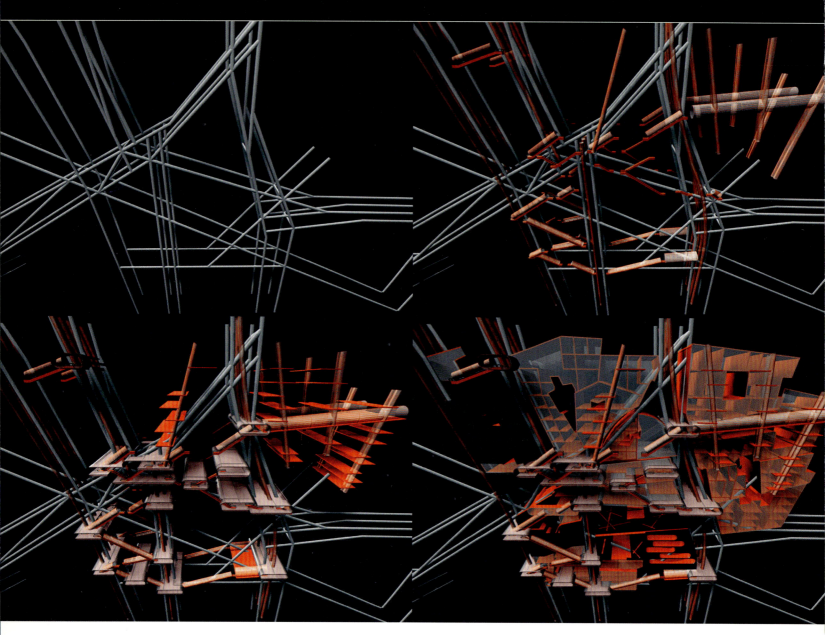

café soleil

sam's bar
+166m

+180m

+172m

music archive

film archive

casino

garden

+130m

laing's hotel

film & music
archive

skylobby
+121m

auditorium

shoppingcenter

café-bar

hotel milton
+96m

restaurant du théâtre
+96m

museum for contemporary arts

+66m

"the factory"

O.W. theatre

café

library

exhibition

+66m

vestibule

ligne roset

+53m

O. W. seminar
ballroom

administration

+46m

foyer

offices

archive

studios

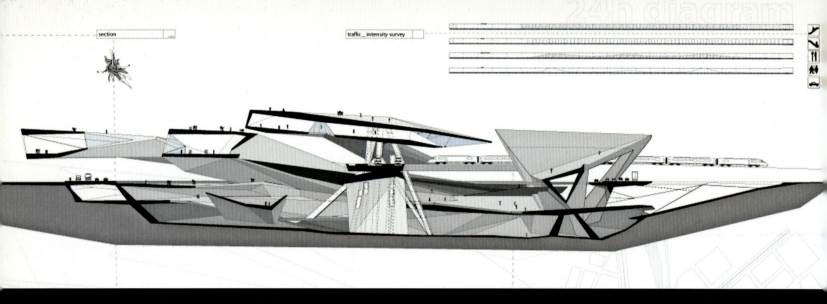

▲ Urban Sink

Matthias Bär, Klaus Ebner, Jörg Hofstätter

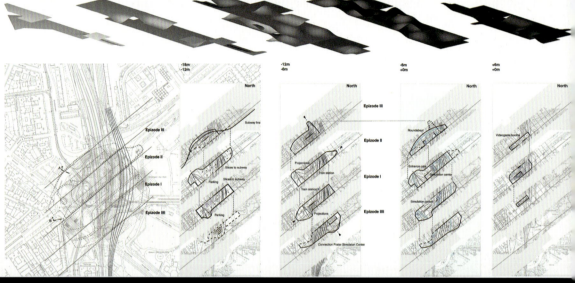

▲ Praterstern

Robert Grössinger, Peter Stec

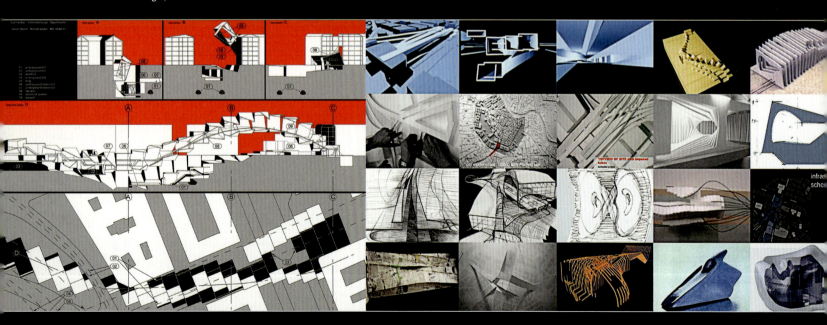

▲ Karlsplatz

Michael Gruber, Daniel Steindl, Thomas Vietzke, Michaela Weisskirchner

- enlargement of the existing university
- enlargement of existing museum
- bar, restaurant
- sports
- performance, exibition, great hall
- lecture hall, conference room,

▲ Chain

Petra De Colle, Ivana Jug

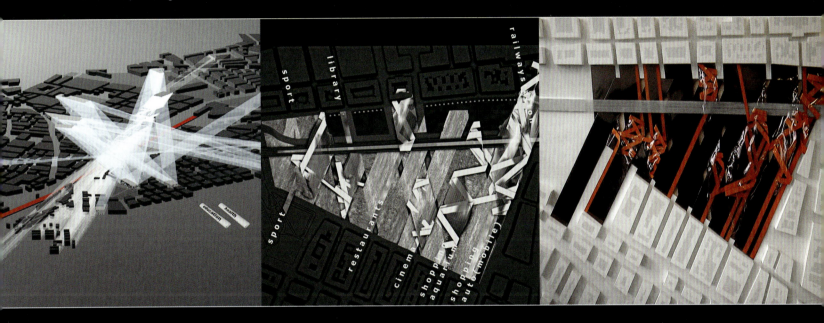

▲ X-Change City Weaver

Carmen Hammerer, Marion Lubitz, Katharina Mayr

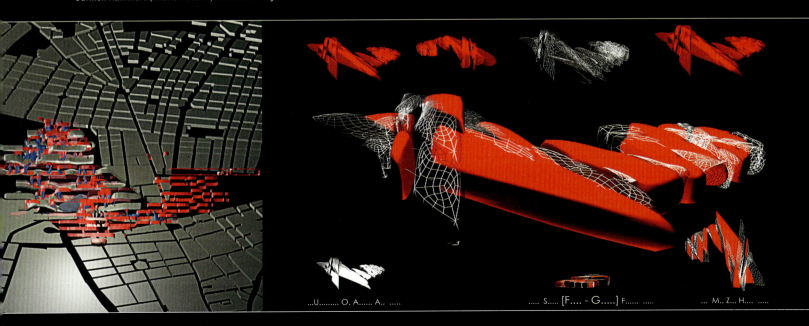

...U........ O. A...... A.. .... S..... [F.... - G....] F...... .... M.. Z.. H.... .....

▲ Fusion of Urban Spaces

Simone Fuchs, Florian Gypser

New York's World Trade Center was one of the largest and most ambitious structures ever built.

This large complex was designed by Minoru Yamasaki in the mid and late sixties, at the peak of the Fordist era, Fordism referring to a system of assembly-line mass production that led to a modern mass society organized around huge corporations. Construction of the towers started in 1969 and was completed in 1973. The Twin Towers alone offered 1 million square meters of office space spread over 110 stories. The entire center offered working space for 50,000 people. This is equivalent to the population of a medium-sized city.

Fordism in general was marked by large-scale endeavors. Everything was produced in bulk quantities, based on standardization and reproduction. The serial aesthetic of Mies van der Rohe's American period was the most pertinent expression of Fordism in architecture. Yamasaki's twin towers developed this principle to its ultimate symbolic conclusion. Even such an enormous, iconic structure like the great American skyscraper could be subordinated to the principle of repetition. The repetition of the same operates between the two towers as well as within each tower.

The tragic destruction of the World Trade Center raises the question of what could replace it. What kind of organizational structure would satisfy contemporary business life, what kind of formal language would articulate it? What is the functionality and aesthetics of the city of contemporary business?

The epoch of the skyscraper is over – not primarily due to concerns about security – but because the skyscraper's organizational structure is too simple and constricting. Towers only grow in one dimension. The strict linearity of its extension accounts for its characteristic poverty of connectivity. Towers are hermetic units, which are themselves arrays of equally hermetic units (floors). These features of linearity and strict segmentation are contradictory to contemporary business relations and to contemporary urban life in general, where much higher levels of complexity and spatial order are required.

ARCHITECTURE AS URBANISM
The demise of Fordism and of the skyscraper as its urban archetype does not imply the retreat from the large scale or from high density. Both bigness and density are increasing within the contemporary metropolis. The demise of historical city centers and the bankruptcy of comprehensive city planning in the face of market uncertainty means that architecture has to carry the burden of urbanism within large single developments. New spatial models must be able to organize higher levels of complexity and integrate significantly more

simultaneous programmatic agendas and processes. But how can appropriate spatial patterns be invented and how can the required spatial complexity be build up?

FROM ANALYSIS TO SYNTHESIS
The task is to develop strategies that can produce large building structures fulfilling the urban functions of communication and exchange. The aim is to conceive spatial entities of a higher order than what one usually considers as "building" or even "ensemble", an entity that recreates within itself approximations of the multiplicity, complexity and effectiveness of the urban condition.

In order to assemble the programmatic ingredients, possible spatial patterns and generative formal principles that might be used later in the synthesis of a large urban architecture, an initial exercise in urban analyses needs to be conducted first.

Each team of students was to choose, analyze and model an intriguing urban phenomenon from anywhere around the world, the only requirements being that the phenomenon inspires curiosity, has a certain level of complexity and promises to lead to discoveries that might be usable in the synthetic stage of the project.

The analysis is not geared towards documentary purposes. It is rather generative and should focus on the extraction, abstraction and re-formulation of key principles that might become the driving force of the later project. While initially these principles might be principles of formal (spatial) organization the analysis should reveal the functional performance of the spatial structures in question.

The design phase (synthesis) of the project is itself divided into two parts: the systematic and the pragmatic phase.

First abstract models are to be devised on the basis of the principles extracted from the urban analysis. All principles should be systematically explored through a thorough series of systematic variations, exhaustive recombinations, etc.

Once an abstract system or prototype has been developed, the pragmatic implementation of this system or prototype can be tested on the site of the former World Trade Center in downtown Manhattan. This symbolically significant site should only be tackled after having developed systems and architectural principles that suggest that the planned intervention has a chance to articulate the essential operations and ambitions of the contemporary metropolis with the same poignancy and profundity that made the World Trade Center such a powerful symbol of modern civilization.

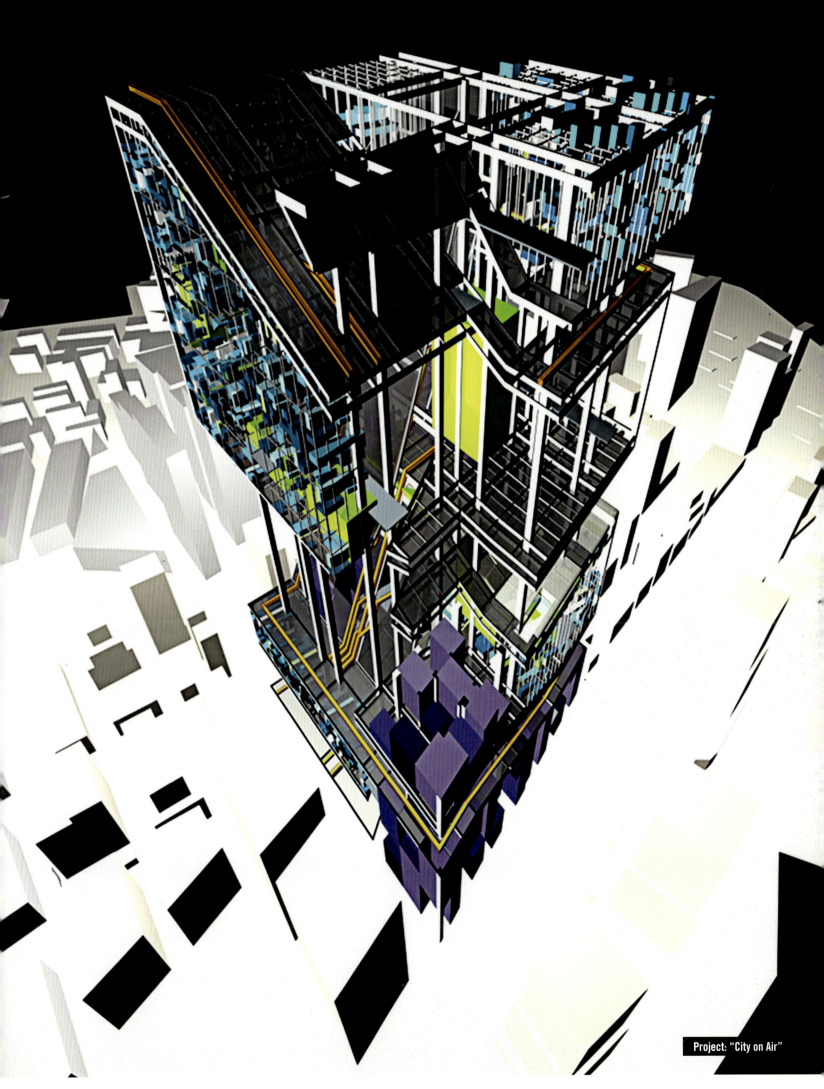

Project: "City on Air"

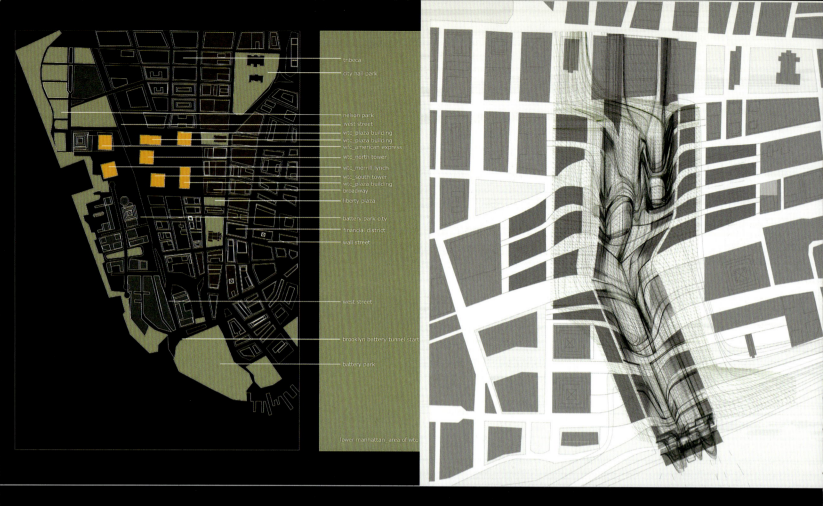

tribeca
city hall park

nelson park
west street
wtc_plaza building
wtc_plaza building
wfc_american express
wtc_north tower
wtc_merrill lynch
wtc_south tower
wtc_plaza building
broadway
liberty plaza

battery park city
financial district
wall street

west street

brooklyn battery tunnel start

battery park

lower manhattan_area of wtc

Funnel City

Daniel Baerlecken, Judith Reitz, Peter Stec

Rather than constituting the city as an array of additive elements the project proposes a coherent urban surface system allowing for horizontal as well as vertical urban conditions. The proposed geometry of the new urban center is able to react adaptively to the existing city fabric as well as to accommodate different programmatic requirements.

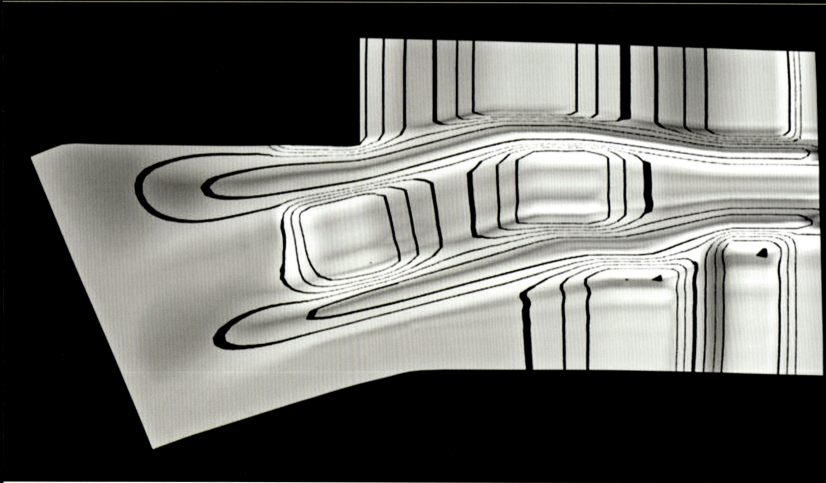

NOMADSLAND
BIG VOLUME STRUCTURE

SUBURBIA
LOWRISE HOUSING ZONE

WORKSTATION
DIFFERENT TYPES OF VOLUMES

KASBAH
HOUSING WITH COLLECTIVE
PATIOS

City Sex

Matthias Bär, Daniel Grünkranz, Florian Pucher

Examining the architectural potential of programmatic differences the proposed urban complex refers to the large-scale urban context by allowing programmatic differentiation and offering a wide range of spatial specifics.

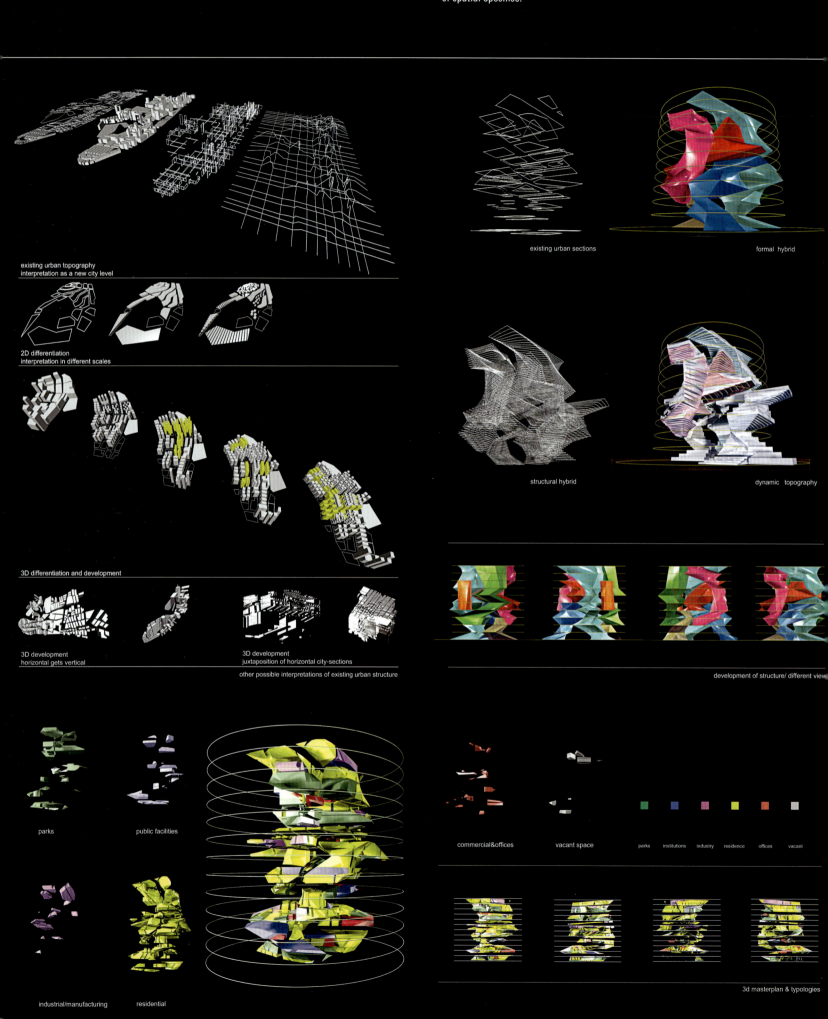

existing urban topography
interpretation as a new city level

existing urban sections

formal hybrid

2D differentiation
interpretation in different scales

3D differentiation and development

structural hybrid

dynamic topography

3D development
horizontal gets vertical

3D development
juxtaposition of horizontal city-sections

other possible interpretations of existing urban structure

development of structure/ different view

parks

public facilities

commercial&offices

vacant space

parks   institutions   industry   residence   offices   vacant

industrial/manufacturing

residential

3d masterplan & typologies

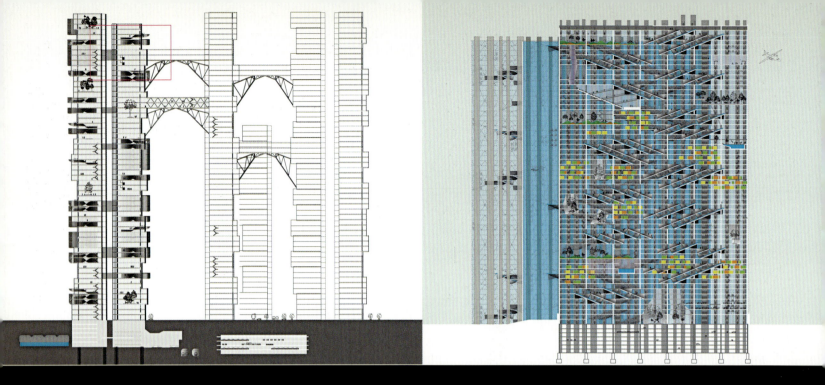

Denseclub, New York

Paul Fürst, Robert Grössinger, Paul Peyrer-Heimstätt

The project is based on the architectural contrast of a grid system versus a "soft" circulation system. The duality of both systems offers a wide range of potential usage.

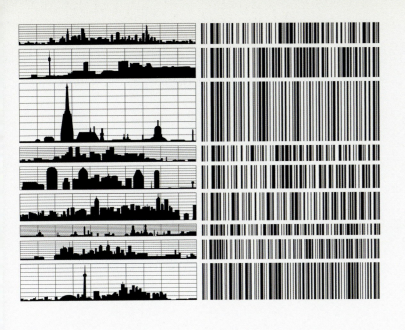

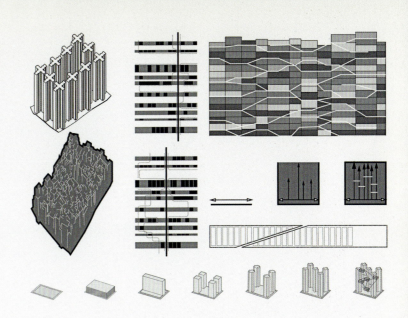

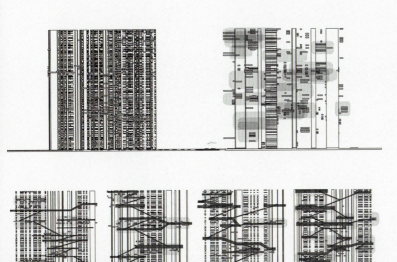

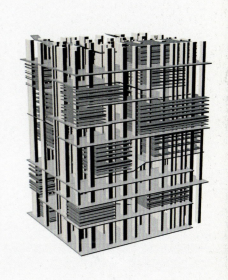

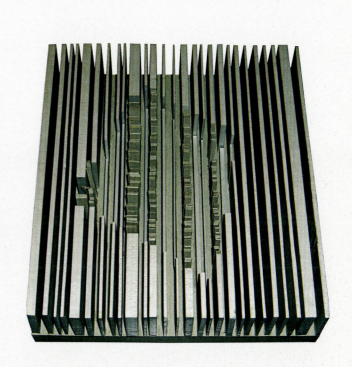

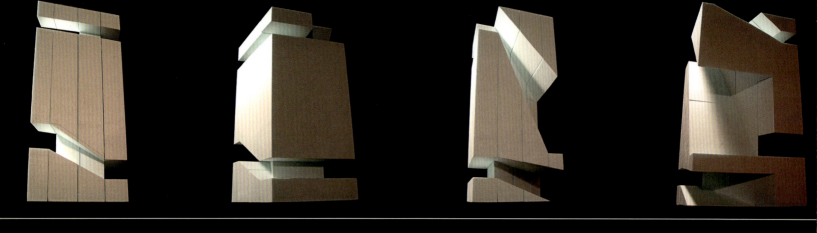

City on Air

Sandra Riess, Daniel Steindl, Barbara Ziegerhofer

The project proposes an urban super-block, in which a public vertical spiral passage is inscribed as an extension of the existing street system. The resulting attractive spatial qualities constitute the basis for the new urban center.

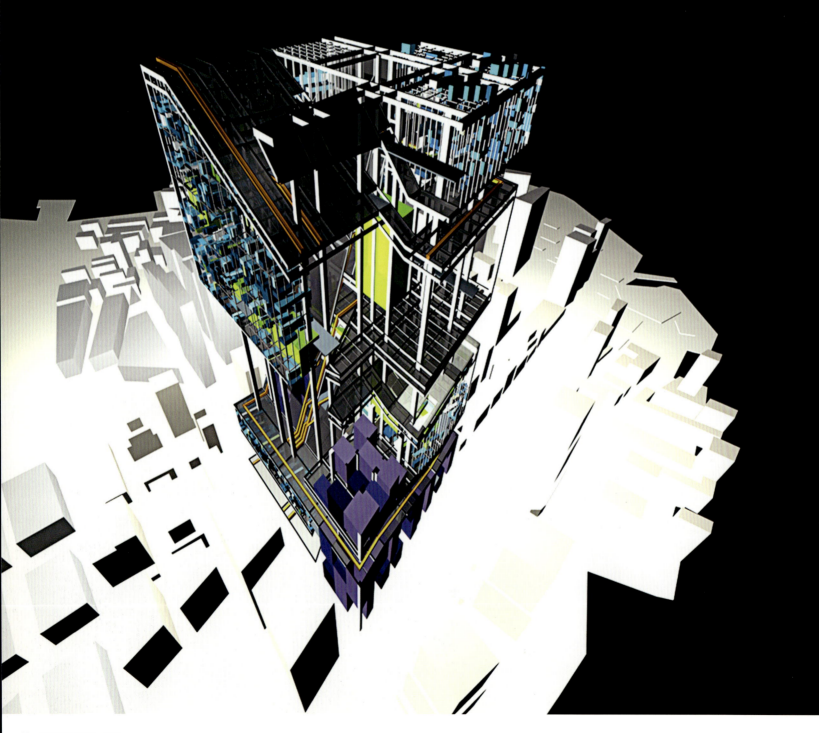

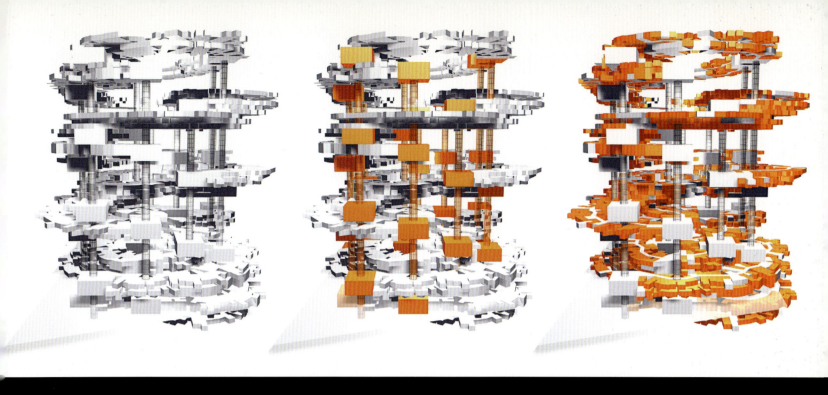

WTC, N.Y.C

Sebastian Gallnbrunner, Eva Scheucher

Looking at urban growth patterns as a first step, the project proposes a continuous vertical urban spiral as a contemporary urban center.

november, day: 15
3800 sqm office
100 sqm shopping
0 sqm cafe/restaurants
0 sqm parks

january, day: 60
23000 sqm office
1500 sqm shopping
1100 sqm cafe/restaurants
0 sqm parks

may02, day: 180
102000 sqm office
12000 sqm shopping
5000 sqm cafe/restaurant
3000 sqm parks

november02, day: 360
320000 sqm office
20000 sqm shopping
10500 sqm cafe/restaurant
22000 sqm parks

possible state february 2003, day: 450
592000 sqm office space (~34000 employees)
26800 sqm shopping 18800 sqm cafe/restaurants
35000 sqm parks

basics connectable pileable unities

staircase
public parks
offices
cafe/ restaurant
shops
elevators

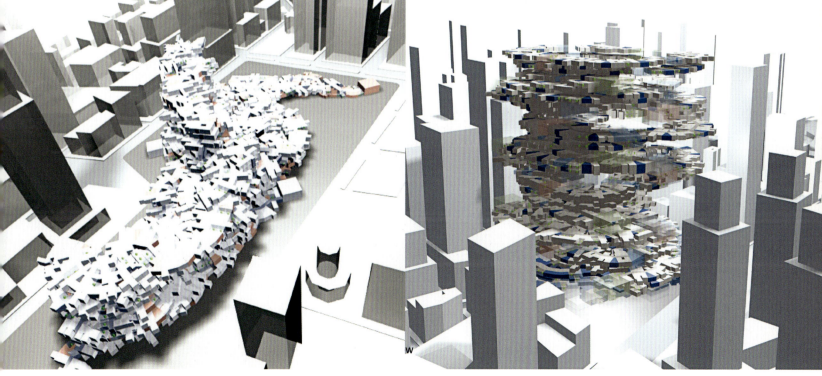

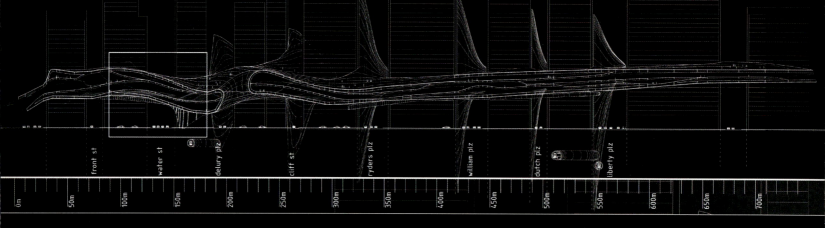

Light Density

Pietro Gellona, Jörg Hugo, Jens Mehlan

'Light Density – Metropolis Beyond the Skyscraper' investigates New York City's zoning regulations from 1916 and 1982 and develops a speculative model for further densification of currently unused spaces within the city fabric. It seeks to outline novel solutions with regard to maximizing light intake, alleviating car traffic and creating public spaces.

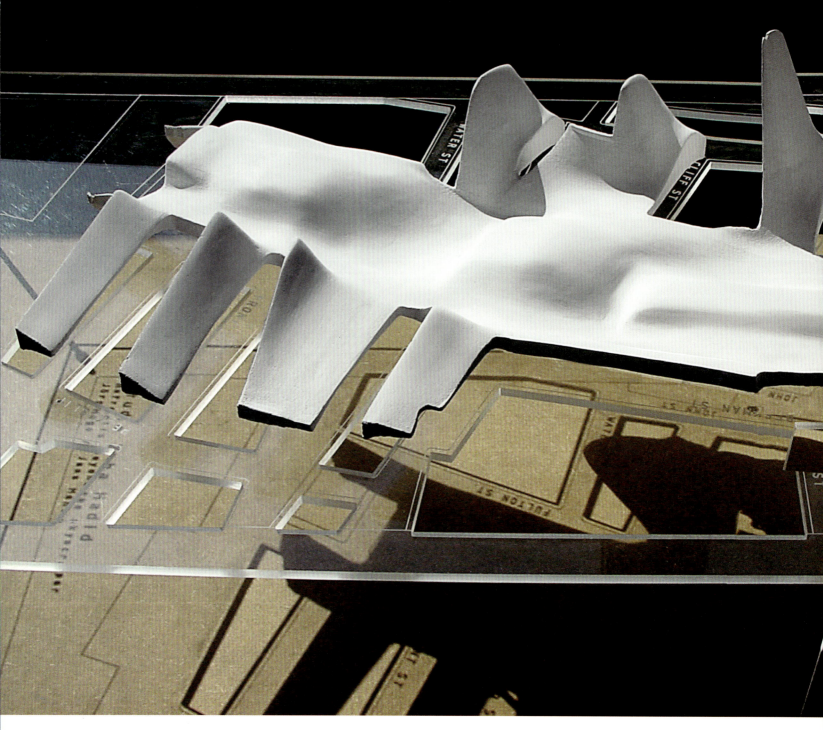

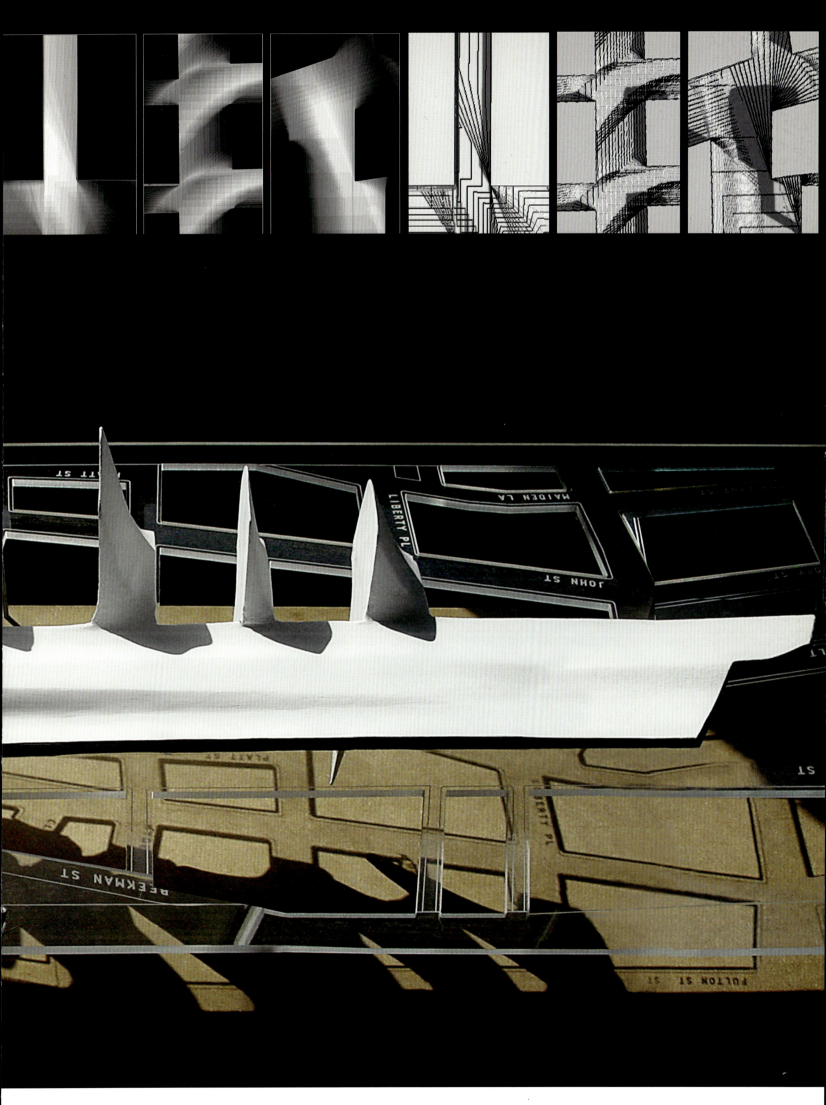

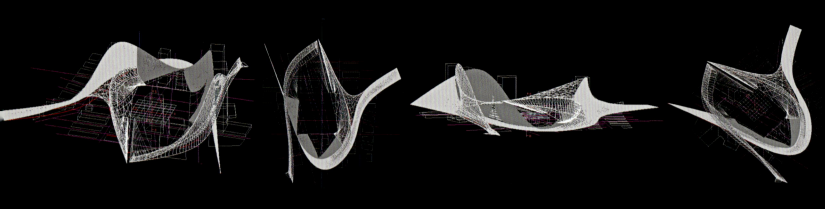

▲ New York Harbour
Andrea König

▲ Liberty Pier
Nina Gorfer, Andrea Kessler, Carola Stabauer

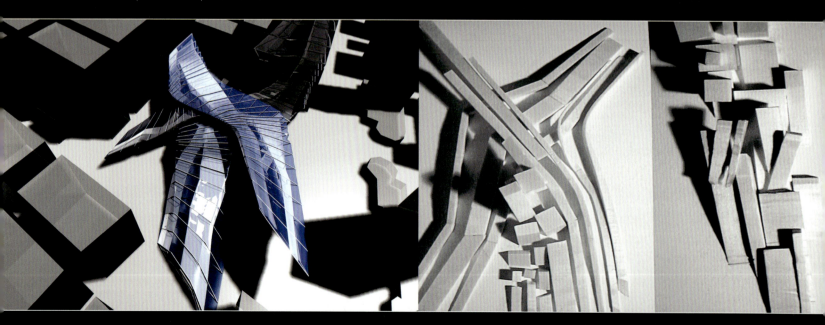

▲ Birdflight
Petra De Colle, Mario Gasser, Ivana Jug, Panajota Panotopoulou

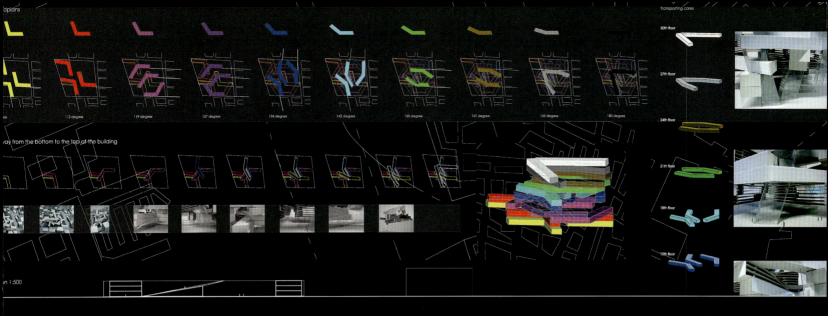

▲ Inside Outside
Cornelia Klien, Gerhild Orthacker

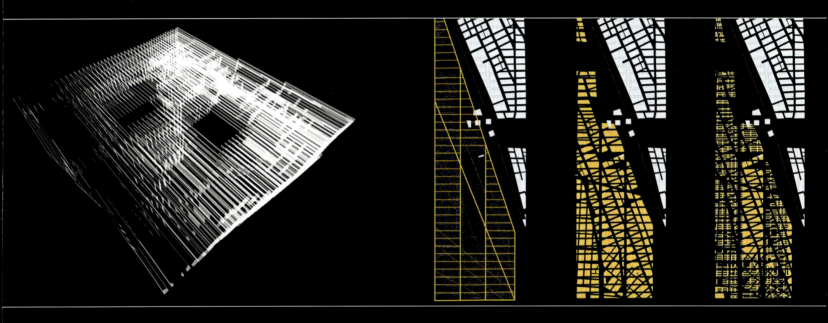

▲ New York - WTC
Christoph Opperer, Florian Unterberger

▲ New York Strip
Kaloyan Erevinov, Mario Gasser, Peter Schamberger, Flemming Svendsen

FORMS OF METROPOLITAN LIVING

2002 - 2003

This year's investigations will be dedicated to the possibilities of applying the rich formal vocabularies that have been developed in recent years to the design of new forms of urban living.

LONDON INTENSIFIES
London is the fastest growing city in Europe, with an influx of about 70,000 people per year. In recent years London has been able to absorb such numbers by transforming former derelict industrial areas into dense mixed-use quarters.

Offices as well as apartments (lofts) have been created by converting warehouses, workshops and small factories in an uncoordinated small-scale development process. Now the British government is promoting the further development of so-called "brown field sites", i.e., the utilization of derelict sites within the cities.

This strategy favors high-density urbanity instead of low-density sprawl. For the studio this debate serves as an opportunity to explore new concepts of urban living on a scale with urbanist implications.

ARTICULATING THE COMPLEXITY OF CONTEMPORARY DEMOGRAPHICS
The task is to design a large urban complex in London with a focus upon residential functions. The studio's goal is to make an innovative contribution to the contemporary repertoire of residential typologies and to offer convincing solutions to a number of complex urban sites in London taking into account the contemporary diversity of household-types and life-styles.

After the decline of the age of mass production today's society is witnessing a strong stratification and differentiation of incomes, types of occupation, and a multicultural diversity of ethnic groups. Architecture should strive to organize the full demographic spectrum of the modern metropolis within a complex whole.

NEW HOUSEHOLD CONFIGURATIONS
The private household serves as the point of departure, its geometry becoming more complex as the traditional model of the nuclear family is disintegrating. Within the private household we might assume differentiation into further subsystems. Therefore, the definition and demarcation of the residential unit can no longer be taken for granted. In some or most of the cases this demarcation might not be clear-cut anymore. A deliberately ambiguous articulation of what might be read as a dwelling unit at various occasions might be called for.

MODERN LIFE VERSUS TRADITIONAL COMMUNITY
In order to increase the probability of achieving a sense of communal life within the context of a modern metropolis, the first task might be to devise a demographic matrix that allows a certain ordering of the expected residential population in terms of age, interest, marital status, type of occupation, etc.

THE DESIGN TASK
With respect to the design of a contemporary, metropolitan residential complex we place equal emphasis upon the organization and articulation of spaces and furnishings within the interior of the dwelling as well as upon the organization and articulation of the urban space that is created between the dwellings. However, a strict definition of what is inside or outside a dwelling unit might be neither possible nor desirable. Instead a hierarchy or even network of nesting or overlapping territories might be articulated.

Two key aspects of architectural design will be pursued:
Firstly, the definition of territory by means of a system of various spatial demarcations that operates across the whole spectrum of boundary definitions – from the establishment of private and public zones to the definition of residential units and their further subdivisions into territorial subunits. And, secondly, the facilitation of specific activities by means of appropriate furnishings.

The initial furnishing elements might be used to articulate boundaries (boundaries are not necessarily walls nor even spatial concepts) and initially territorializing devices might be used to facilitate various activities as the designs become more complex and interwoven.

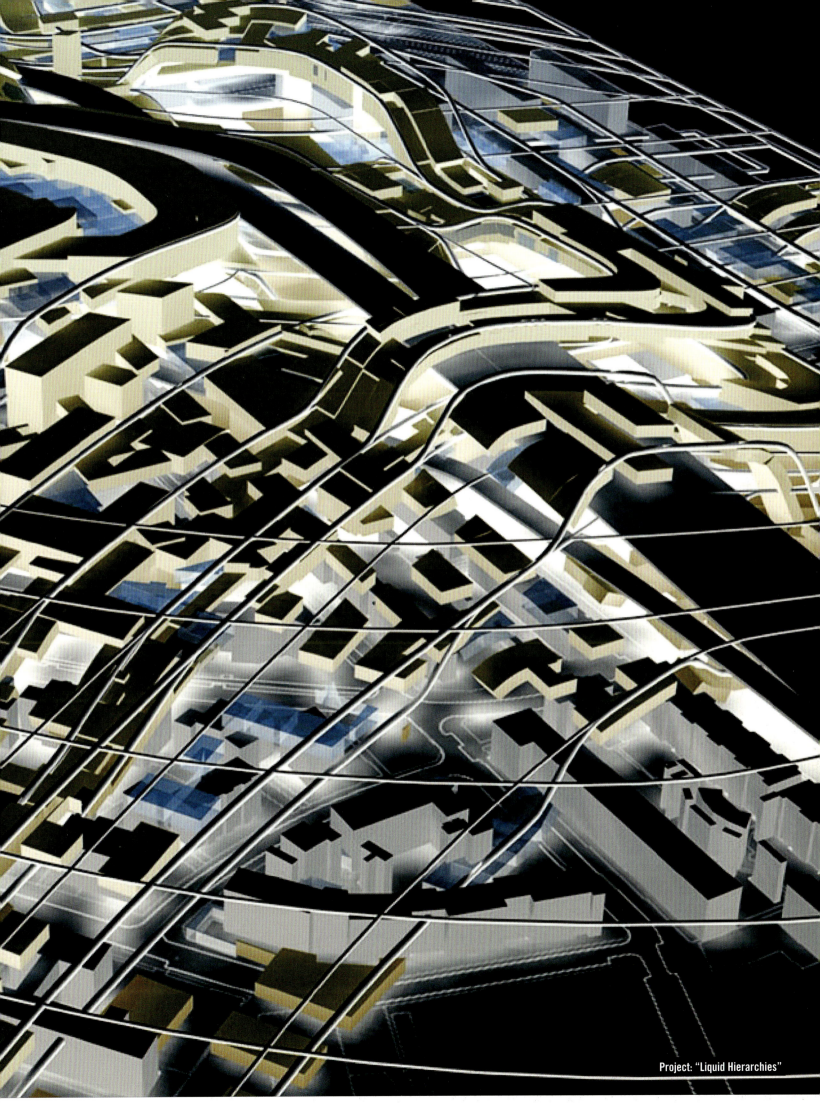

Project: "Liquid Hierarchies"

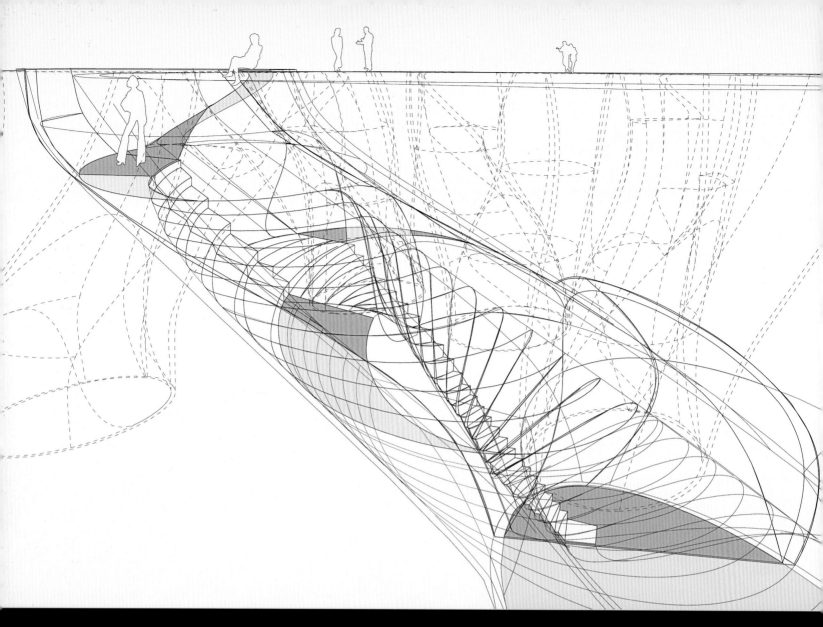

Metropolitan Forms of Living

Matthias Bär, Jörg Hugo, Jens Mehlan, Christoph Opperer

Developed for a specific site in Rotterdam, the project targets the spatial and social challenges connected with dense agglomerations in low-rise environments. It aims at leveraging the benefits of generative design tools in order to find an alternative architectural model within the constraints of such settings.

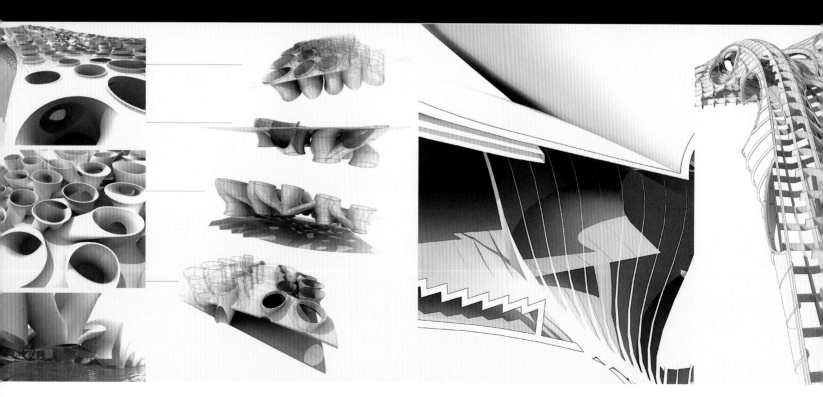

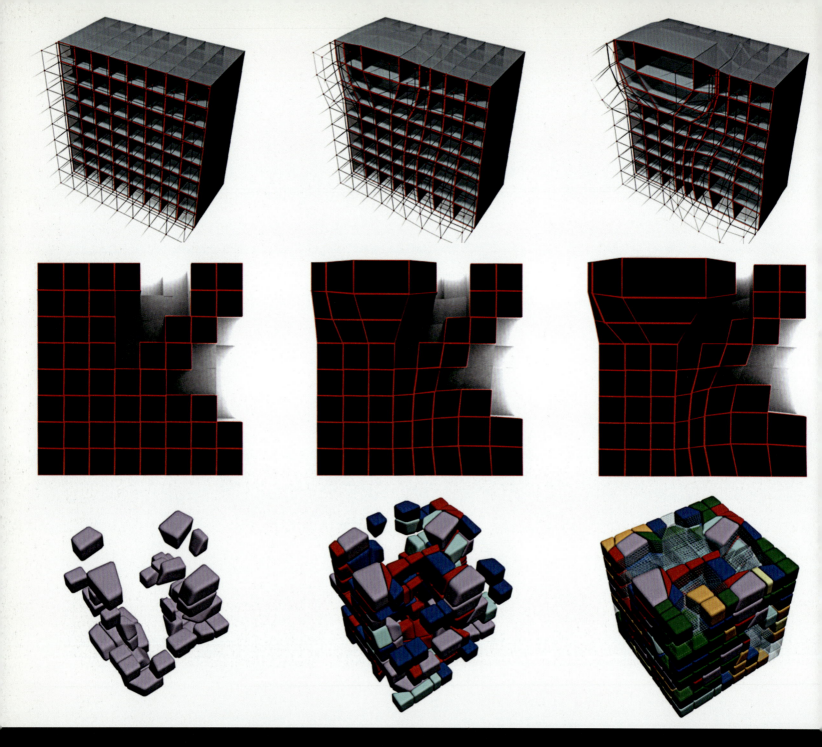

Liquid Hierarchies

Ivana Jug, Florian Medicus, Felix Strasser, Katharina Tanzberger

This project represents an early experiment, testing which parameters could be used to trigger and then control an urban growth process. Located along a highway between Rotterdam and Delft this structure shows an evolutional state reflecting traffic, existing urban fabric and the dependence on natural light. This program has been 'successfully' tested in various scales and environments (London, Patagonia).

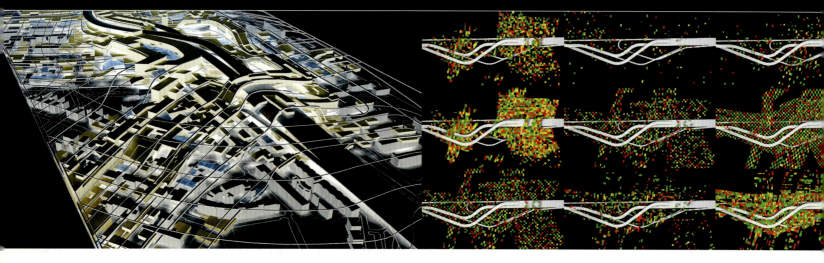

Metropoli_X

Simone Fuchs, Florian Gypser, Felix Lohrmann, Johannes Schafelner

The project conceives a new city block based on different programmatic and urban requirements. Spatial continuity and a complementing rectangular structure allow new and unexpected forms of living.

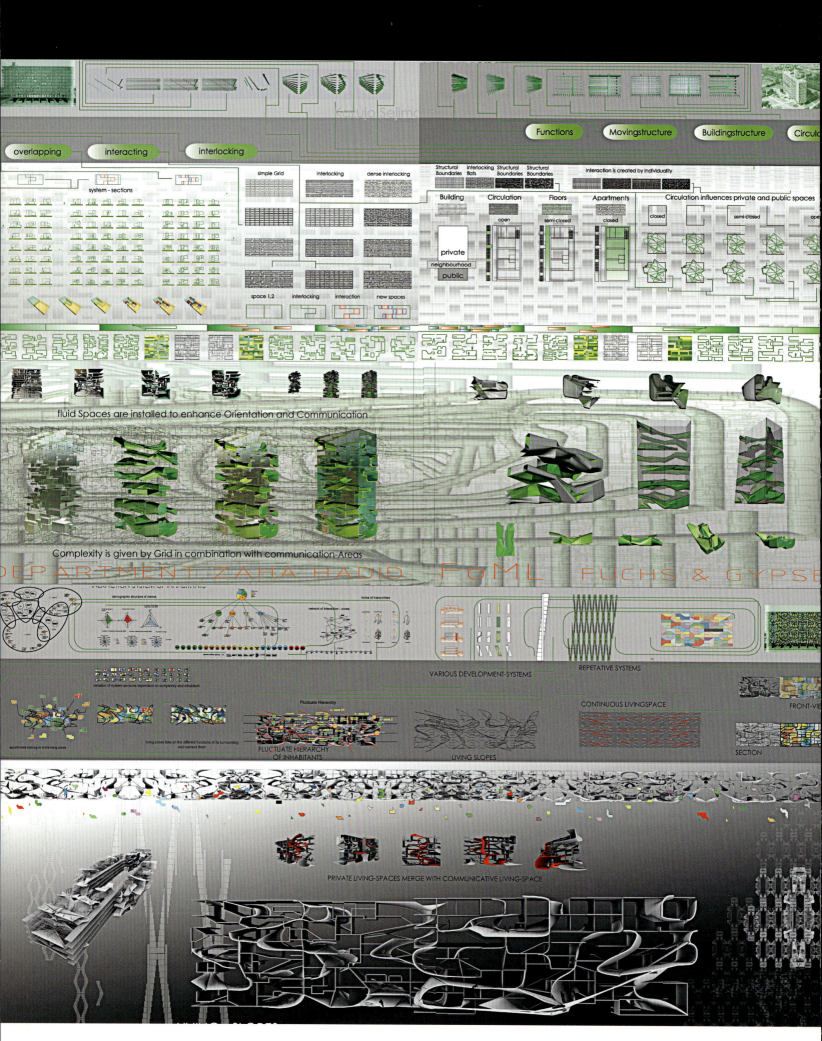

overlapping   interacting   interlocking

Functions   Movingstructure   Buildingstructure   Circul

system - sections

simple Grid   interlocking   dense interlocking

space 1.2   interlocking   interaction   new spaces

Structural Boundaries   Interlocking flats   Structural Boundaries   Structural Boundaries   interaction is created by individuality

Building   Circulation   Floors   Apartments   Circulation influences private and public spaces

open   semi-closed   closed   closed   semi-closed   ope

private   neighbourhood   public

fluid Spaces are installed to enhance Orientation and Communication

Complexity is given by Grid in combination with communication-Areas

DEPARTMENT ZAHA HADID   FoML   FUCHS & GYPSE

VARIOUS DEVELOPMENT-SYSTEMS   REPETATIVE SYSTEMS

Fluctuate Hierarchy   CONTINUOUS LIVINGSPACE   FRONT-VIE

FLUCTUATE HIERARCHY OF INHABITANTS   LIVING SLOPES   SECTION

PRIVATE LIVING-SPACES MERGE WITH COMMUNICATIVE LIVING-SPACE

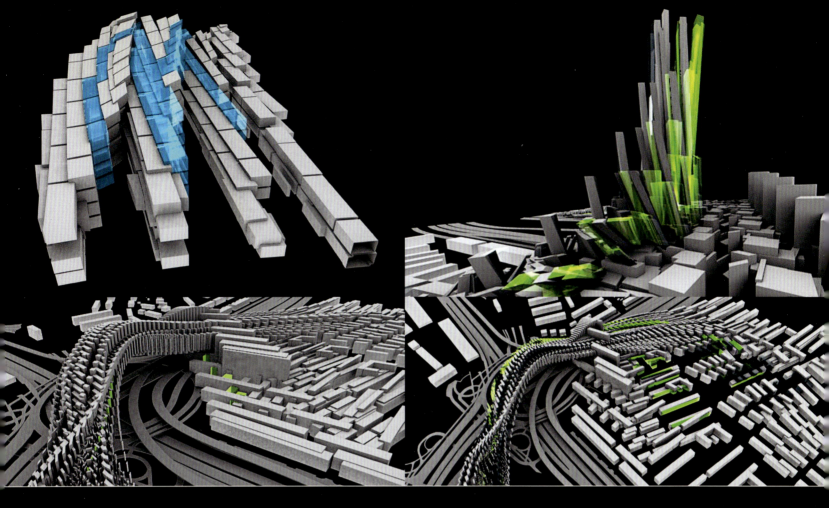

Z-Pattern / Iteration Matrix

Robert Grössinger, Katharina Mayr, Paul Peyrer-Heimstätt,
Eva Scheucher, Gabriel Zirm

The project refers to the existing urban structure and uses the given urban typologies as a basis for different digital "sweep" operations. The proposal thus respects the existing city structure while offering radically new complex urban structures with a high degree of spatial and programmatic diversity.

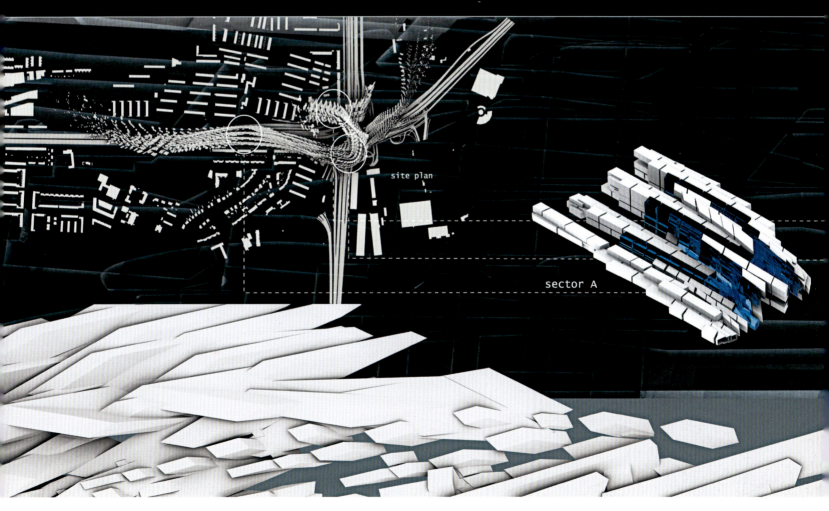

site plan

sector A

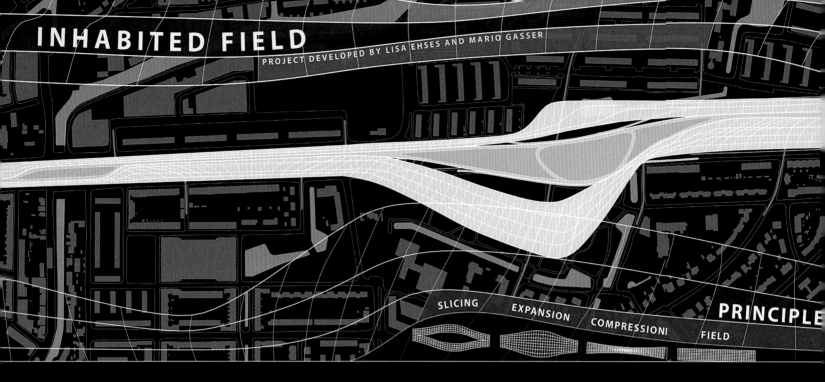

INHABITED FIELD

PROJECT DEVELOPED BY LISA EHSES AND MARIO GASSER

SLICING EXPANSION COMPRESSIONI FIELD PRINCIPLE

Inhabited Field

Lisa Ehses, Mario Gasser

A grid spanning the highway is deformed by the edge of adjacent buildings, sliced to allow sun exposure and folded in order to form separate units. Ramps connect the structure to the existing circulation paths.

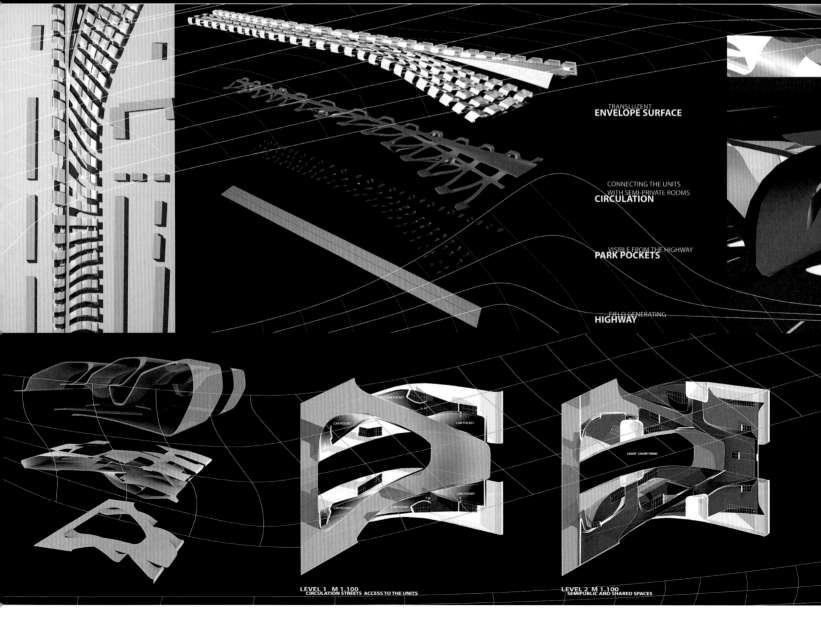

TRANSLUZENT
ENVELOPE SURFACE

CONNECTING THE UNITS
WITH SEMI-PRIVATE ROOMS
CIRCULATION

VISIBLE FROM THE HIGHWAY
PARK POCKETS

FIELD GENERATING
HIGHWAY

LEVEL 1 M 1:100
CIRCULATION STREETS ACCESS TO THE UNITS

LEVEL 2 M 1:100
SEMIPUBLIC AND SHARED SPACES

INSIDE RIBBON
STRUCTURES AND CONNECTS THE UNITS

ENVELOPE SURFACE
CREATES FOLDED AND SHARED SPACES

STRUCTURING THE FIELD

PRINCIPLES FOR COMPRESSION

EXPANSION AND COMPRESSION OF THE FIELD CREATES ENCLOSED AND OPEN
SHARED SPACES

SECTION M 1.100

1.100
EAS

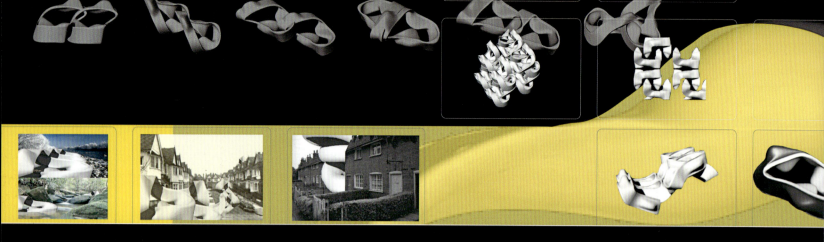

Infinite Living

Eldine Heep, Gerhild Orthacker

The qualities of coherence and continuity of Mobius loops is seen as a basis for new contemporary forms of metropolitan life: continuous open spatial structures allowing for differentiated programmatic usage.

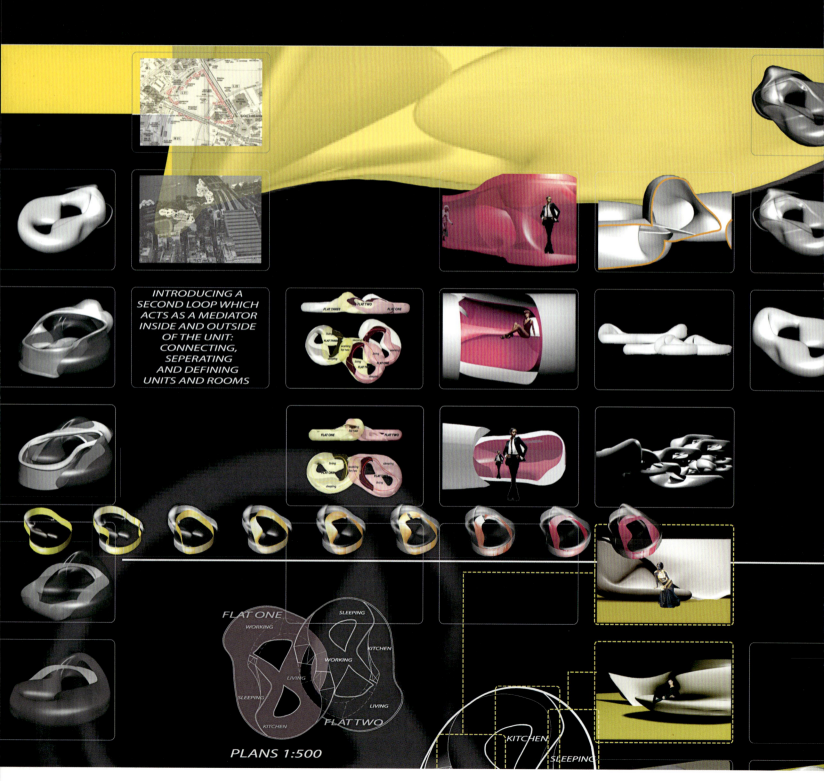

INTRODUCING A
SECOND LOOP WHICH
ACTS AS A MEDIATOR
INSIDE AND OUTSIDE
OF THE UNIT:
CONNECTING,
SEPERATING
AND DEFINING
UNITS AND ROOMS

FLAT ONE
WORKING
SLEEPING
WORKING
KITCHEN
LIVING
SLEEPING
LIVING
KITCHEN
FLAT TWO

PLANS 1:500

KITCHEN
SLEEPING

24 Hours Min Max Housing

Petra De Colle, Sophie Luger, Peter Schamberger

The concept of a constantly changing city constitutes the basis of the project. The required programmatic change during a day is taken into account as well as the creation of flexible, new housing types.

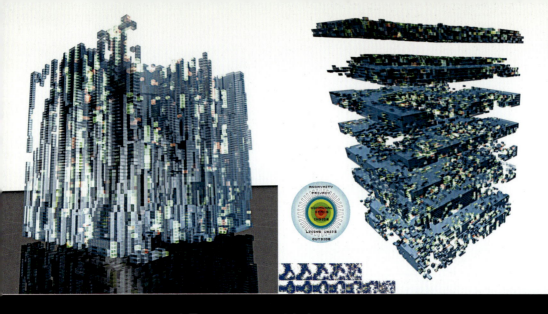

▲ Mobile and Temporary Living
Andrea Kessler, Eva Scheucher

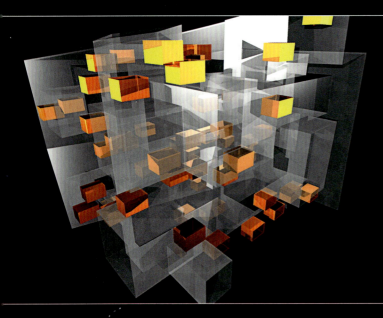

▲ Arabic Cities and Cultures
Peter Schamberger, Georg Wizany

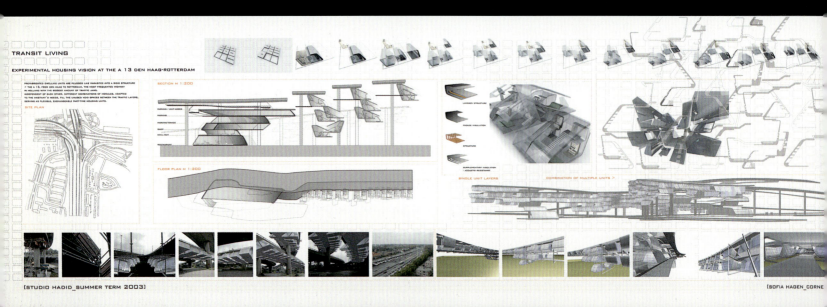

▲ Flexible Housing Typologies
Sofia Maria Hagen, Cornelia Klien, Michaela Weisskirchner

▲ **Loos Remixed**

Yonka Dragomanska, Kaloyan Erevinov, Katherina Ortner

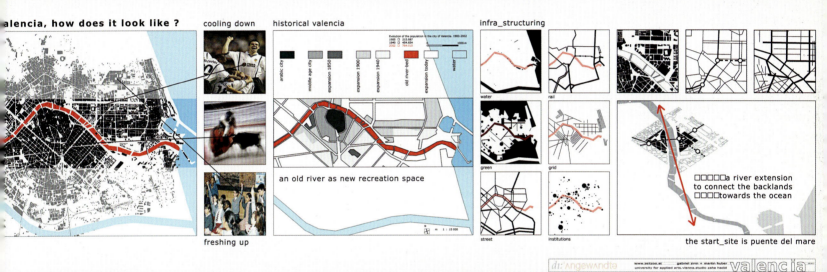

valencia, how does it look like ?

cooling down

historical valencia

infra_structuring

an old river as new recreation space

freshing up

water

rail

green

grid

street

institutions

□□□□□a river extension
to connect the backlands
□□□□towards the ocean

the start_site is puente del mare

▲ **Bofil Walden / Residential Building Barcelona**

Martin Huber, Gabriel Zirm

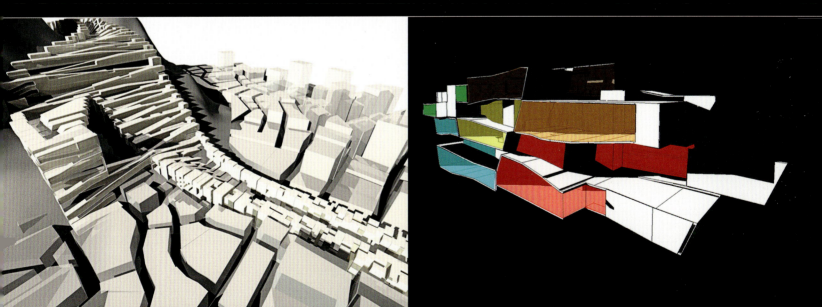

▲ **Forms of Metropolitan Living**

Julian Breinersdorfer, Markus Innauer, Andrés Schenker

BIOMIMETIC

2003 - 2004

Rather than falling back upon well-rehearsed spatio-kinetic systems, like striated of folded surfaces, a whole new range of physical systems should be generated on the basis of biological analogies. The world of organic life might be scanned on many scales, from large organisms or even biotopes to individual microbes, in search of models and principles that can meaningfully transferred to the domain of architecture.

IN PARTICULAR THE FOLLOWING TYPES OF SYSTEMS SHOULD BE INVESTIGATED:

1. envelope and boundary systems
2. structural systems
3. kinetic systems
4. systems of aggregation and organization

As a result of the investigation of biological systems, different bio-mimetic approaches, isolated from these systems, will be used to expand the repertoire of architecture along these four above-mentioned dimensions. Each of these systems might be taken from one and the same organism or each of these systems might be taken from a different organism. The analyses, syntheses and elaboration of a biological model as an architectural system might proceed in three steps:

1. The selective, but authentic, modelling of the organism's system.
2. The proposition of technological or artificial equivalents – quasi-prosthesis.
3. The transfer of isolated aspects, models and principles of the organism's system, extracted into the construction of a new architectural system that might at a later point function in the context of the project scenario.

This analogical method relies on a very precise initial investigation of the respective biological models and principles. Quick metaphorical or superficial applications should be avoided.

During the course of investigation one should always keep in mind the organisational differences between the classical notion of an organism and the more contemporary notion of the assemblage:

definite type (idea, ideal form) vs. no a-priori form, fixed number of parts in fixed relations vs. loosely coupled networks of elements, closed systems vs. open systems, clear purposes and functions vs. temporary unexpected functions, organized and well-proportioned systems vs. unpredictable self-organisations.

AT THE END OF THE TERM TWO INVESTIGATIONS HAVE TO BE PRESENTED:

First, the bio-mimetic models, which have been analysed, have to be presented as physical and digital responsive systems.

Finally, a sketch design has to be presented, executed as an STL model: the first attempt to synthesise the bio-mimetic systems into a tectonic or architectural model.

"One side of a machinic assemblage faces the strata, which doubtless make it a kind of organism, or signifying totality, [...] it also has a side facing a body without organs, which is continually dismantling the organism, causing asygnifying particles or pure intensities [...]"
(Deleuze/Guatarri, A Thousand Plateaus, p.4)

"The ant's path is irregular, complex and hard to describe. But its complexity is really a complexity in the surface of the beach, not a complexity in the ant."

"Man as a behaving system, is quite simple. The apparent complexity of his behavior over time is largely a reflection of the complexity of the environment in which he finds himself."
(Herbert Simon, The Sciences of the Artificial)

" [...] a profound alteration in the structure and function of the vital organs, an alteration such that it constitutes a new way of life for the organism, new behavior which prudent therapy must take into account" (p.84)

"[...] understanding the sense and value of the pathological act for the possibilities of existence of the modified organism [...]"(p.86)
(Georges Canguilhem, The Normal and the Pathological)

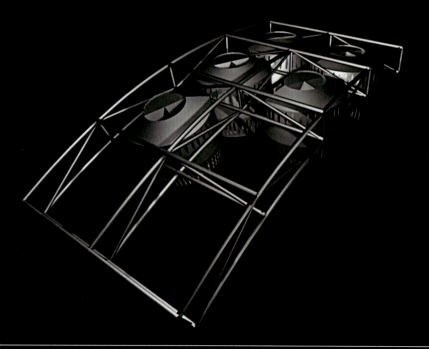

Softcell-Biomorphology versus Biomimetic

Simone Fuchs, Felix Lohrmann, Johannes Schafelner, Eva Scheucher

Looking at the adaptive qualities of biological soft cells as a first step the project proposes a villa as a coherent formal system with a high degree of contextual and programmatic differentiation.

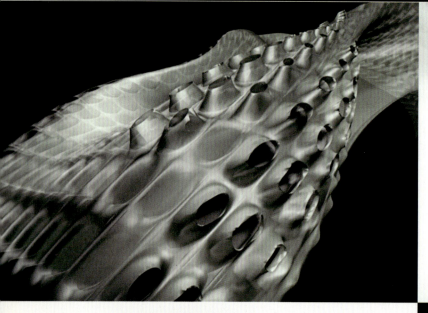

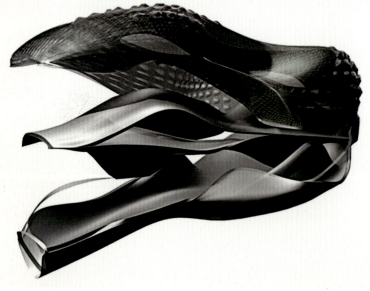

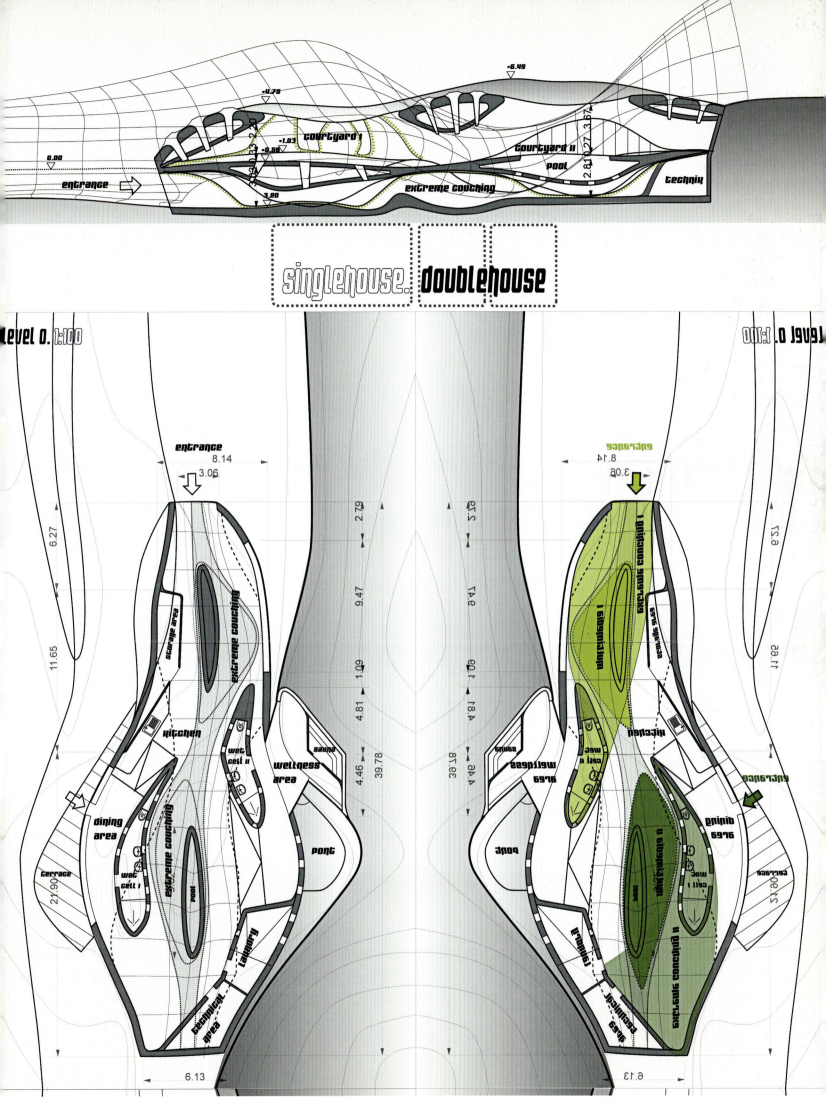

singlehouse. doublehouse

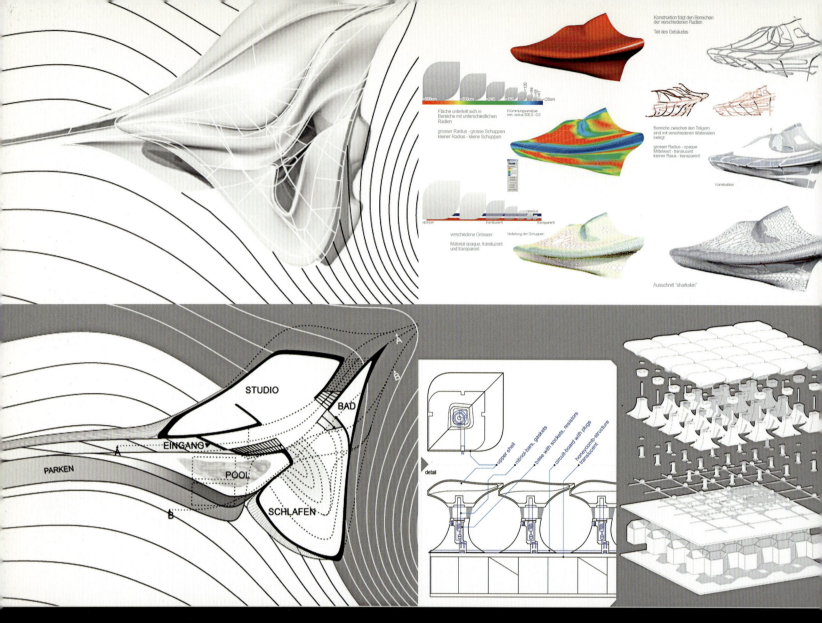

Sharkskin

Sebastian Gallnbrunner, Mario Gasser, Peter Schamberger

The generating force of the project is the analysis of streamline principles on a shark's skin. Out of this research a catalogue of different behaviors of scale aggregations has emerged. These principles were applied to the design of the building — following the main wind direction — as well as the facade — distributing the air among the surface of the building as natural ventilation.

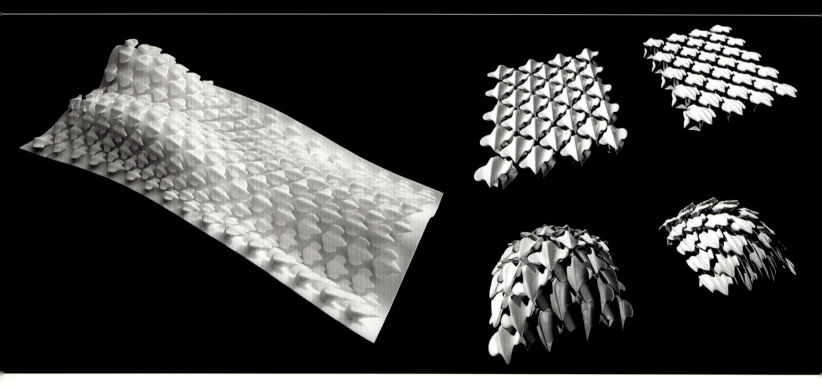

Leaf / Tree

Agnieszka Grochowska, Peter Mitterer, Ewelina Wojtkowiak

The project "Leaf Tree" concentrates on two key properties of foliage: Firstly, on the arrangement of leaves which allows for maximized light intake and, secondly, their microstructure which lends each leaf astounding structural performance. These two references are then translated into the context of a villa typology located in extreme topographic conditions.

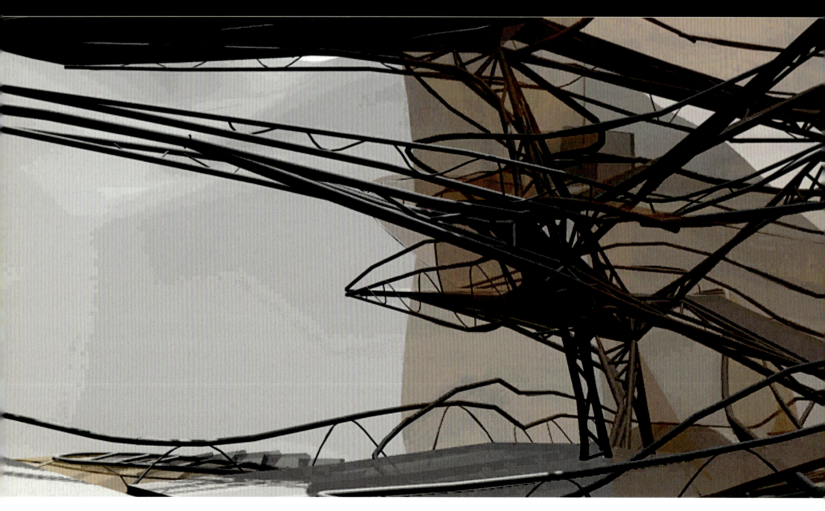

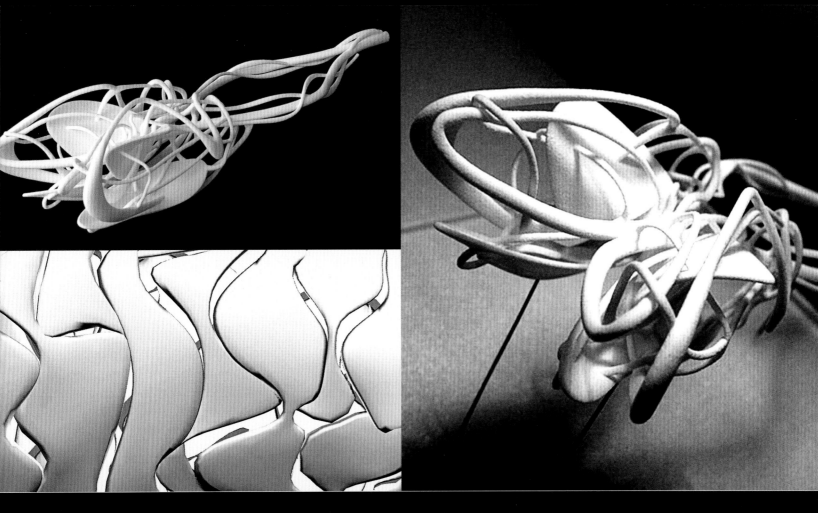

Dragonfly

Eldine Heep, Matthias Moroder, Ariane Stracke

Investigation of morphological, structural, and functional analogies between biological system of the dragonfly tracheids and technical application of its properties in architecture especially on such as performative property of stiffness control and shape adaptation driven by fluids/air-pressure.

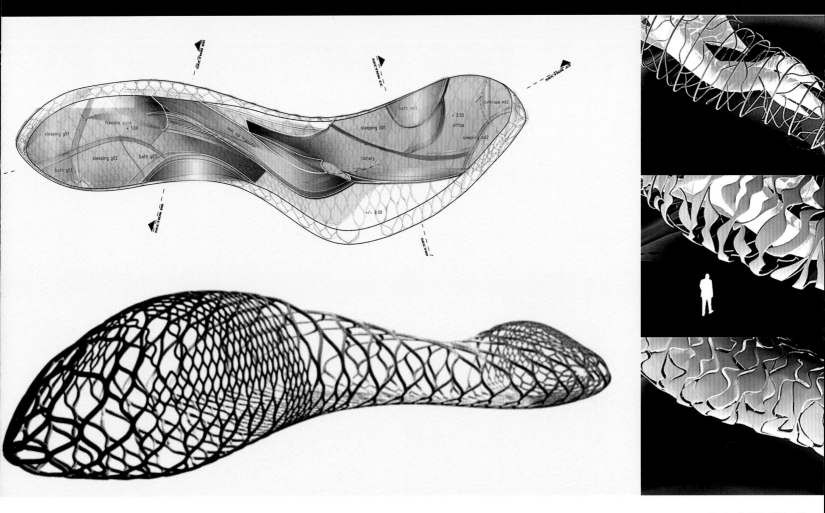

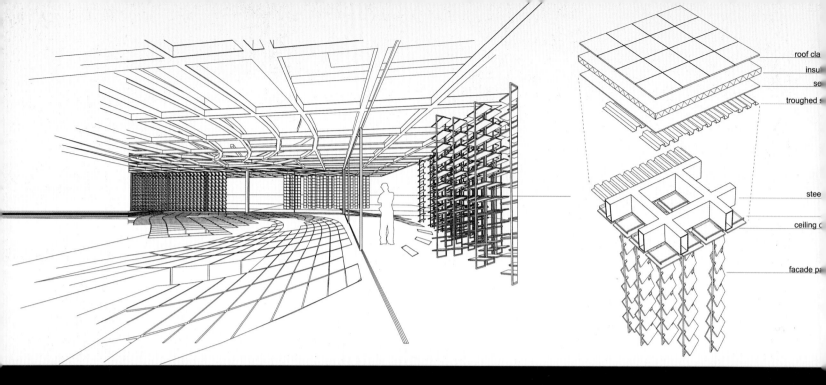

roof cla
insu
se
troughed s

stee

ceiling

facade pa

Swarms – Forms of Aggregation

Nina Gorfer, Daniel Grünkranz, Markus Innauer

The project studies swarm and flocking behavior in nature and investigates possible fields of application within the domain of architecture. The key interest is not only the aesthetic capacity of multiplicities, but also the idea of developing an architectural model that allows for adaptive behavior and changes in overall performance through local reactions of individual components.

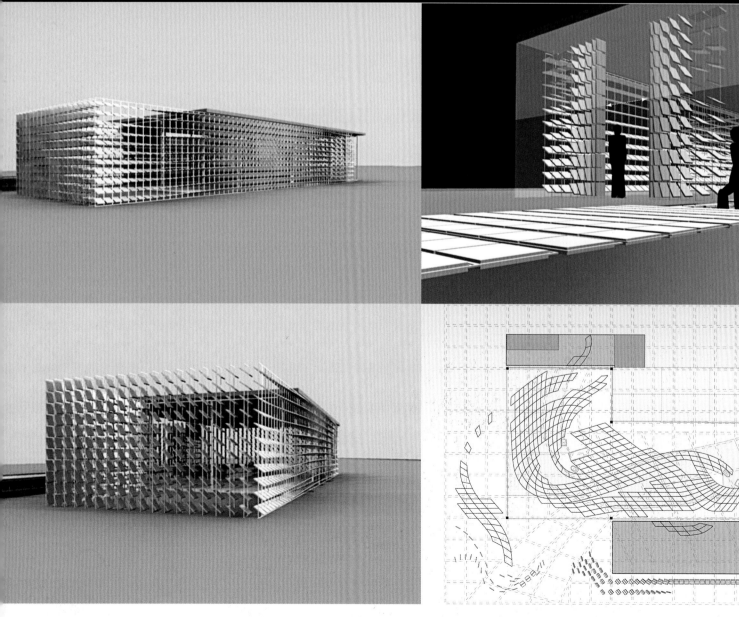

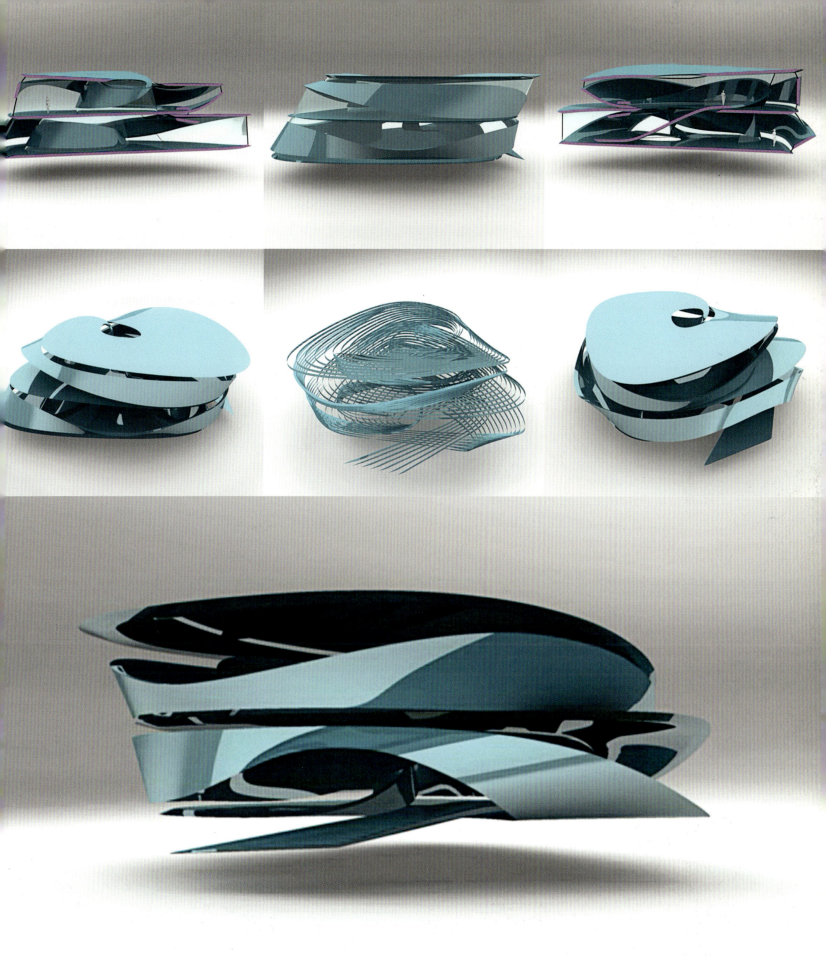

Shells / Epitonium

Kaloyan Erevinov, Tamara Friebel, Christo Penev

The project focuses on the key property of all spiral forms and seeks to transfer it as an abstract architectural concept: Always growing, yet never covering the same ground the spiral is not merely an explanation of the past but is also its own prophecy of the future. While it defines what has already happened, it also keeps leading to new discoveries.

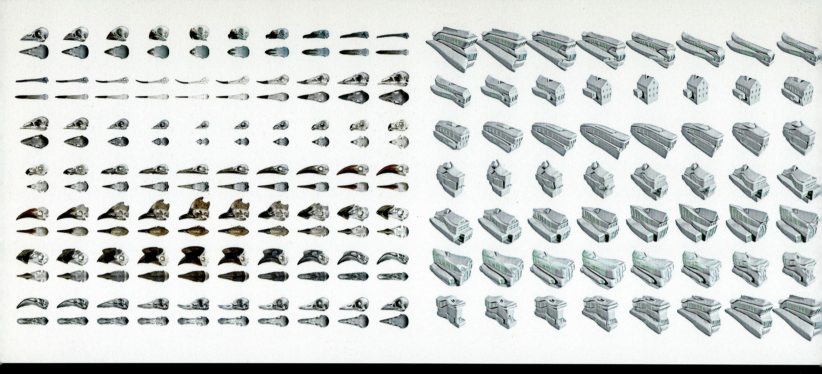

Bird Skulls / Morphogenese

Robert Grössinger, Paul Peyrer-Heimstätt, Florian Pucher

The project was conducted as an exercise to analyze, understand and transform natural forms and principles into architecture. Even though birds look completely different from each other, their bone structure is alike and only different in size, shape and proportion. 'Bird Skulls' applies this insight to houses and builds up a diverse catalogue of villa-phenotypes.

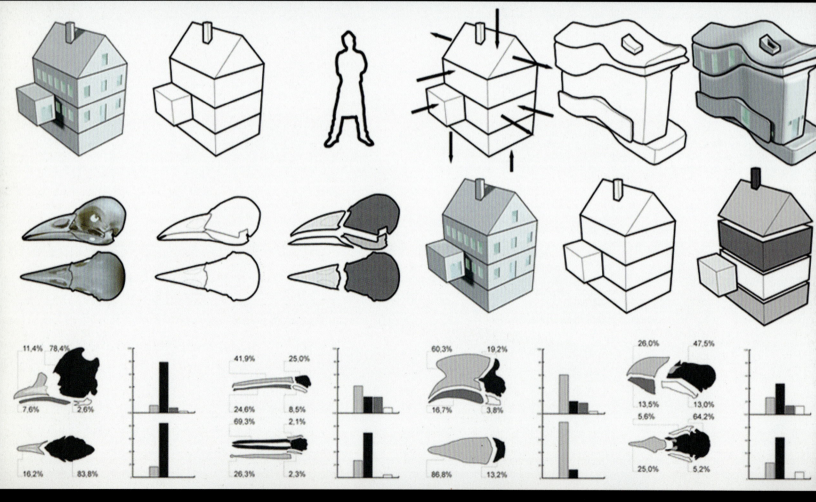

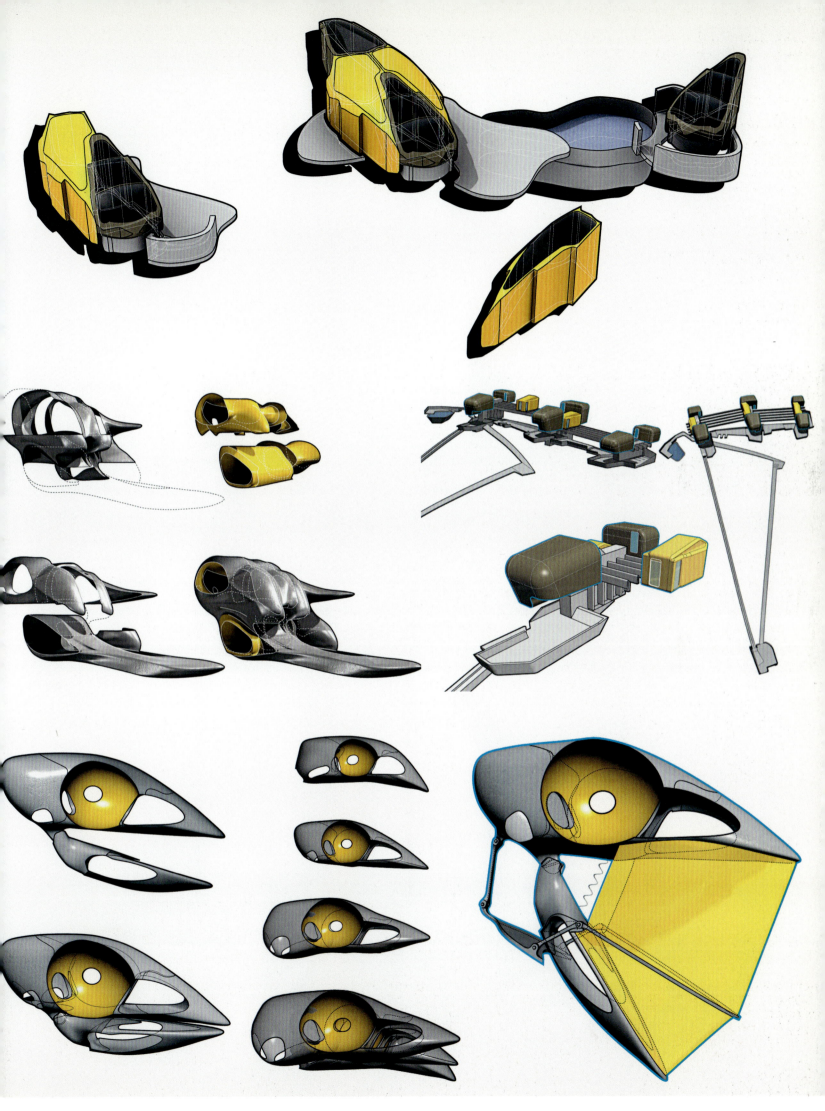

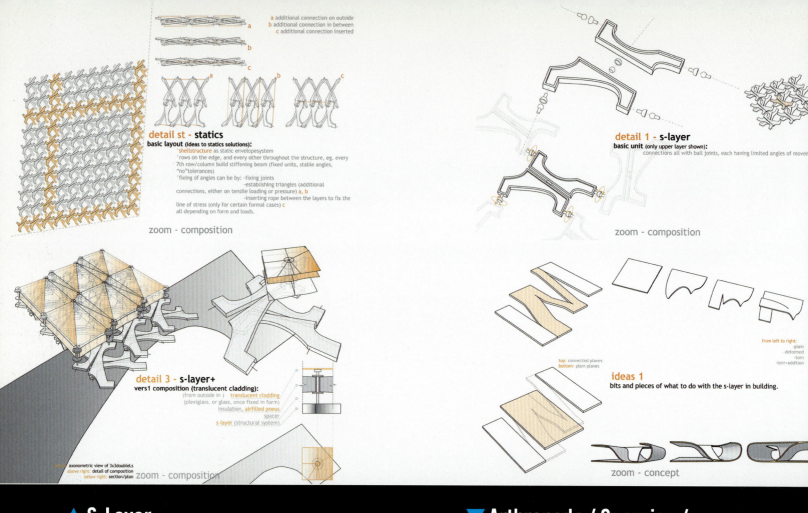

a additional connection on outside
b additional connection in between
c additional connection inserted

detail st - statics
basic layout (ideas to statics solutions):
- shellstructure as static envelopesystem
- rows on the edge, and every other throughout the structure, eg. every 7th row/column build stiffening beam (fixed units, stable angles, "no"tolerances)
- fixing of angles can be by:
  - fixing joints
  - establishing triangles (additional connections, either on tensile loading or pressure) a, b
  - inserting rope between the layers to fix the line of stress (only for certain formal cases) c
  all depending on form and loads.

zoom - composition

detail 3 - s-layer+
vers1 composition (translucent cladding):
(from outside in) translucent cladding
(plexiglass, or glass, once fixed in form)
insulation, airfilled pneus
spacer
s-layer (structural system)

above: axonometric view of 3x3doubleLs
above right: detail of composition
below right: section/plan
zoom - composition

detail 1 - s-layer
basic unit (only upper layer shown):
connections all with ball joints, each having limited angles of movement

zoom - composition

from left to right:
-plain
-deformed
-torn
-torn+addition

top: connected planes
bottom: plain planes

ideas 1
bits and pieces of what to do with the s-layer in building.

zoom - concept

▲ S-Layer
Marion Lubitz, Katharina Tanzberger, Georg Wizany

▼ Arthropoda / Scorpion / Horseshoe Crab
Julian Breinersdorfer, Markus Innauer, Tyan Masten (UCLA), Andrés Schenker

The Horseshoecrab Family (Arthropoda):
Chapter one: the crab herself
fig. 1
usual Appereance

The Horseshoecrab Family (Arthropoda):
Chapter two: it's favourite blue ancestor
fig. 1
usual Appereance

The Horseshoecrab Family (Arthropoda):
Chapter three: the shell stadium
fig. 1
usual Appereance

The Horseshoecrab Family (Arthropoda):
Chapter four: the cousin from china
fig. 1
usual Appereance

▲ Plankton
Irina Busurina, Sabrina Miletich, Birgit Schmidt

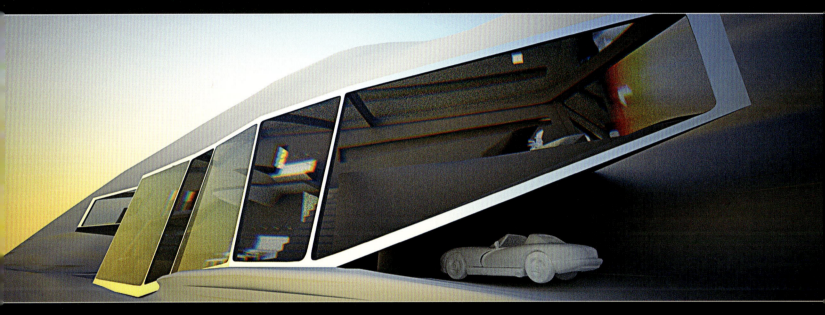

▲ Human Spine
Maren Klasing, Cornelis van Almsick

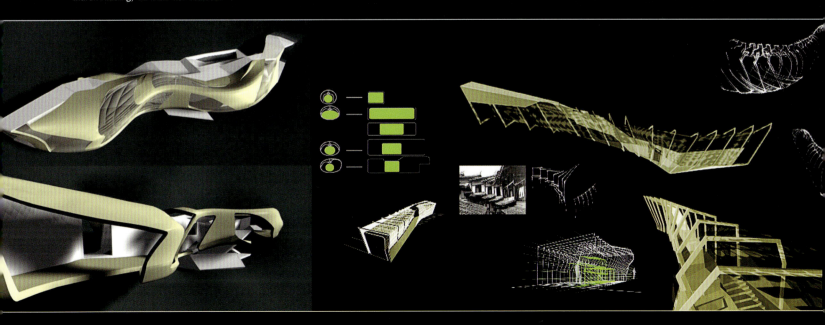

▲ Snakes / Scale
Cornelis van Almsick , Lukas Haller, Katharina Mayr, Gerhild Orthacker, Judith Schafelner

NEW URBAN GEOMETRIES
From Typology to Topology

2004 - 2005

Up to this day architecture and urbanism have relied on the same formal geometric resources since the inception of western civilization in ancient Greece.

Classical architecture privileged clear and distinct Platonic figures such as squares, triangles and circles. Symmetries and simple proportions ruled all spatial compositions. Modern architecture allowed for asymmetry and stretched proportions in so called "dynamic equilibrium" compositions. However, orthogonality and modularity (grids) were still privileged. Deconstructivism opened architecture to the full range of angles, allowed for broken figures, interpenetration and incomplete compositions. Folding in architecture introduced the dynamic use of curve linearity, splines and nurbs. Figures started to emerge as modulations of a continuous surface.

RESEARCH PHASE
In order to systematically expand the repertoire of urban geometries, the discipline of geometry will be investigated to discover what it has to offer beyond the classical canon. The appropriation of complex geometric patterns and the mathematical concepts, which describe these patterns, will become a source for the experimental development of new complex urban geometries. Due to their large scale nature, urban geometries – in distinction to architectural geometries – normally privilege two of the three dimensions of space. Therefore 2D patterns will be the first objects of investigations. The mathematical fields that might be investigated as source domains include Topology, Fractal Geometry and Combinatorics.

The main interest lies in both, the recursive generation as well as the organizational properties of the patterns investigated. For the analysis of urban patterns with respect to organizational concepts Bill Hillier's "Space is the Machine" and Frei Otto's work on the optimization of path networks will be researched.

The task is to achieve a high degree of legible organizational complexity within a single plane through an intricate system of order. The key challenge is to produce complexity that can still be grasped and navigated on the basis of its laws of formation.

In order to stay in touch with urban reality and to avoid getting lost in mathematical abstractions, these investigations are paralleled with urban case studies. They should focus on geometry in relation to spatial organization. Each student team is encouraged to select a suitable urban example to investigate, among which might be the Forbidden City (Beijing), Broadacre City (by Frank Lloyd Wright), Magnitogorsk (a Soviet urban master plan), Tokyo, London or Chicago.

As complex urban patterns are developed one should keep track of the various ways in which the structured field is used by the urban population. Particle animations should be used to simulate the urban flows within the system.

DESIGN PHASE
The design phase will involve the development of an urban structure, either the intervention within an existing urban fabric or the invention of a new town.

The abstract patterns will be confronted with the task of organizing an urban life cycle through the allocation and relation of different components for habitation, production, administration and consumption. We expect that the imposition of a new urban geometry will have an impact upon the architectural elements placed within such a system. Therefore the design will include the development of new architectural typologies. Each student team will first develop an urban master plan defining the three primary layers of any urban field: Urban Massing, Circulation patterns and Land Use.

The urban massing describes a swarm-formation of many buildings. These buildings form a continuously changing field, whereby no two buildings are exactly the same and there are lawful continuities that cohere this multiplicity of buildings. The results of this process may be analyzed by means of the concept of genotype/phenotype. The genotype(s) are to be constructed as parametric models whereby the systematic variations of its parameters produce a multiplicity of phenol-types, which constitute the urban field. The variation of parameters should not be randomized, but should rather follow defined laws of transformation that give coherence to the field. Such laws which give an internal logic to the field should also be correlated to contextual conditions, to the system of circulation, and to the laws of programmatic distribution.

In a next step, design work will go beyond the mere shaping of building mass. The genotype become complex, organized systems that should define the following subsystems:

- *Systems of internal subdivision, i.e. sub-volumes,*
  floors, walls, voids, etc.
- *Structural systems*
- *System of internal circulation*
- *Building envelopes (defining opaque and transparent areas)*

A genotype should be developed, that defines and integrates all these systems across the whole range of phenol-typical variation. This task should ideally be solved by means of a single complex parametric model whereby the different sub-systems are parametrically linked with each other.

Depending upon the overall scope of difference within the field, it might be appropriate to establish more than one parametric genotype as underlying generators of the field.

Phase changes might occur beyond certain parametric thresholds or critical values. Speciation – the splintering of a population into different species – might occur when quantitative variation turns into qualitative difference.

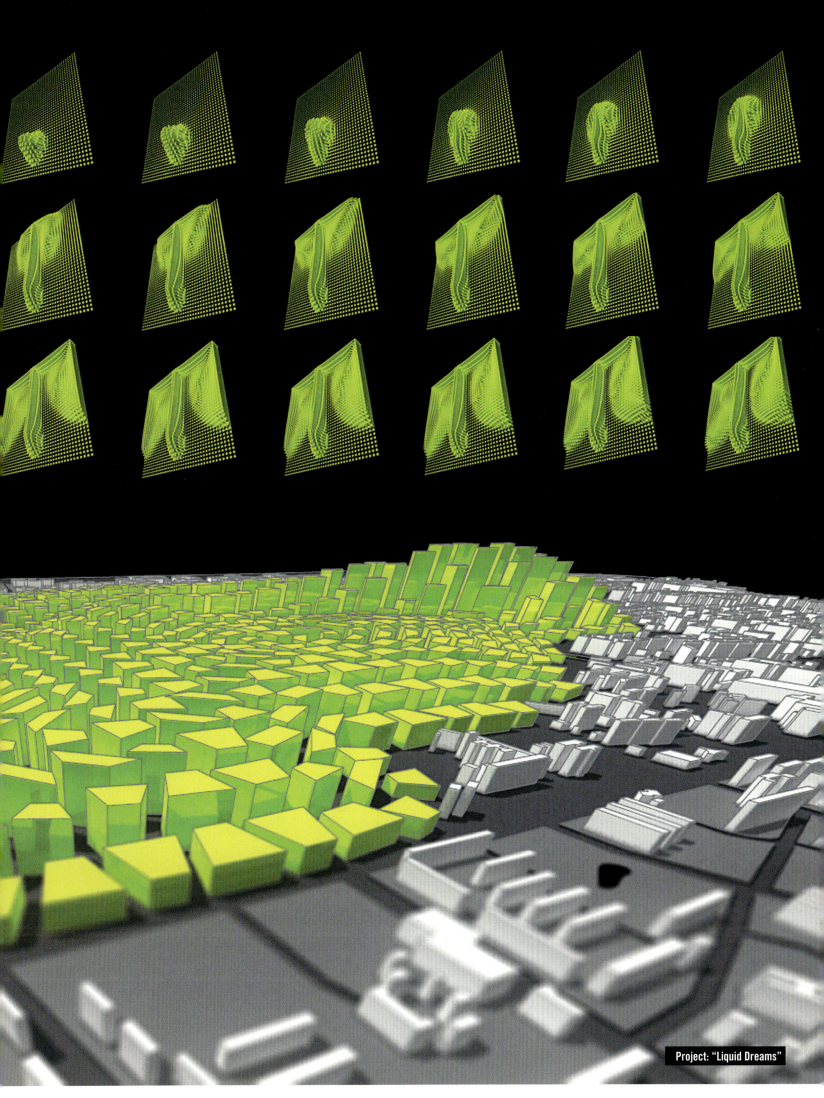

Project: "Liquid Dreams"

Shift Expectations

Agnieszka Grochowska, Birgit Schmidt, Ariane Stracke

Investigations of grid-based urban patterns in American cities and studies of Op-Art painters like Bridget Riley provide the initial impulses for an unexpected complex urban project. Irregularity within regularity is the basic principle for a continuously changing pattern that offers a great variety in generating an urban district for a Moscow site.

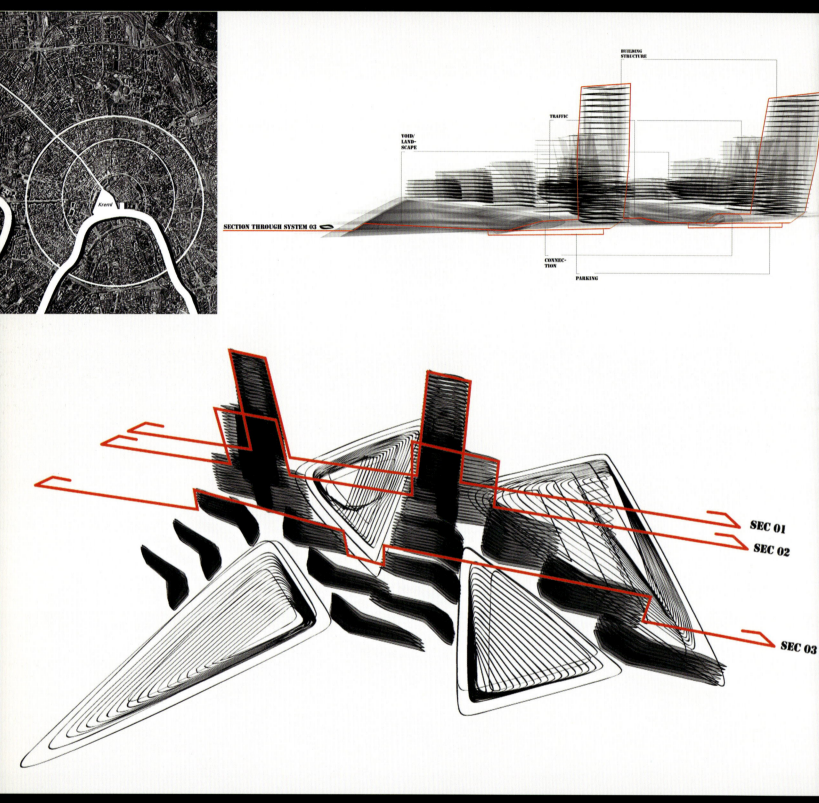

SECTION THROUGH SYSTEM 03

BUILDING STRUCTURE

TRAFFIC

VOID/ LAND-SCAPE

CONNEC-TION

PARKING

SEC 01

SEC 02

SEC 03

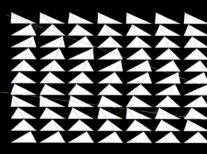

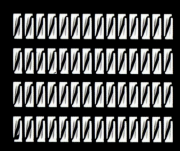

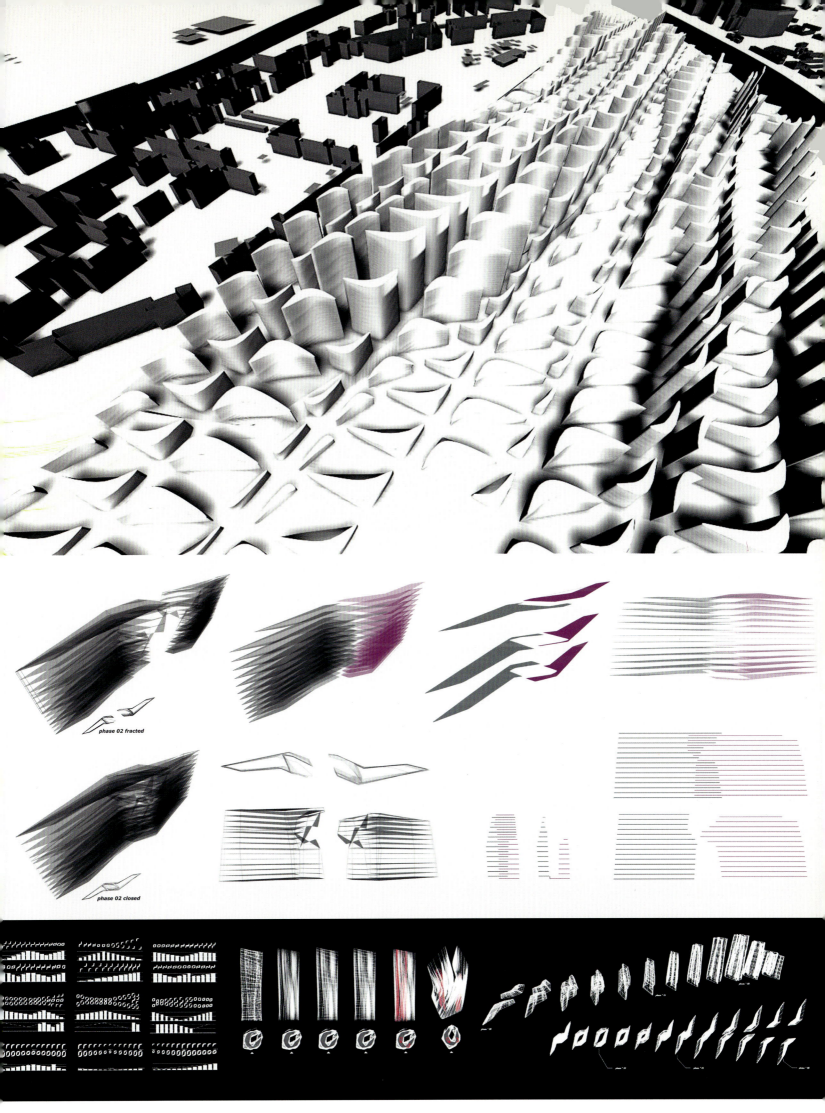

phase 02 fracted

phase 02 closed

Liquid Dreams

Peter Mitterer, Matthias Moroder, Peter Pichler

+5,00
Shopping 3200m²

+100,00
Office 860m²

+150,00
Housing 1550m²

The project refers to fluid dynamics for generating an urban master plan. Attributes like density, velocity or directionality are interpreted accordingly in further transformations to create an urban field. Additional manipulation through magnetic field conditions helps to establish a controlled pattern. The principles are applied even on the facades on a smaller scale.

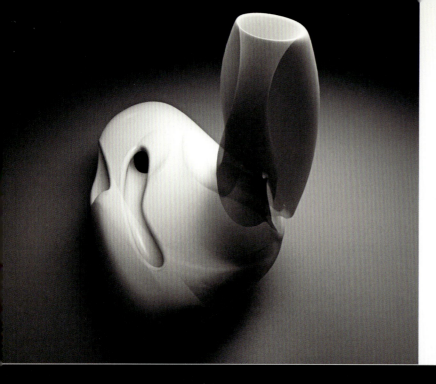

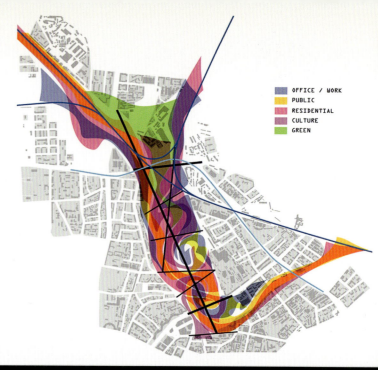

OFFICE / WORK
PUBLIC
RESIDENTIAL
CULTURE
GREEN

Sublime Attractors

Will Carson (UCLA), Kaloyan Erevinov, Tom Wünschmann

The project rejects the binary conventions of urban mapping and the divide between streets and blocks, adopting instead qualitative surveying techniques to generate a complex urban field. Beyond eidetic reduction, the depiction of the distinct importance of elements in an urban environment creates a certain spatial metaphor of attraction and interaction to be outlined as a new urban geometry.

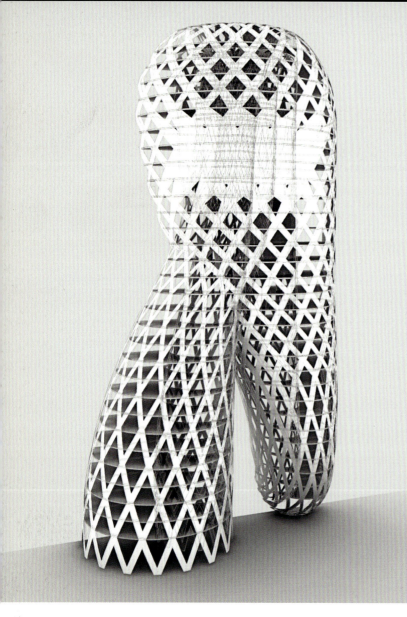

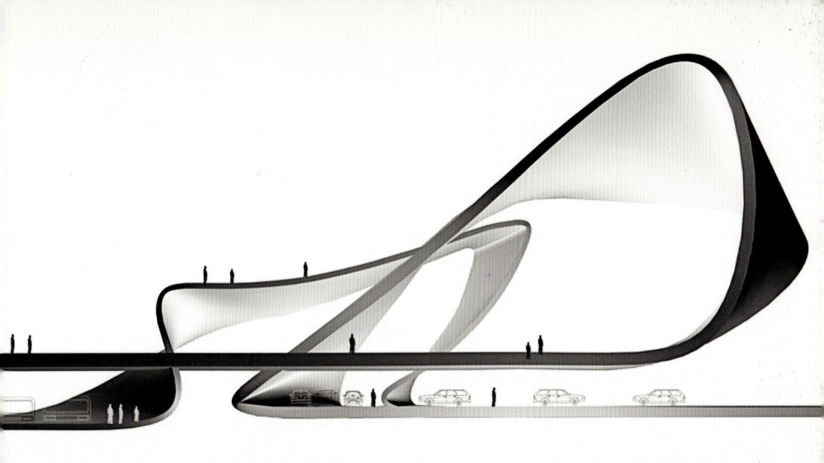

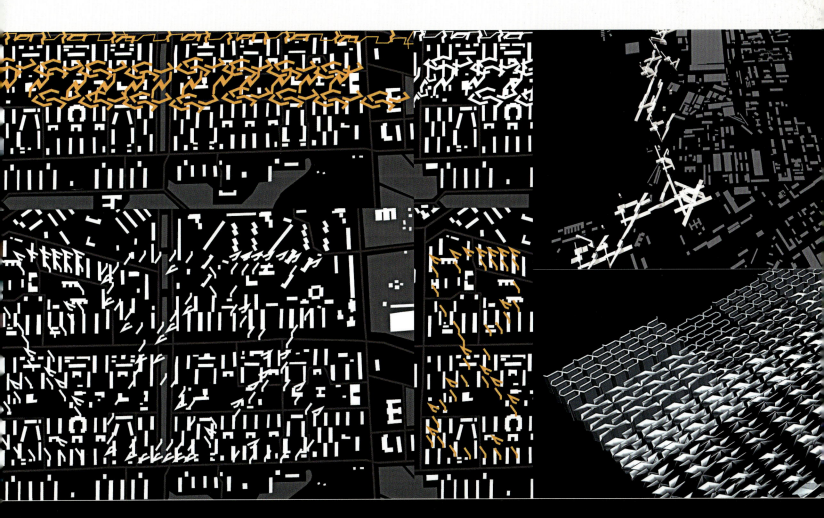

Ornamentic Loops

Martin Kleindienst, Anna Weilhartner, Philipp Weisz

Targeting urban voids in Moscow, the project investigates the potential of urban patterning and visual gestalt grouping as unifying principles in disperse and heterogeneous (sub)urban quarters. The developed set of tools operates on multiple scales (urban grid, building envelope, structure, deep facade, ornament) to achieve a cohering, yet differentiated scheme.

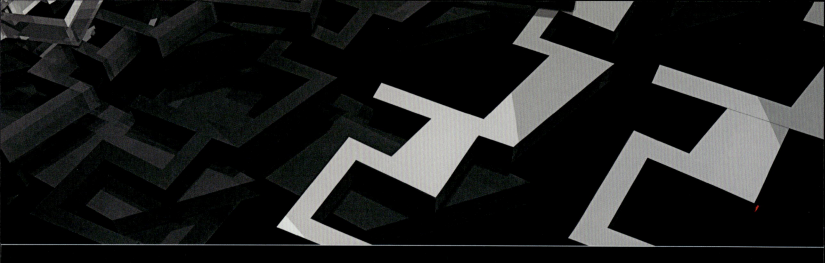

Fracts

Jasmina Frincic, Nino Tugushi

The principles of fractal scaling and complex infinity were explored to develop a set of rules, which would operate coherently on different scales. The idea of repetitive geometric characteristics and spatial organization principals was systematically tested scaling down from urban field to building typologies, to interior spaces.

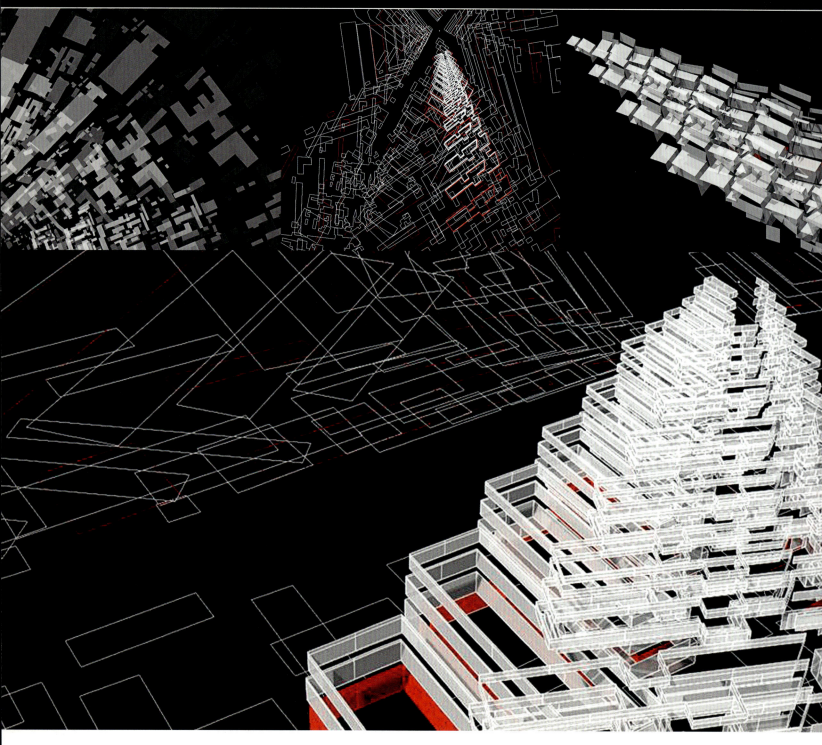

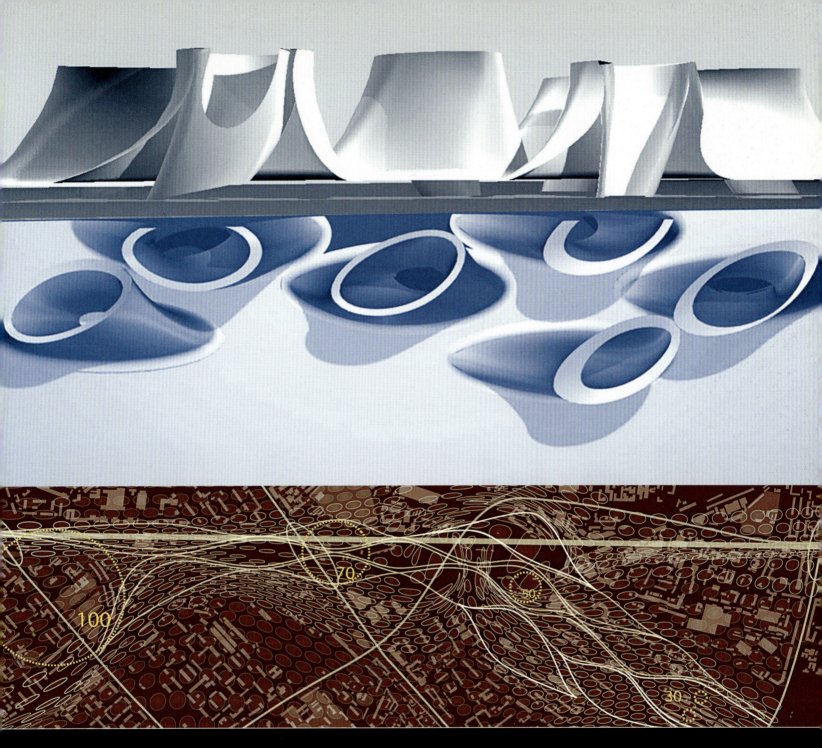

Velocity

Simone Fuchs, Konrad Hofmann, Johannes Schafelner

Based upon an extensive analysis of the existing urban circulation patterns this project explores the potentials of a homogeneous fluent urban geometry generated through the various force fields, seeking to optimize the overall city flow.

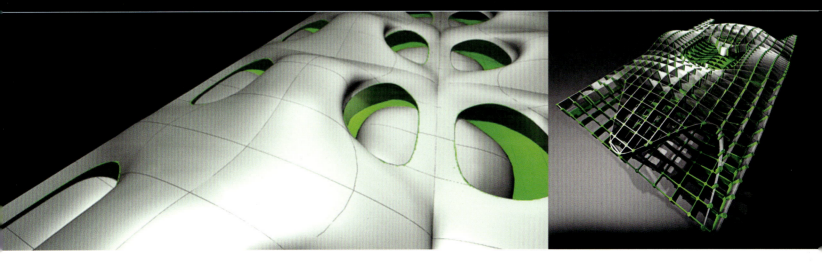

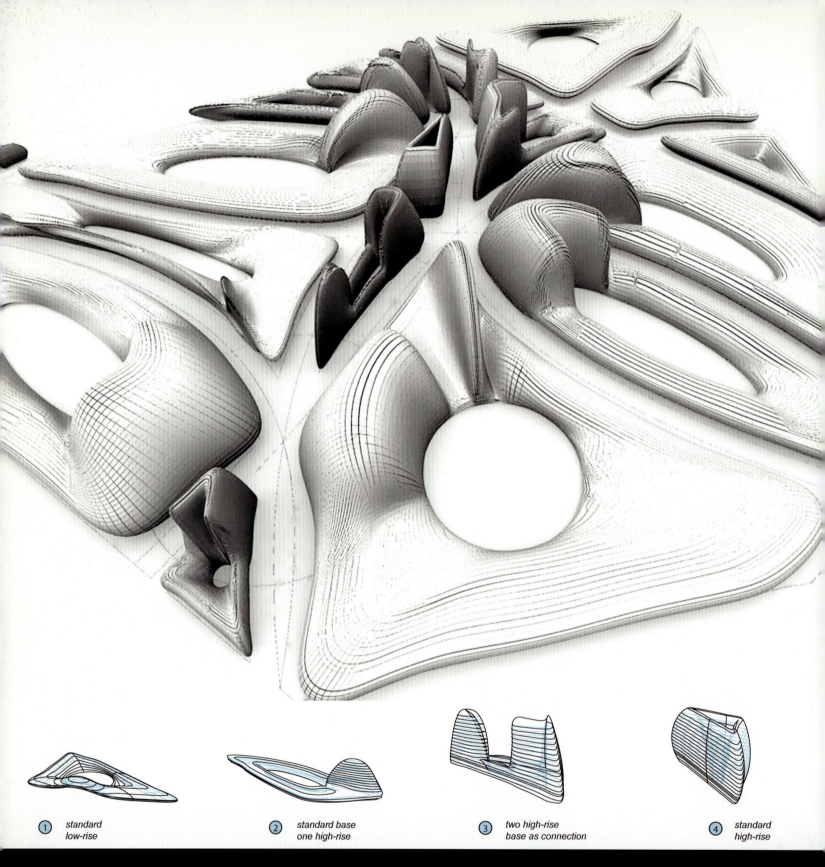

 ① *standard low-rise*

 ② *standard base one high-rise*

 ③ *two high-rise base as connection*

 ④ *standard high-rise*

Blob Box

Cornelis Van Almsick, Mirek Vavrina, Tom Wünschmann

The project is based on the idea of a "soft" city block, allowing one to react adaptively to urban and contextual density parameters by maintaining a coherent urban structure.

M:Scraper

Markus Innauer, Martine Nicolay

Stimulated by porous systems such as foam and sponges, elements were created which produce a continuous field with integrated open spaces. Delving into the world of minimal surfaces and their geometric identities, an understanding for the precious aesthetics of a non-interrupted urban space emerged.

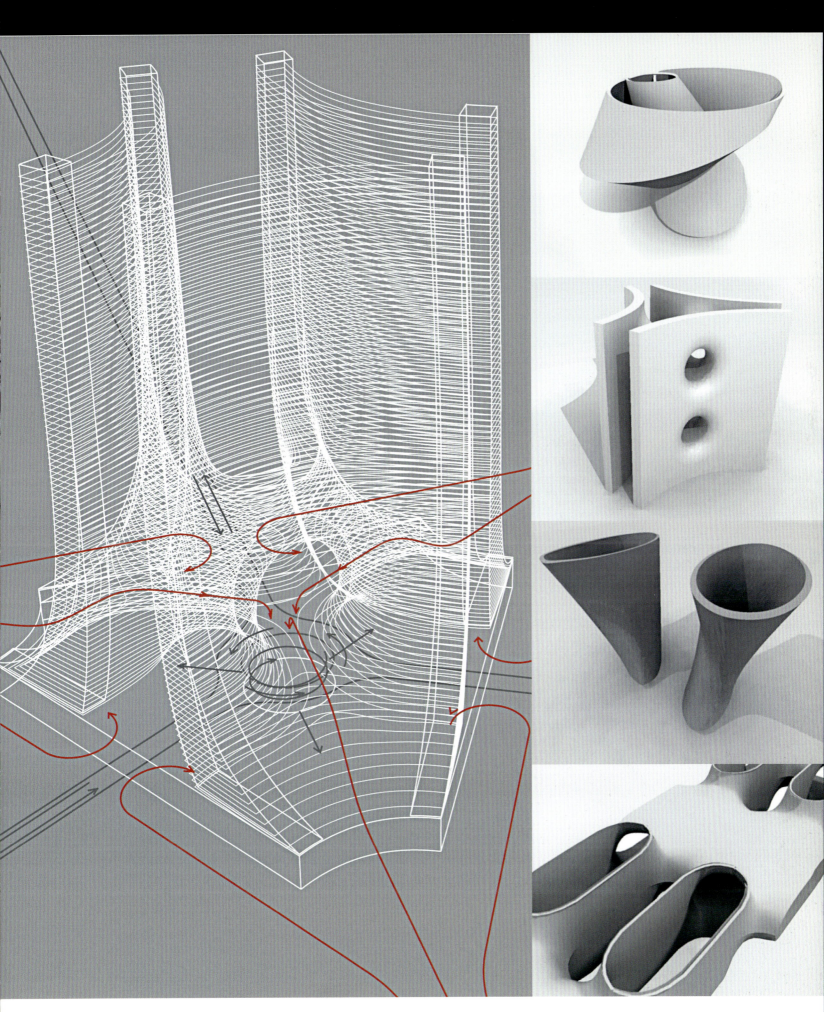

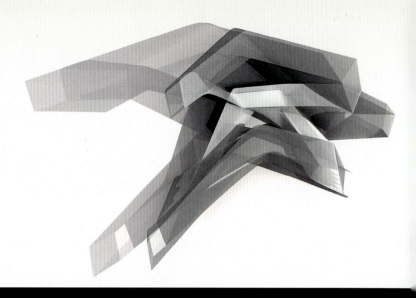

▲ Zoomliners
Petra De Colle, Maren Klasing

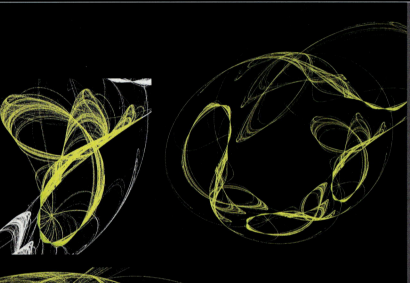

▲ Allegory of a Strange Attractor
Tamara Friebel

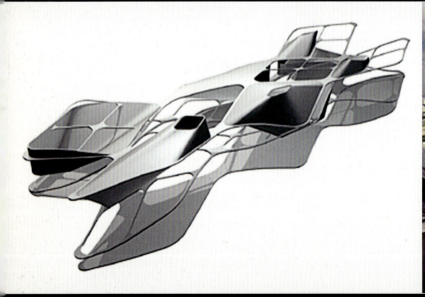

▲ Linear Interweaving
Ivana Bzduchova, Cornelia Klien, Philipp Weisz

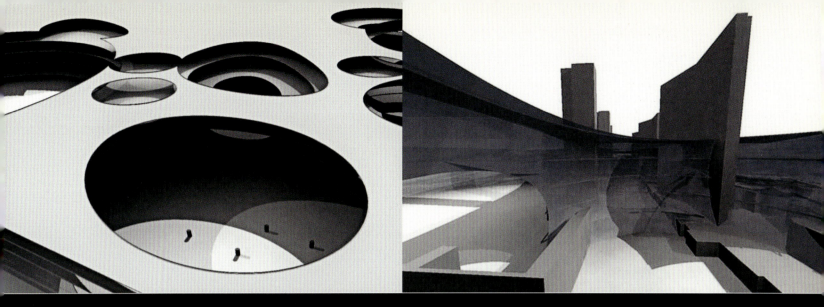

▲ **Box Superbe_**
Martine Nicolay, Bengt Stiller

▲ **Linear Cities**
Eldine Heep, Sophie Luger

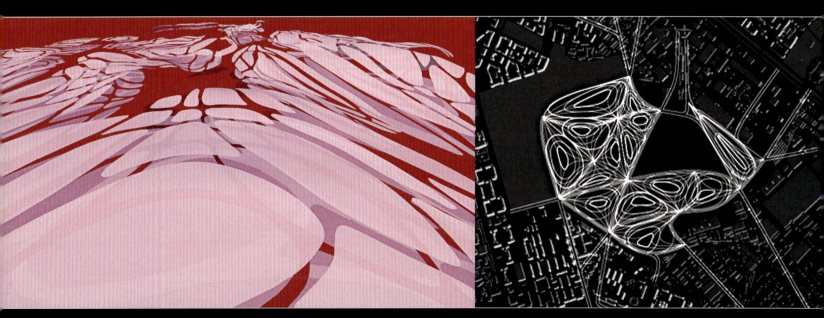

▲ **Controllable Complexity**
Andrea König, Nicole Stöcklmayr

COMPRESSED COMPLEXITY
Density-Diversity-Complexity-Unity

2005 - 2006

This year's studio agenda focuses on the application and development of parametric concepts, methods and techniques, moving from urban scale to the detailed articulation of a single complex building, to the design of a mixed used tower for Istanbul.

Mixed-use implies the related presence of the three primary programmatic categories: retail, commercial, and residential. The task is to vertically organize and coordinate these three fundamentally different programmatic categories in a condensed single tower. Each of the three program categories might in itself be further differentiated, which offers a chance to establish correlations, mediations, adaptations, or other forms of interarticulations between them. Parametric techniques should be developed and applied for the proliferation and differentiation of these units.

PROTO-TYPING – THE INTERARTICULATION OF SUB-SYSTEMS
The first step is the design of a proto-type that demonstrates the principle of interarticulation and comprises the co-development of the following related sub-systems:

Spatial accommodation: Develop a specific spatial distribution logic for each programme category and propose modes of interarticulation that integrate or unify these different domains.

Navigation: Develop a circulation system that is guided by the requirements of orientation with a reference to perception, visual penetration and mental maps. This system of navigation provides orientation and access.

Stabilization: Design a structural system that affords the structural stabilization of the spatial systems composed in the previous steps.

The developed formation of the accommodation system provides the selection criteria for possible navigational and structural systems. However, navigation and structure cannot be derived from spatial organization. The development of each sub-system requires additional invention, which contributes in each step to a changing character of the overall composition

PARAMETRIC INTERARTICULATION
Interarticulation is to be achieved on two levels: firstly on the level of spatial accommodation between the three programmatic domains (retail, commercial, residential), and secondly with respect to the composition of the tower's three subsystems (accommodation, navigation and stabilization).

Each of the subsystems should inflect and be inflected by the other two subsystems to build up an elaborated design complexity. This might result in a complex parametric model (with scripted functions) where the variations of relevant parameters are correlated across subsystems.

CONTEXTUALIZATION
An appropriate site within the rich cityscape of Istanbul needs to be selected. The local topography plays a big role, making it necessary to devise an effective mode of interfacing with the ground. The tower has to work with its immediate surroundings and at the same time to exploit the wider cityscape for monumental effects. It affords views, establishes vistas, and provides orientation within the urban fabric. The large tower thus has multiple contexts, calling for contextual interarticulation on various levels.

ACHIEVING ELEGANCE
Elegance articulates complexity. An elegant building or urban design should be able to manage considerable complexity without descending into disorder. The elegance we are talking about is not the elegance of minimalism. Minimalist elegance thrives on simplicity. The elegance we are promoting here instead thrives on complexity.

As ordered complexity the elegant composition is highly differentiated, yet this differentiation is based on a systematic set of lawful correlations that are defined between the elements and subsystems. These correlations establish a visible coherence across the overall system. In this way, elegance ensures the legibility of a complex formation and facilitates orientation within a complex arrangement. Just like organic and inorganic natural systems, elegant compositions are so highly integrated that they cannot be easily decomposed into independent subsystems – a major point of difference in comparison with the modern design paradigm of clear separation of functional subsystems.

A specific aspect of this integrated nature of elegance is the capacity to adapt to complex urban contexts. Achieving adaptive capacity is another key element of the design process, suggesting comparison with natural organic systems. An architectural system that has the capacity to adapt to its environment will result in an intricate ensemble that has – out of initial contradictions – developed into a new complex synthesis that further enhances the overall sense of sophisticated elegance.

FACADE ENVELOPE AS FOURTH SUB-SYSTEM
To express the aforementioned elegance, an external envelope has to be developed as a fourth sub-system. This facade system needs to interact with the tower's other three sub-systems (spatial accommodation, navigation and stabilization). It needs to filter the internal complexity and interface with the ground-surface.

The internal complexity of the mixed-use towers needs to be selectively articulated on the exterior of the building. The facade may act as a smoothing agent, thus reducing the complexity of the underlying complex organisation. In the end the facade itself will be a very elegant surface.

Project: "Compressed Complexity"

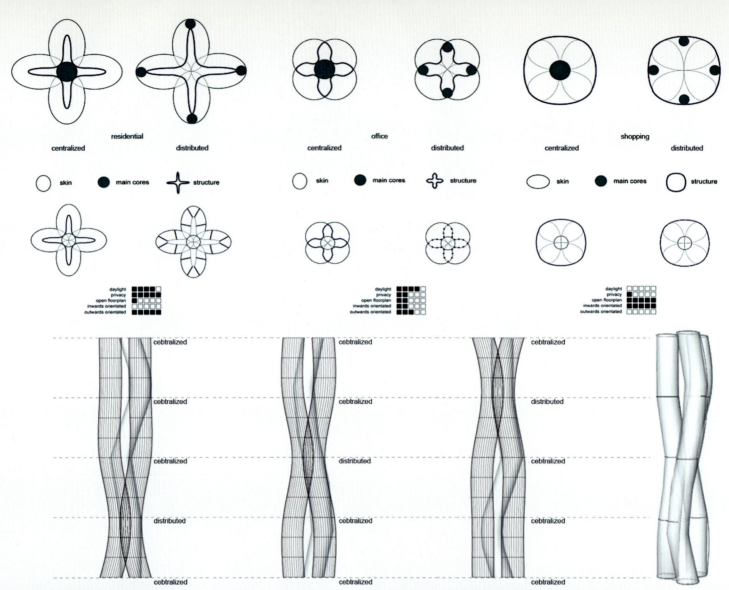

residential — centralized — distributed

office — centralized — distributed

shopping — centralized — distributed

○ skin   ● main cores   ✛ structure

○ skin   ● main cores   ✛ structure

○ skin   ● main cores   ○ structure

daylight / privacy / open floorplan / inwards orientated / outwards orientated

daylight / privacy / open floorplan / inwards orientated / outwards orientated

daylight / privacy / open floorplan / inwards orientated / outwards orientated

cebtralized · cebtralized · cebtralized
cebtralized · cebtralized · distributed
cebtralized · distributed · cebtralized
distributed · cebtralized · cebtralized
cebtralized · cebtralized · cebtralized

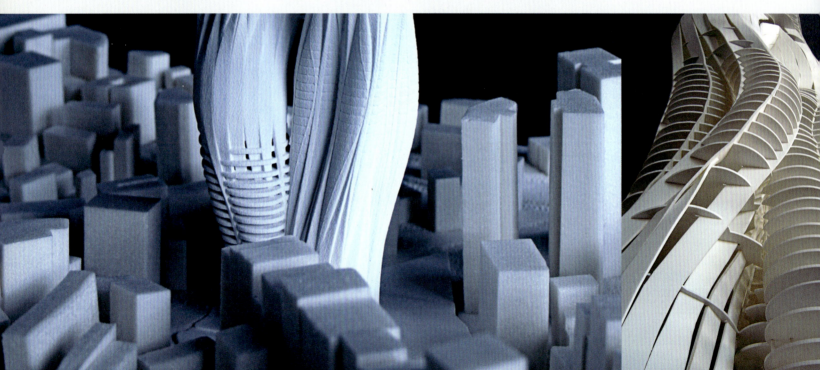

Compressed Complexity

Eldine Heep, Gerhild Orthacker, Ellen Przybyla (UCLA), Judith Schafelner

The project demonstrates a variety of complementary strategies which allow for an effective introduction of typological heterogeneity within a vertically stratified design. The lawful differentiation between the different subsystems (facade, structure, spatial partitioning) enables it to continuously adapt to specific requirements and establishes the overall tectonic system as an inter-articulated surface.

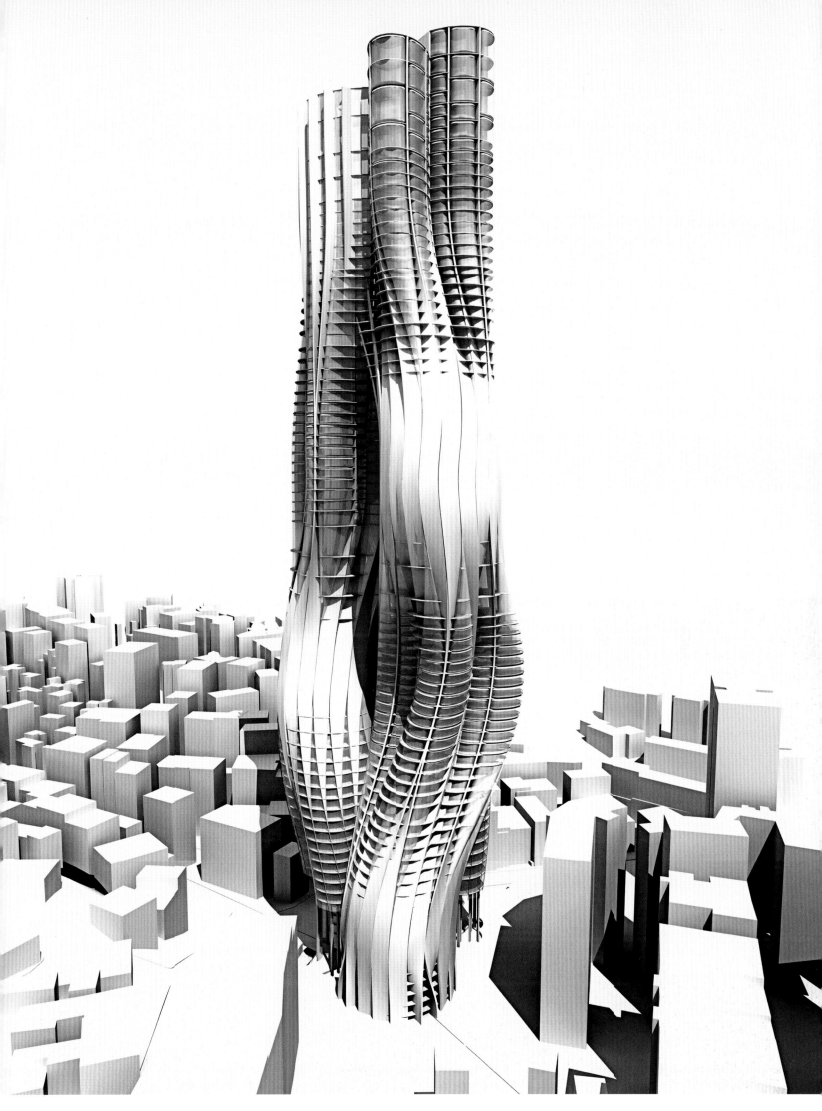

Positive-Negative Space

Clemens Nocker, Baris Önal, Peter Pichler

Investigating in maximized interrelations between functions, new ways of connectivity and corresponding manifestations emerge on the facade. The structure allows different functions to work simultaneously. It adapts itself according to space requirements and defined interaction rules.

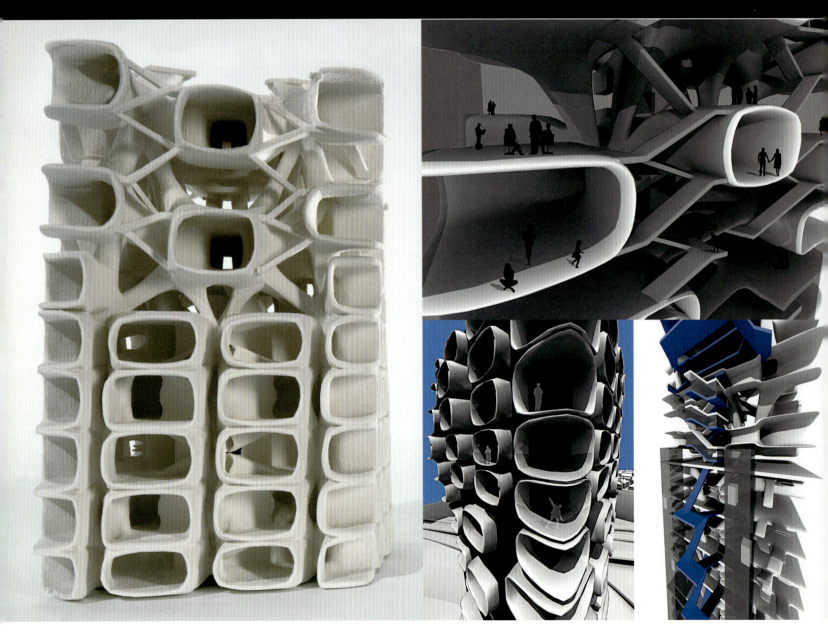

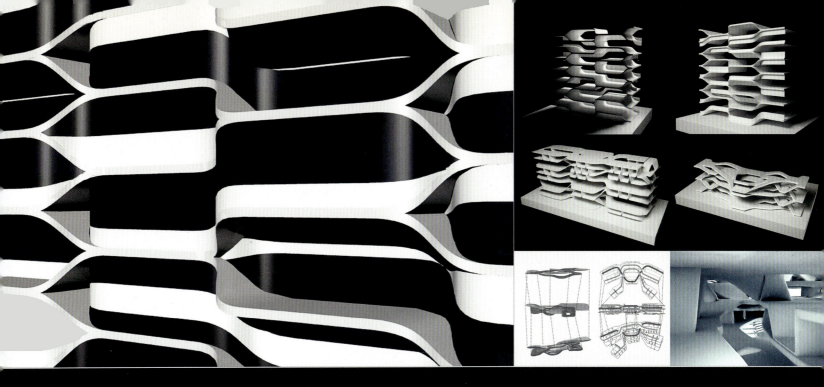

Vertical ORIENT.ation

Christoph Hermann, Konrad Hofmann, Daniel Köhler, Raffael Petrovic

The project seeks to achieve complex spatial interrelations and interactions between the given programs within a high-rise typology and their corresponding manifestation in the building structure and shell.

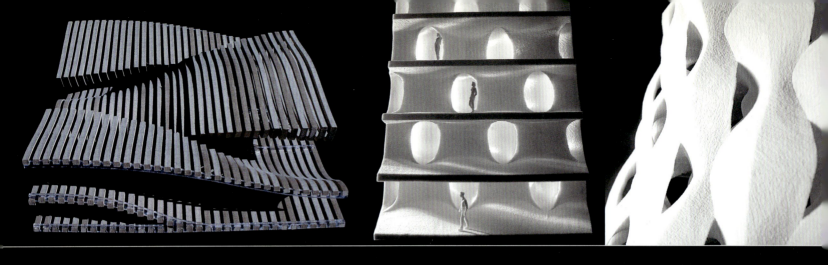

Bendscraper

Jasmina Frincic, Mario Gasser, Peter Schamberger, Philipp Weisz

Horizontal, spatial components morph into vertical facade elements. Variations of the same geometric component become an inhabitable field on the ground, incorporating surrounding directions and multiplying the layers of activity. On the facade the components adapt to program-specific requirements and blend between programmatic clusters.

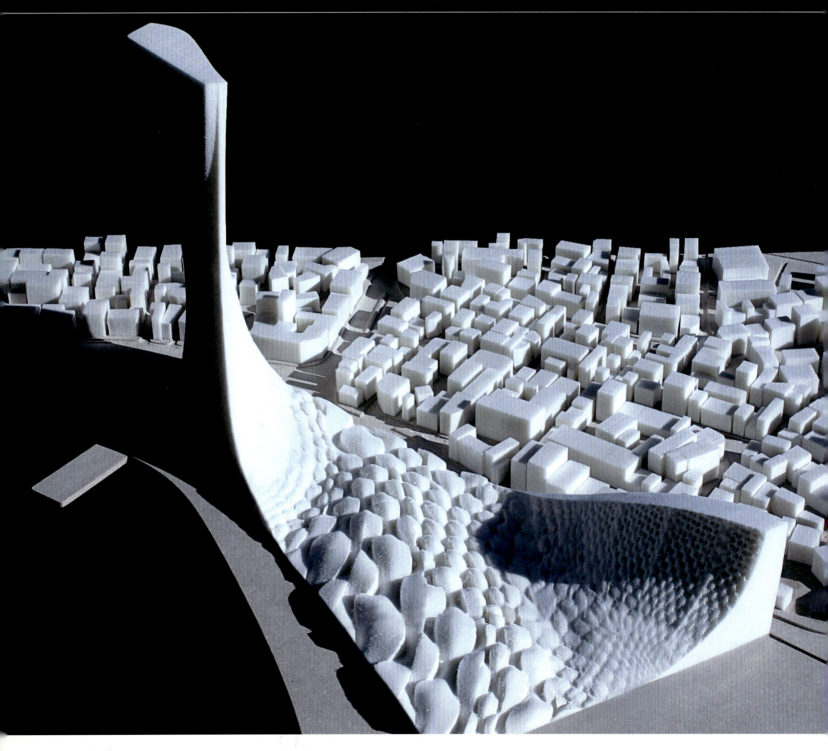

Vertical Shopping

Peter Mitterer, Matthias Moroder

Merging the typological characteristics and organizational systems of a classical skyscraper with those of a linearly organized shopping street or mall the group developed an interconnected diagonally organized two-level type. Its vertical sequence allows a continuous circulation flow within the entire tower. Various functional formations are developed through parametric adaptations of the basic type.

CIRCULATION RETAIL

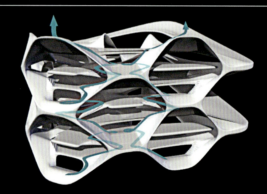

CIRCULATION COMMERCIAL

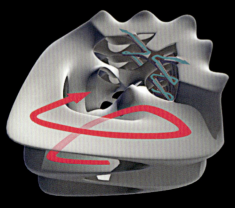

CIRCULATION RESIDENTIAL1

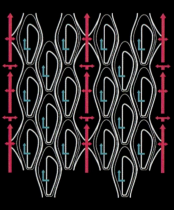

CIRCULATION RESIDENTIAL2

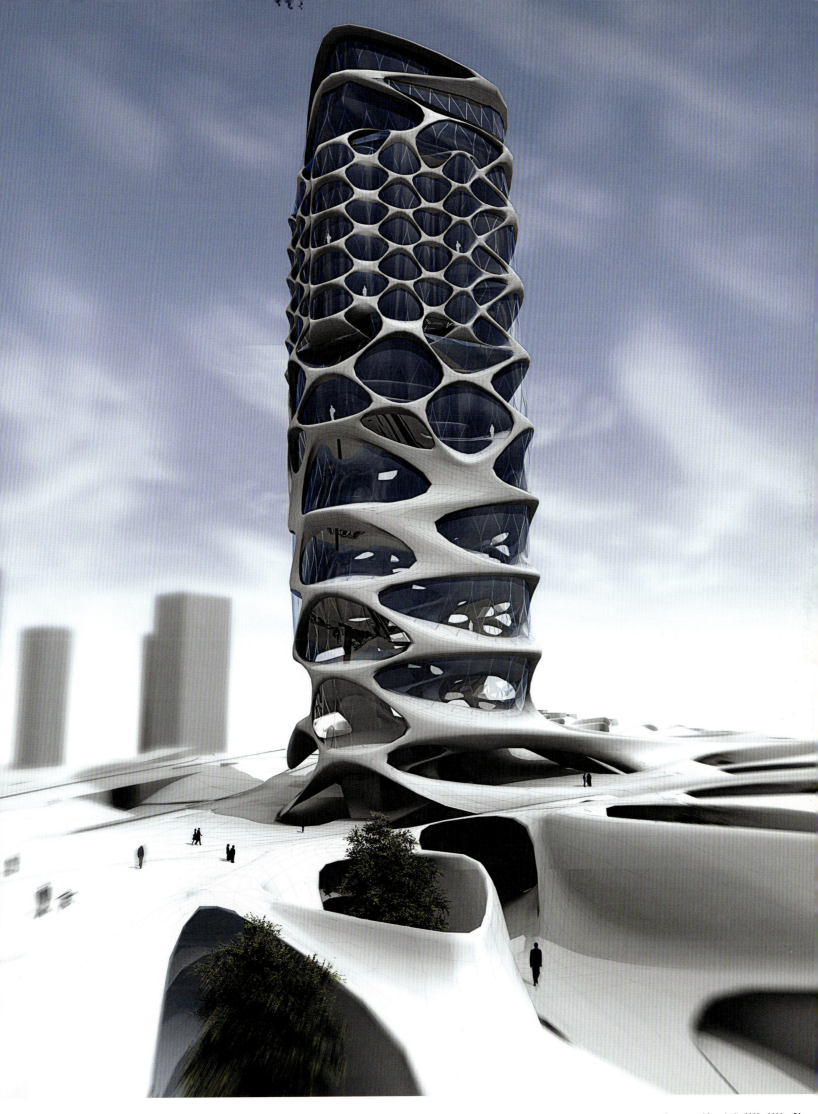

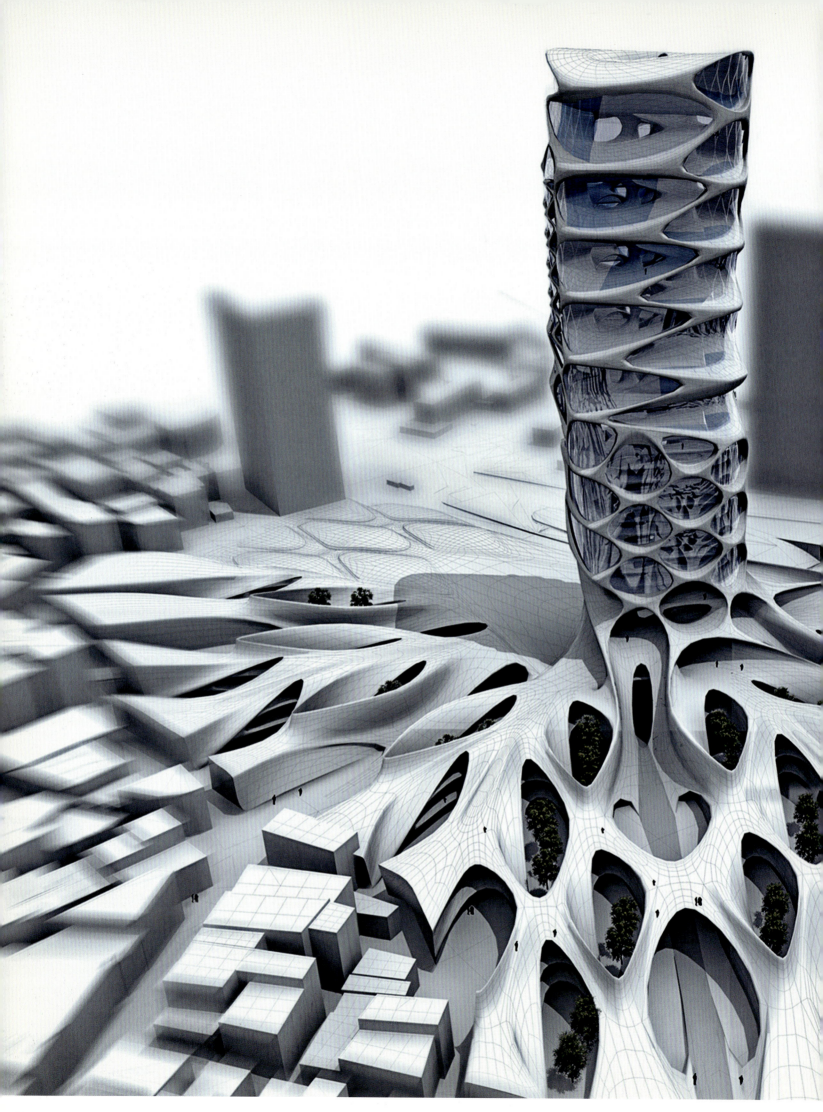

Oriented Modulation

Vladimir Ivanov, Irina-Elena Preda,
Lisa Sommerhuber, Nino Tugushi

The Skyscraper consists of three convoluted towers containing different programs. Each of the programs predominates a certain sector of the tower transforming the shape of the tower accordingly. The programs overlap vertically, gradually developing new spatial properties.
The facade mirrors this distribution with differentiated structures stretching across the volumes.

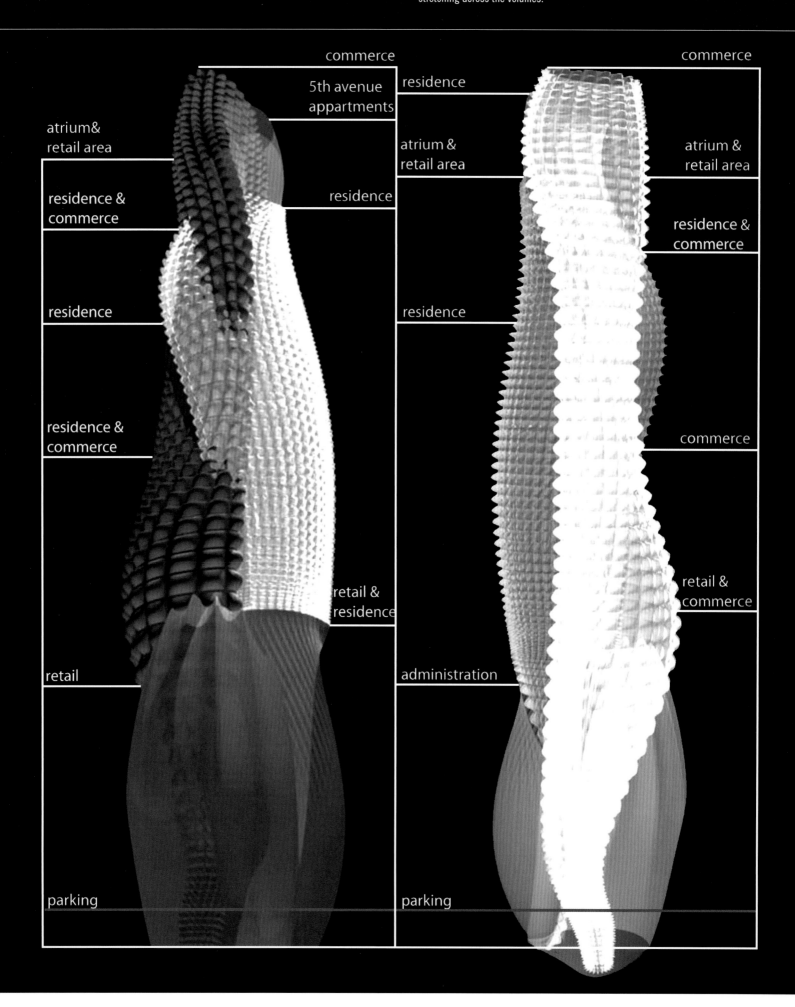

commerce

5th avenue
appartments

residence

atrium&
retail area

residence &
commerce

residence

residence &
commerce

retail

parking

commerce

residence

atrium &
retail area

atrium &
retail area

residence &
commerce

residence

commerce

retail &
residence

retail &
commerce

administration

parking

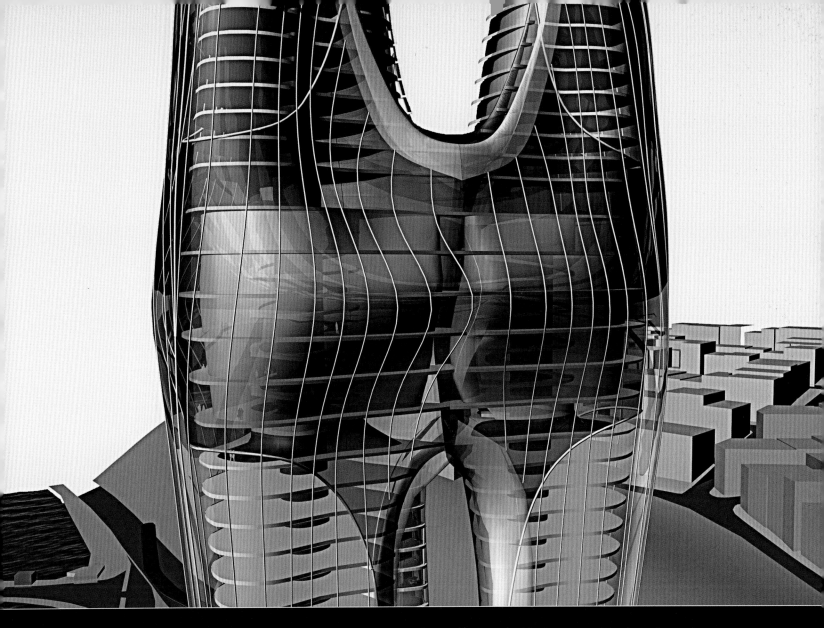

Trident Tower

Mirta Bilos, Manuel Fröschl, Gilles Greis

By separating the parts of the skyscraper and then fusing them back together, a different condition is created that allows more natural light to enter the tower and more privacy for residential areas. Smaller floor plans reduce the number of rooms but increase the angle of perspective. The fused parts of the tower create larger floor plans in which the programs interact without interfering with each other.

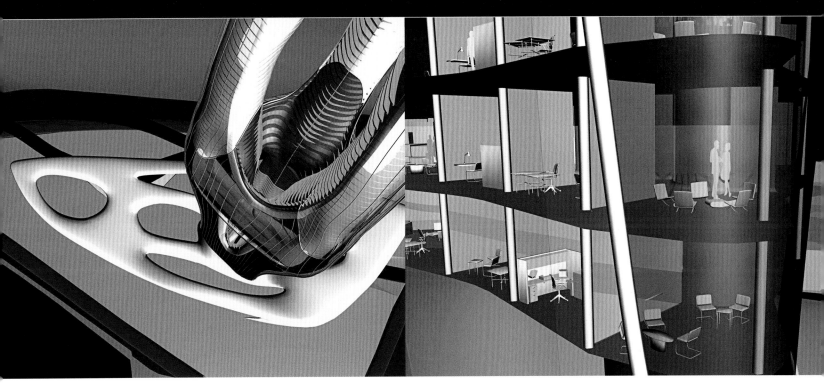

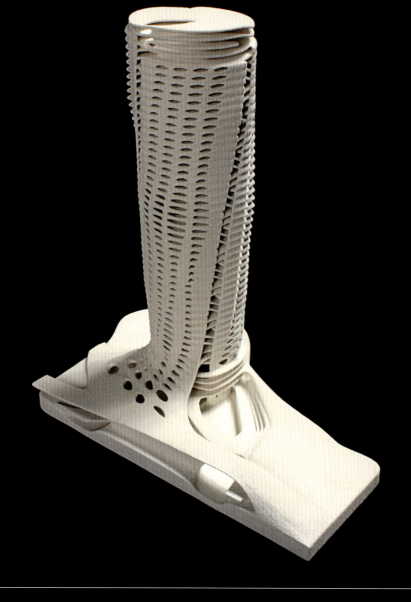
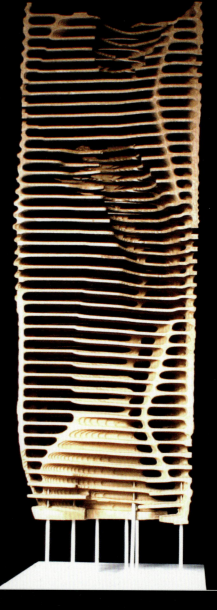

VERTICAL elastiCITY

Johannes Elias, Christoph Hermann, Nuray Karakurt,
Martin Kleindienst, Thomas Milly

By introducing the principles of the horizontal urban fabric into the verticality of the high-rise this proposal seeks to enhance the building by means of higher connectivity, a blend and inter-linkage of the different programs and a differentiation of the spaces.

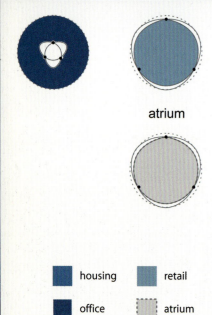

atrium

- ■ housing
- ■ retail
- ■ office
- ◻ atrium

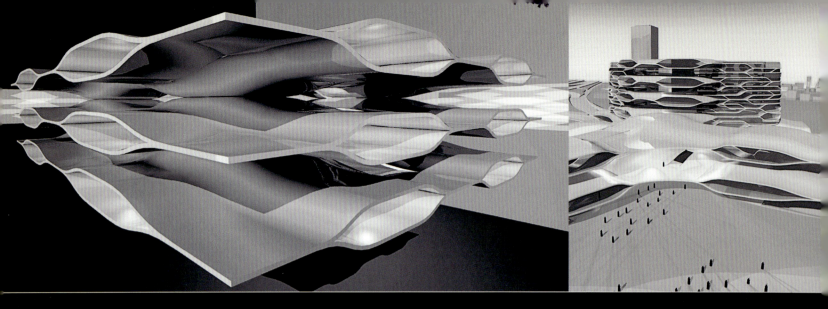

▲ Surface Bazaar
Niran Büyükköz, Uli Schifferdecker

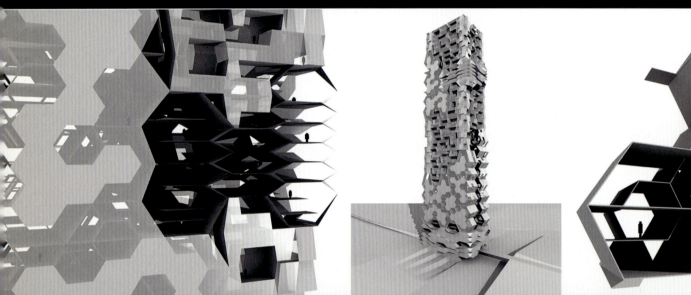

▲ Hexametric Complexity
Siri Ulrikke Hoye, Uli Schifferdecker, Lisa Sommerhuber

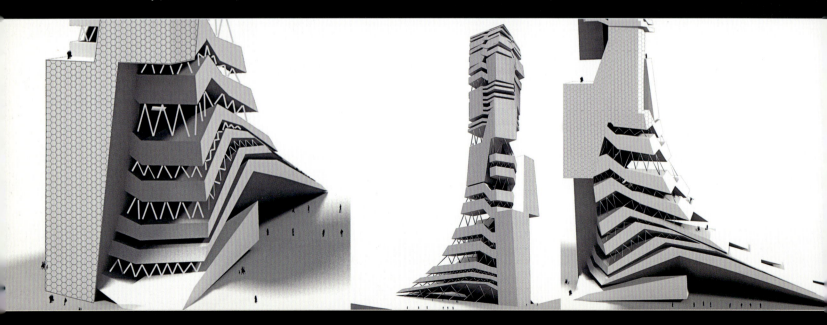

▲ Integrated Community in Vertical Continuity
Niran Büyükköz, Andrea König, Baris Önal

▲ Systematic Mesh Management

Oskar Hanstein, Katharina Hieger, Martin Krcha, Saman Saffarian

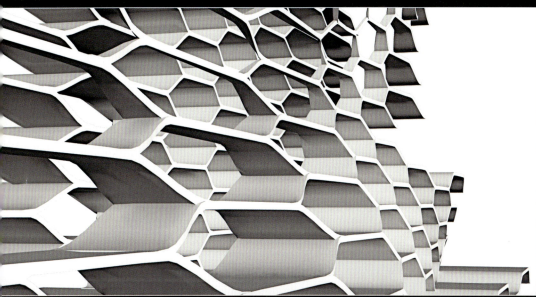

▲ Segments

Christoph Hermann, Konrad Hofmann, Daniel Köhler, Raffael Petrovic

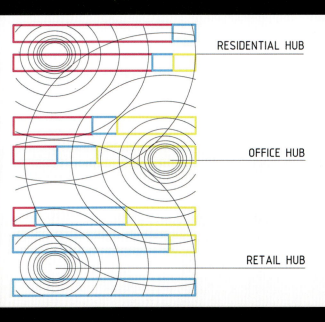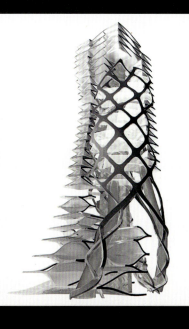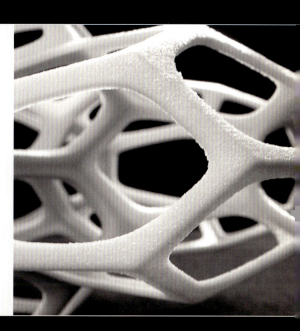

RESIDENTIAL HUB

OFFICE HUB

RETAIL HUB

▲ Hybrid Tower

Andrew Bryant (UCLA), Markus Jacobi, Andrés Schenker

SIMULTANEITY & LATENCY
Perception-Insight-Orientation

2006 - 2007

This year we are investigating our capacity to *perceive* spatial complexity. Design experiments will focus on the attempt to increase the complexity of a specific spatial configuration without losing its instant recognizability as an integrated whole. We will call this instant recognizability the iconic condition or iconicity of the configuration.

Rather than creating simple iconicity we are striving for *multiple iconicity*.

Multiple iconicity implies that one configuration has the capacity to produce at least two (or more) iconic conditions by associating its parts in different ways. These different iconic conditions are either simultaneously present (like the famous ambiguous figures or flip-images discussed in the psychology of perception) or they might be triggered successively, either by the shifting relative position of the observer, by ephemeral, dynamic conditions like the change of lighting, or by kinetic manipulations like the reorientation of louvers etc.

The primary measure of complexity is therefore the number and diversity of iconic conditions that are manifest or latent within a given configuration.

Multiple iconicity is a special case of the perceptive simultaneity effect that Colin Rowe called Phenomenal Transparency. Phenomenal Transparency implies the multiple recombination of different parts

of a given formal arrangement. Ambiguous figures are the perfect example. But we can also observe this phenomenon in three-dimensional space.

We want to work with the effect of multiple iconicity in relation to a large tower (or a cluster of towers). In towers it is the elevation and section rather than the plan that dominates the design. And it is the elevation rather than the plan that is important for the tower's perception.

In order to sharpen our understanding of the effects we are aiming at, we first study the basic insights of Gestalt psychology.

GESTALT PSYCHOLOGY: THE PRIMACY OF WHOLES
Fast orientation in complex scenes is based on the capacity to perceive configurations as immediate unities, as wholes. Gestalt-grouping principles like proximity (contiguity), similarity, smooth continuation, closure or symmetry regulate how one (rather than another) whole figure is perceived (interpreted) in the face of a certain arrangement of "matter" (we refer to "matter" here, because to speak of parts, elements or even fragments already implies a certain whole as reference).

Parametric Figuration:
We propose that any complex configuration, latent with multiple potential readings, can be constructed as a parametric model to

Project: "Surface Figuration"

control the various Gestalt potentials that are embedded in the configuration. Parametric setups describing the relative form, relative light conditions, relative color modulations, variable transparencies or variable contexts are devised to control the emergent figuration and re-figuration of the arrangement.

Contemporary digital tools (renderings, animations, scripting tools), involving multiple (changing) perspectives, color, light, shadow, transparency, reflection, fade-ins or kinetic capacities, are utilized to explore the effects of various Gestalt potentials.

MULTIPLE ICONICITY AS FACADE ARTICULATION

The multiple iconicity that has been pursued and achieved on the level of the urban field (taking the city of Dubai as an urban testing ground) is then applied to an architectural solution on a building scale, involving first of all the articulation of the facades.

The design is guided by the demands of the desired urban field effect, that of multiple iconicity. This requires a facade strategy that encompasses the totality (or a significant part) of the over-all urban proposal. The articulation of the facades allows us to group and separate the urban mass.

Facades can be designed to draw together and group various buildings within the field into larger, iconic wholes and thus compose larger visual entities or to differentiate urban volumes by applying different facade treatments onto different parts or different sides of the volumes in order to break up and recombine the volumetric constituents of the urban form.

The next step is to move from a global facade pattern to the elaboration of (a range of different) detailed facade articulations. The facade is developed as a deep facade that begins to structure the interior of the volumes. Its multiple appearances and readings correlate with multiple functions inside the building.

The facade is also crucial in terms of exploiting ambient parameters like natural light conditions (sunlight (vertical/horizontal), diffuse light), or artificial lighting conditions (exterior, interior).

All of this can be explored with explicit reference to different observer positions.

GESTALT CATASTROPHES

Display your orchestrated Gestalt catastrophe!

The desired gestalt-catastrophe (a gestalt flip, gestalt transformation, or re-figuration) will emerge from the careful simultaneous orchestration of parameters related to object, ambience and observer. The effect might be most striking if all these registers are engaged in relations of mutual amplification.

Phenomenal Similarity

Mario Gasser, Philipp Weisz

Phenomenal Transparency is used as an urban organizational tool to deform a dense field of towers on the basis of multiple first-person perspectives. While shifting the relative position of the observer different iconic figurations appear. Every tower in the field is shaped by at least two perspectives. The facade grid is following the same rules on a different scale, allowing grouping and highlighting of certain areas of the facade.

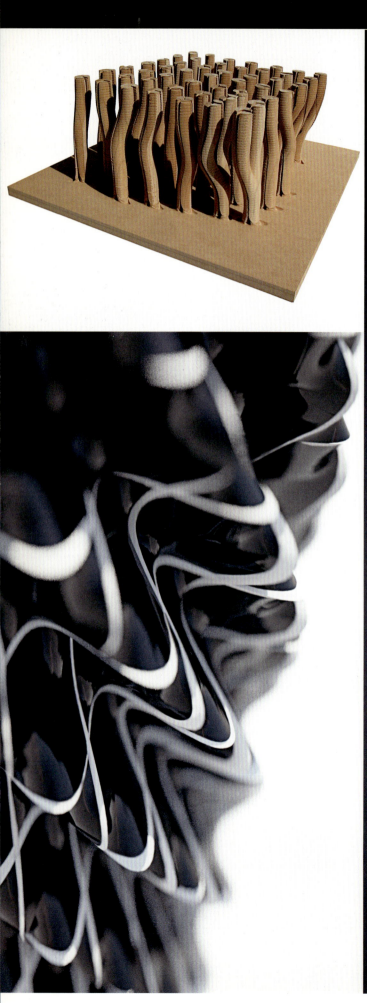

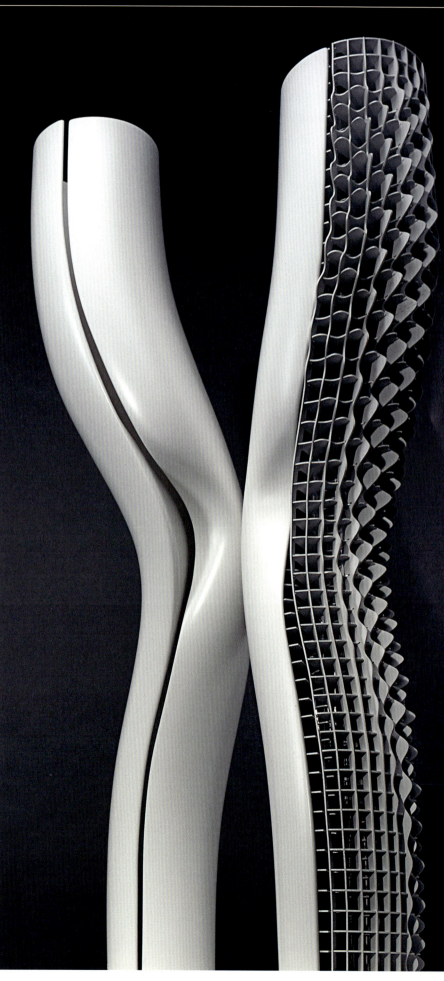

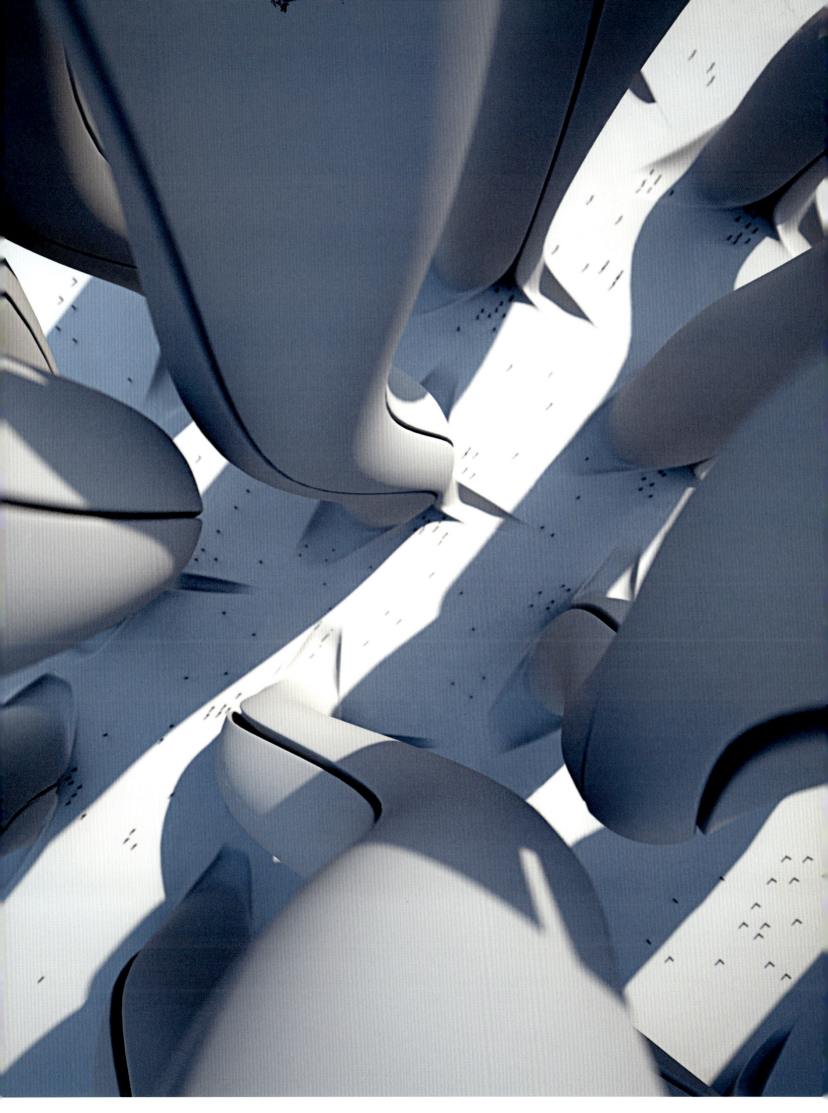

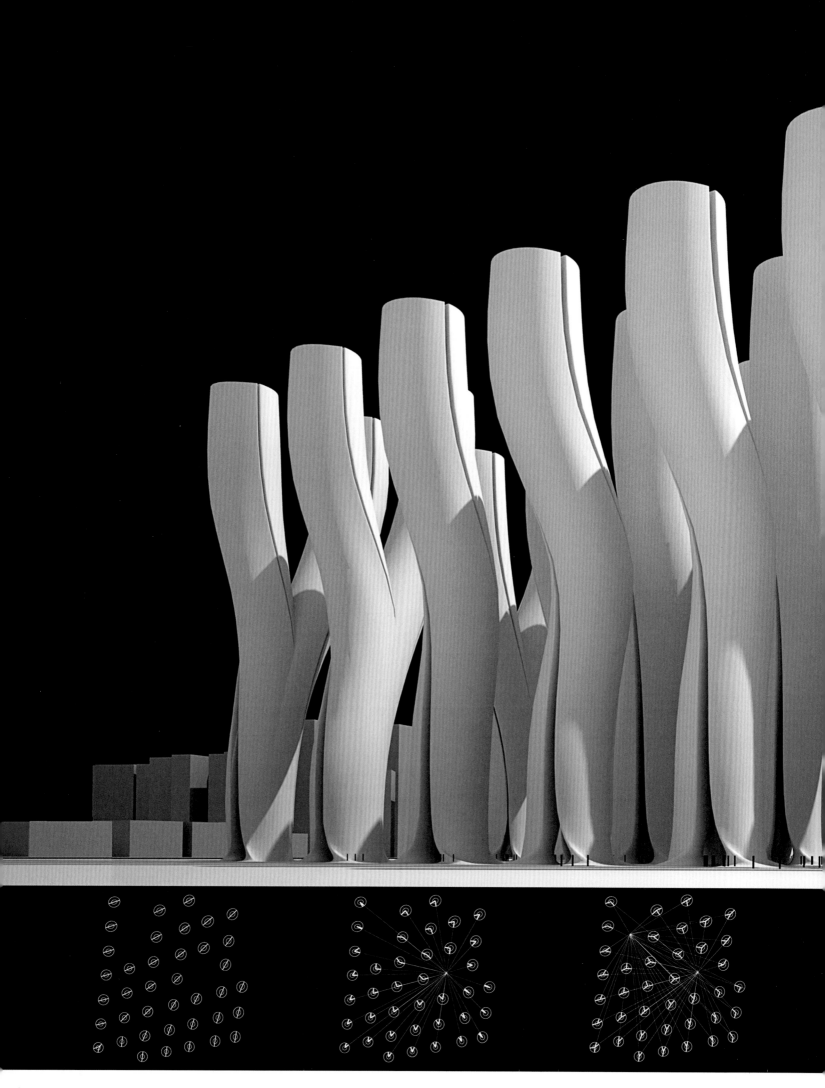

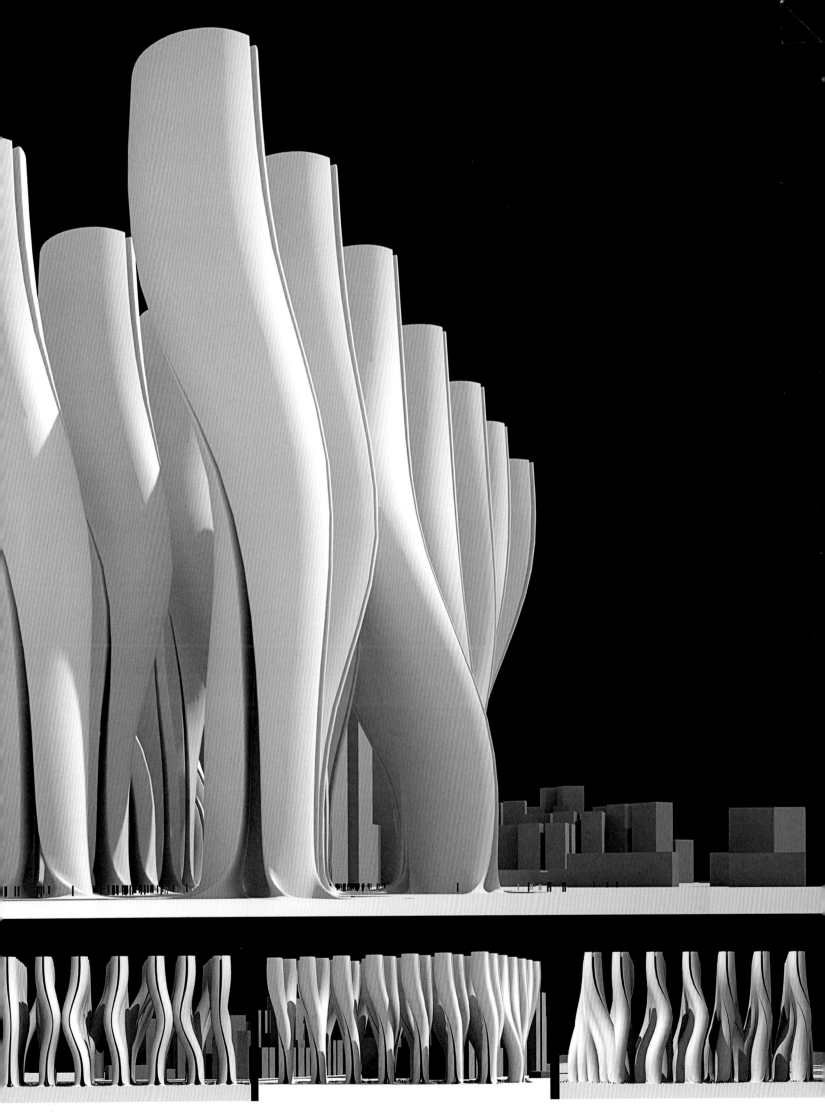

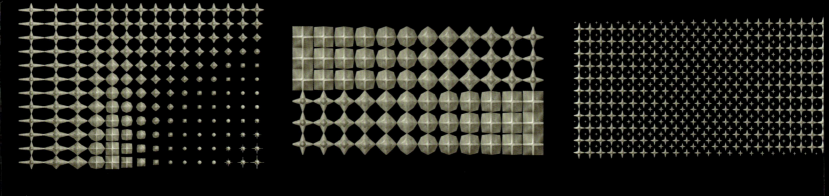

³lements

Daniel Köhler, Rasa Navasaityte, Anna Weilhartner

Taking a structural analysis of Dubai as a point of departure, a component called ³lements was developed. The element can be dramatically altered without losing its recognizability. When integrated into existing situations, the component reacts – on the basis of the Gestalt principle of contrast – alternatively, and thereby offsets the mainly mono-functional island projects in terms of both program and design.

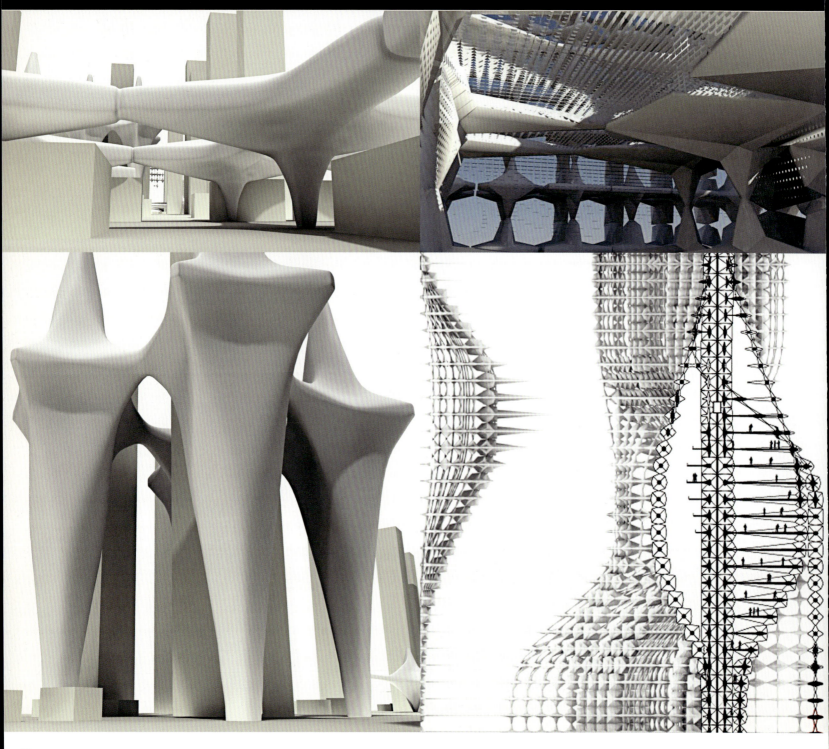

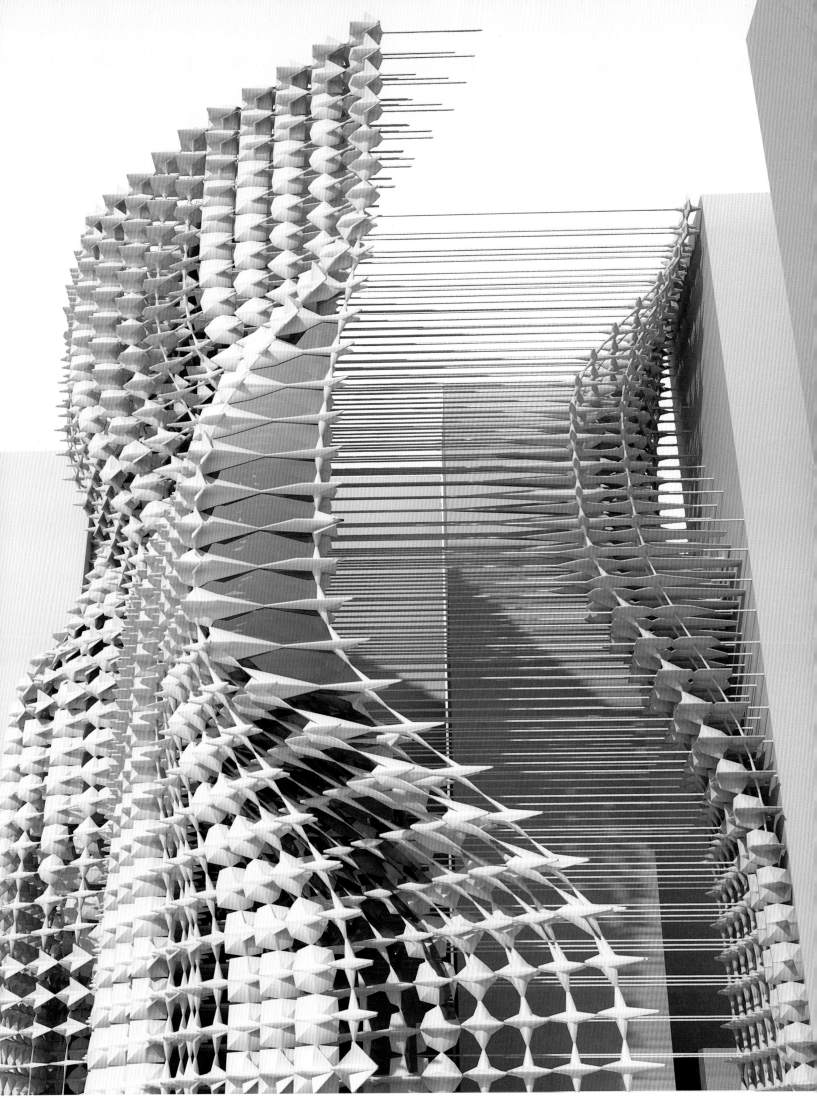

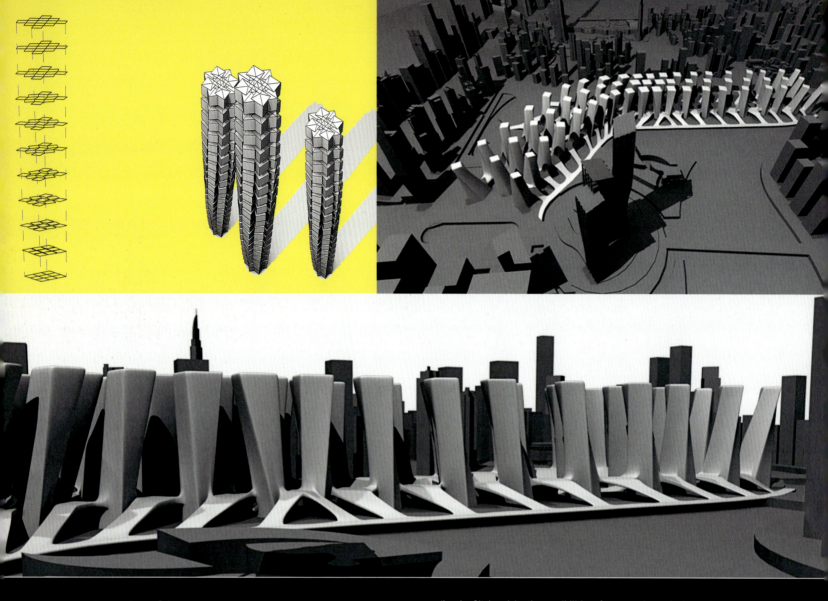

building pattern development

Load a City
Manuel Fröschl, Clemens Nocker, Baris Önal

'Load a City' exploits the possibilities of parametric versioning and phenotypical adaptation in order to create a rich catalogue of multilayered facade articulations. It is the aim of the project to manipulate the involved geometry such that it allows for adaptive differentiation throughout the built volume.

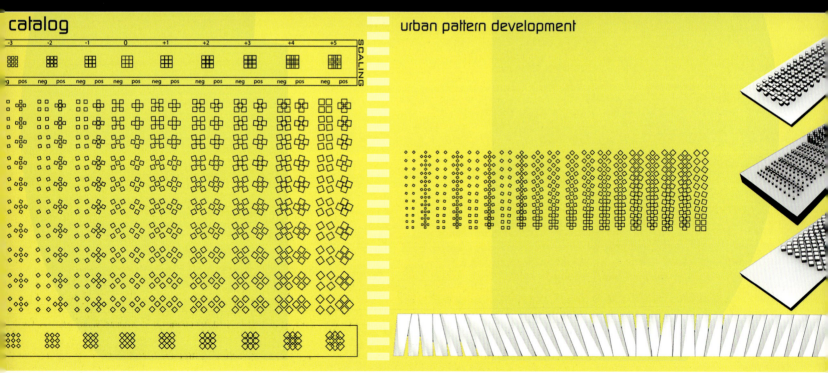

catalog

-3	-2	-1	0	+1	+2	+3	+4	+5	SCALING

neg pos neg pos neg pos neg pos neg pos neg pos neg pos neg pos neg pos

urban pattern development

LowHighRise

Johannes Elias, Christoph Hermann, Thomas Milly, Negar Niku

'Low High Rise' proposes a methodology of generating highly differentiated urban atmospheres within dense fields of skyscrapers. Through methodical change in the silhouette and shape of the individual towers the design achieves a dichotomy between the "real" and perceived height of the building envelopes.

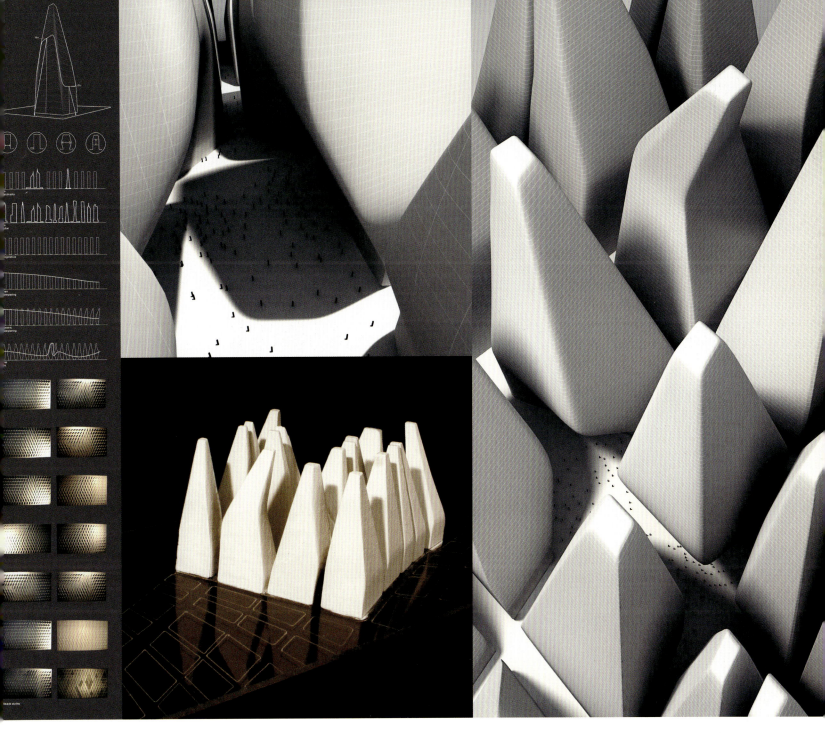

I.nter.CON.i.city

Manuel Fröschl, Konrad Hofmann, Maren Klasing,
Martin Krcha, Judith Schafelner, Antonio Torres (UCLA)

The Dubai-specific iconic potential of extending the coastline is translated into an offshore master plan strategy which is, first of all, able to 'post-contextualize' non-related parts in that area and, secondly, blurs the border between the land and waterside.

Surface Figuration

Katharina Hieger, Florian Puschmann,
Saman Saffarian, Milan Suchanek, Georg Wizany

The capacity to perceive form is largely dependent on the motion and velocity of the observer. The project exploits these changes in human perception and develops an urban model where multiple latent layers of information can be inscribed within the city fabric. The developed tools allow for different readings of the city when it is viewed at certain speeds or along specific trajectories.

Edge Outline

Vertice Outline

Vertice Outline

Linear Outline

Linear Outline

Linear Outline

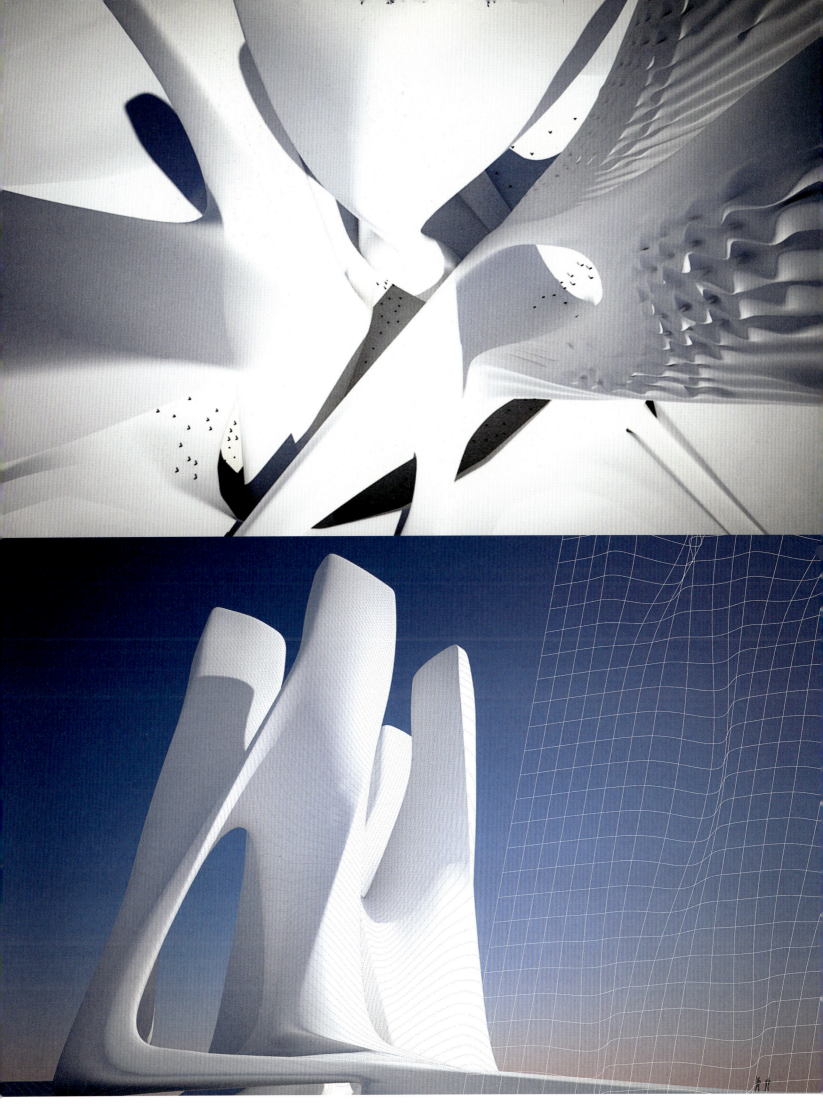

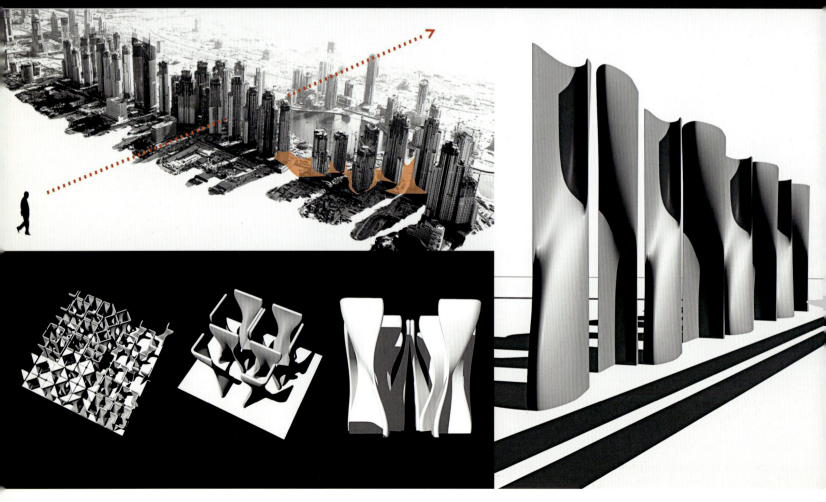

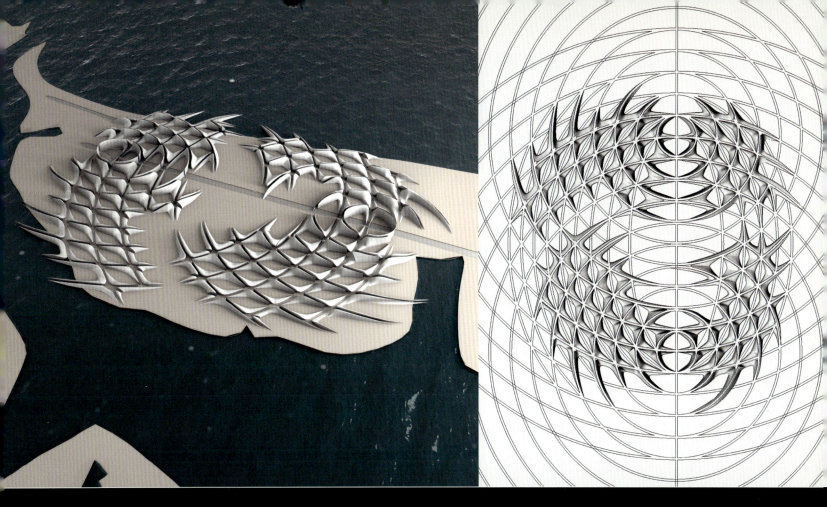

▲ **Magnetic Field**
Nicola Beck, Alexander Karaivanov, Magda Smolinska

▼ **Ipanema**
Raffael Petrovic, Uli Schifferdecker,
Phoebe Stewart, Albrecht von Alvensleben

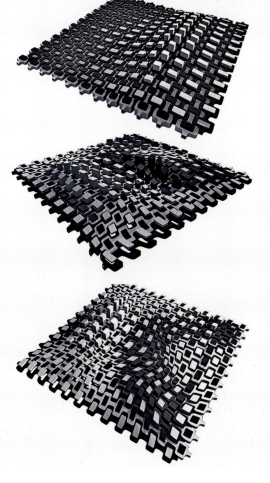

▲ **Anagrammatic**

Sabrina Miletich, Martine Nicolay, Birgit Schmidt

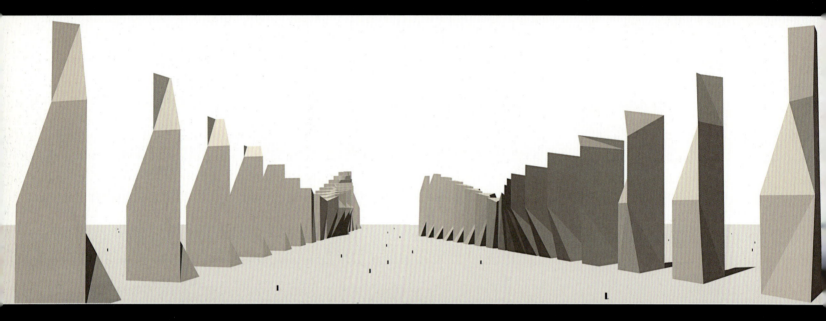

▲ **Edge_Flip**

Vladimir Ivanov, Phoebe Stewart

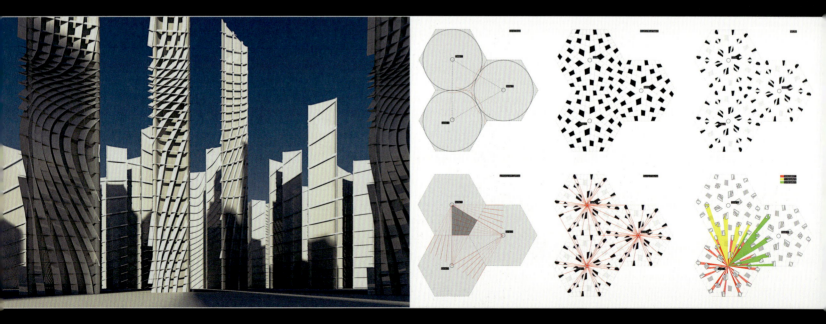

▲ **Projectit**

Linawaty Hasmy (SCI-Arc), Alexander Karaivanov, Philipp Ostermaier

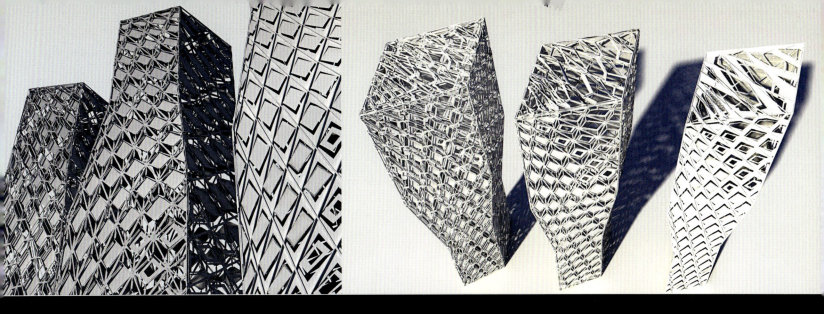

▲ **Multicentered Field**

Stephen Deters (UCLA), Konrad Hofmann, Philipp Ostermaier, Daniel Stockhammer

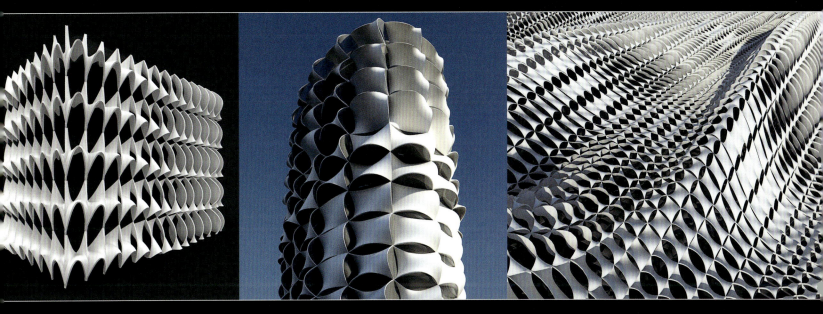

▲ **Distorted Vision**

Niran Büyükköz, Irina-Elena Preda

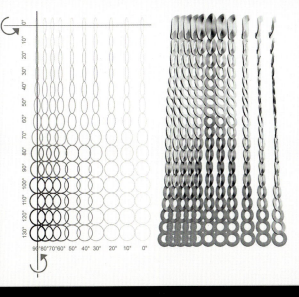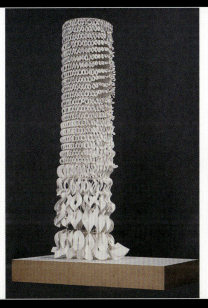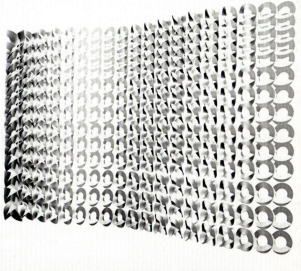

▲ **Annulorum**

Sofia Maria Hagen, Anna Weilhartner

PARAMETRIC URBANISM
Thames Gateway – Urban Laboratory

2007 - 2008

Parametric Urbanism takes the tools of parametric design into the domain of large-scale urbanism. The project specifically exploits the benefits of parametric versioning in order to create urban fields with an unprecedented level of intricacy.

THAMES GATEWAY AS URBAN LABORATORY

London's architectural and urban sensibility has to wake up to the fact that London is one of the epicenters of urban growth in an accelerating world-wide dynamic. We explore how to approach such super-large scale developments with the sensibility of an architect, deploying contemporary digital form- and space-making strategies rather than traditional planning tools. The ability to handle such territories on an architectural level is afforded to us by a series of new and powerful digital design techniques. The application of the thusly retooled architectural sensibility to the design of large scale urban fields results in what we call Parametric Urbanism. Thames Gateway is hailed as Europe's largest urban regeneration project; for us, it holds the potential to become a most potent laboratory for contemporary forms of urbanism.

We start into the project by constructing a fundamental typological catalogue of urban field conditions: point-fields of villas, line-fields of towers, plane-fields of slabs and volume-fields of urban blocks. With respect to these four basic types of fields we go through a series of parametric variations and differentiations before we begin to recombine and cross-breed the individual types, leading to mutations of both, fields as well as components. Through this process we build up a repertoire of sufficient richness and complexity to approach the targeted project site with multiple interlacing strategies.

CONSTRAINED PROLIFERATION:
THE BUILDING AS 'GENERATIVE COMPONENT'

Bentley's "Generative Components" is a parametric-associative design environment. It allows for components to be constructed from discrete elements which are constrained and cohered by associative relationships. These components may then bring the characteristics of any of the embedded elements to the forefront when needed, thus enabling them to adapt to various and changing given conditions in sensible ways. As the components populate fields of alternating local conditions their adaptation should accentuate and amplify this differentiation. This technique can also be replicated in other 3D programs.

The relationship between these initial 'generative components' and their various instances at different points of insertion in an environment may well be conceptualized analogously to the way a single genotype can produce a differentiated population of phenotypes in response to varying environmental conditions that impact the ontogeny of the respective individual organism.

Method: Architectural tectonics generate urban field effects and vice versa.

Initially, each of the aforementioned 'generative components' may be a rather simple building mass which populates a topographically or otherwise articulated urban mesh (parcel array). The resultant differentiation of building shapes through local adaptation translates the varying characteristics of the topography as well as other environmental factors into architecture. This already produces significant urban effects.

The crux, however, of how we would like to use 'generative components' is the ambition to bring multiple architectural subsystems and the attendant tectonic articulation of buildings under the spell of global urban differentiation in a single computational setup. This in turn means that the local architectural features work towards the amplification of urban vectors, facilitating, for example, orientation on an urban scale via an unprecedented level of overall associative integration. The key subsystems that are to be embedded into the 'generative components' are:

1. Systems of internal subdivision, i.e. sub-volumes, floors, walls, etc.
2. Structural systems, i.e. primary and secondary skeletons, etc.
3. Navigation Systems, i.e. void with primary circulation/ orientation, etc.
4. Envelope, i.e. opaque vs. transparent, layered with bri-soleil, balconies, etc.

The attempt should be made to develop a genotype that defines and integrates all these systems across the whole range of phenotypical variation. This task should be solved by means of a single complex parametric model that adapts to the differentiated site-conditions.

Project: "Liquefy La Ville"

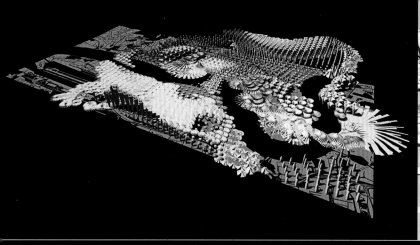

Circavior

Gilles Greis, Oskar Hanstein, Daniel Köhler, Rasa Navasaityte

Departing from the field logic of large scale urbanism this project develops architectural systems of intricate tectonic differentiations, adaptive to various local conditions and highlighting the transitions between varying urban typologies. The gradual shifting from one type to another creates various threshold conditions in correlation with the overall urban master plan.

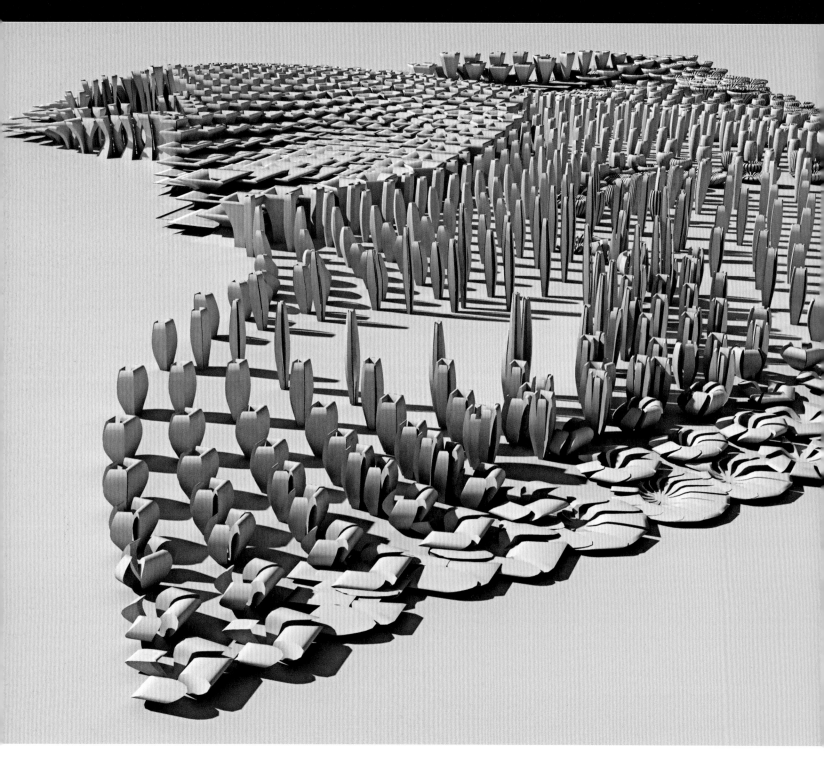

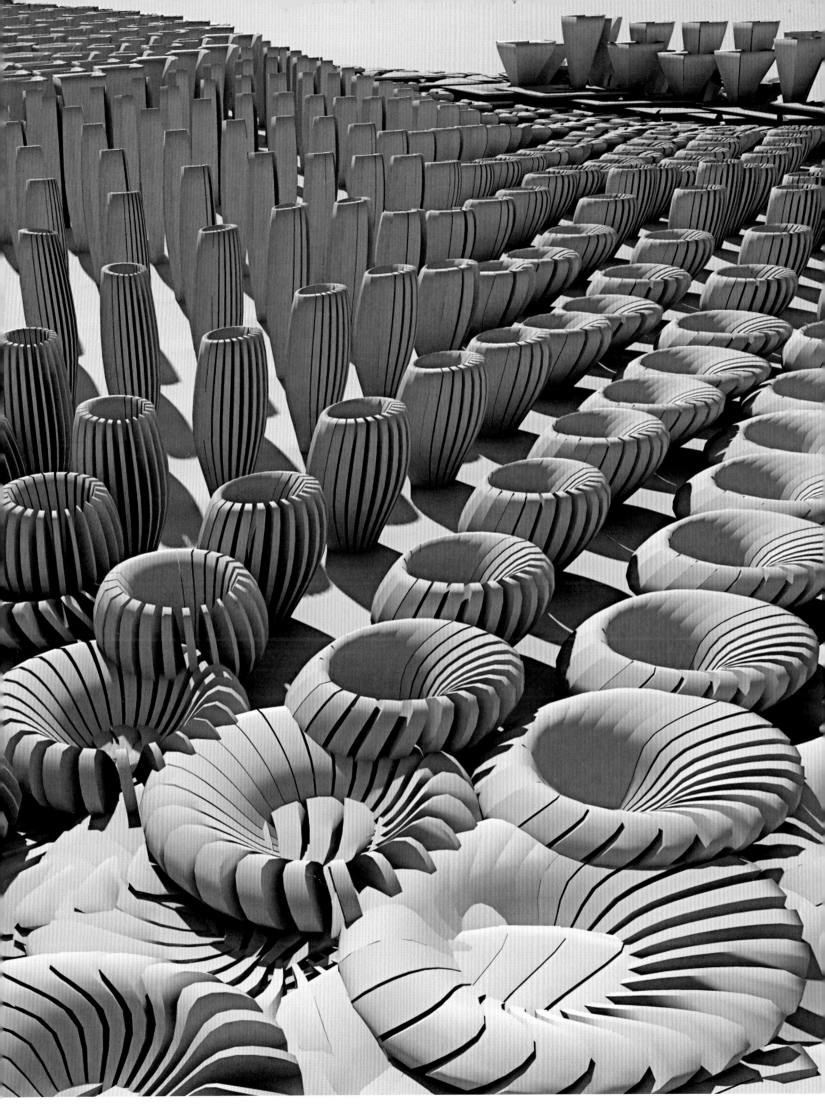

Adaptive Cruise Control System

Katharina Hieger, Martin Kleindienst,
Mitsuhiro Komatsu (UCLA), Thomas Milly

The project's aim is to set up a system to control navigation and diversification within the urban fabric. Based on initial research on Frei Otto's minimal path scheme and the discovery of its limitations, the system's reinterpretation leads to an "optimized" grid, whose singular modules are capable of adapting to actual field conditions, deliberately increasing the field's complexity.

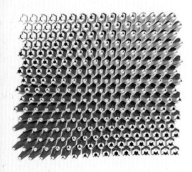
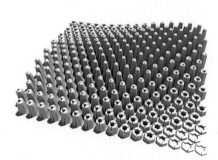
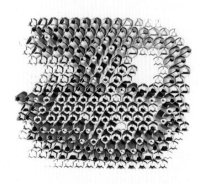
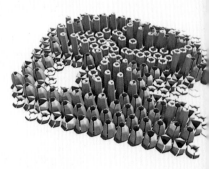

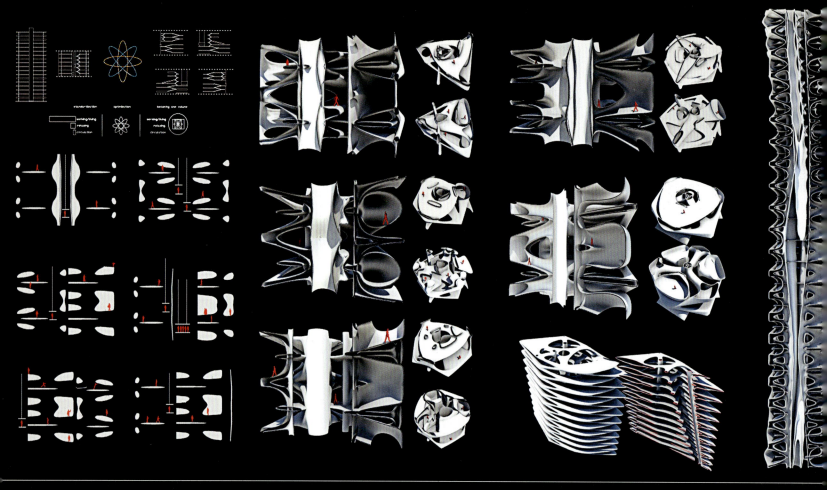

Liquefy La Ville

Martin Kleindienst, Baris Önal, Clemens Nocker,
Raffael Petrovic, Uli Schifferdecker

Assuming that the relationship between transport and density is crucial for any urban setting, a set of parametric systems is developed to generate an urban field in which figure and ground are no longer separated but morph into one another. Urban information is transported through the main axis of the city and distributed to buildings and open public spaces. As the density changes, buildings adapt to this global information.

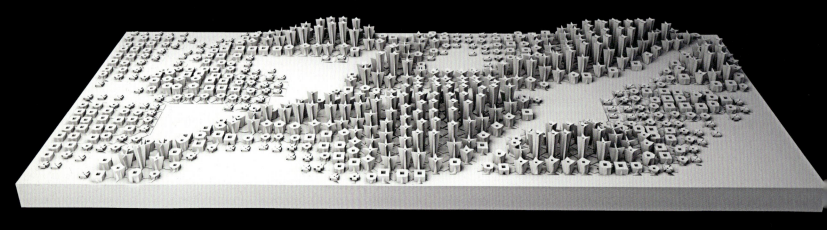

CONNECTIONS
PRIMARY TRAFFIC JUNCTIONS Ⓐ
SECONDARY TRAFFIC JUNCTIONS Ⓑ
TERTIARY TRAFFIC JUNCTIONS Ⓒ
INTER-CONNECTIONS Ⓞ

DENSITY
HIGH DENSE
MID DENSE
LOW DENSE

COLOR MAP
HIGH DENSE
MID DENSE
LOW DENSE

GRADIENT
HIGH DENSE
MID DENSE
LOW DENSE

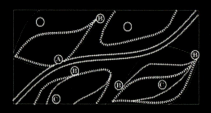

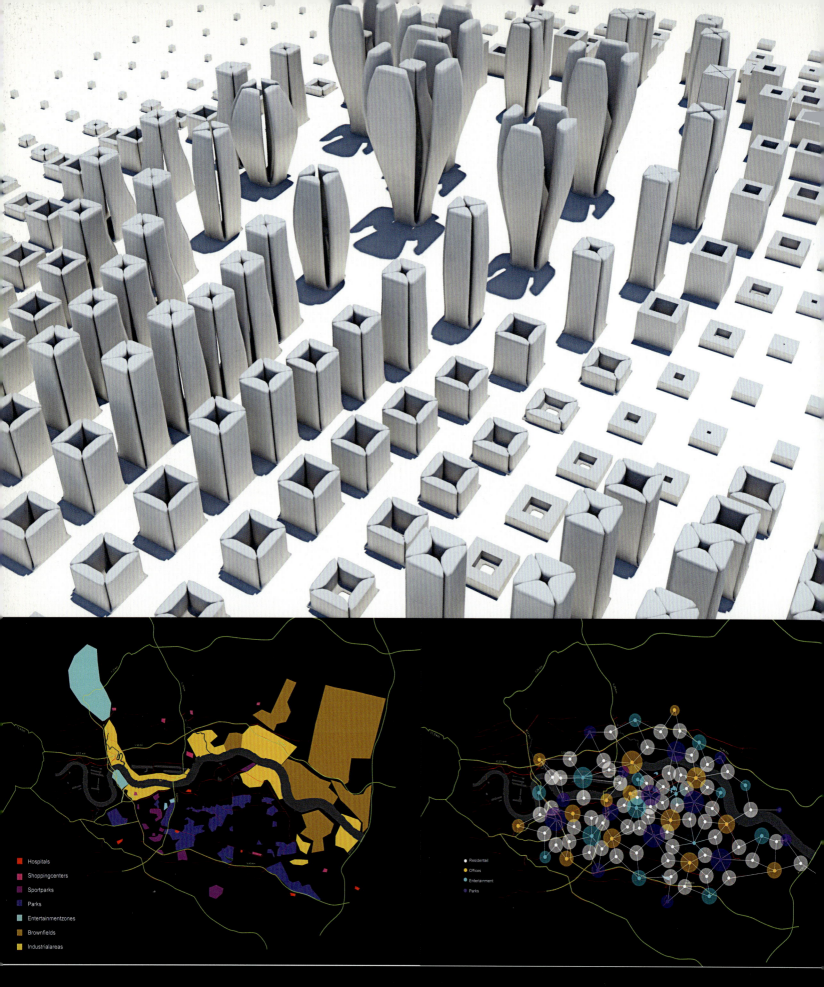

RGB Stripes

Kourosh Asgar-Irani, Josip Bajcer, Vladimir Ivanov, Christoph Zimmel

Having analyzed the Seoul commune 2026 project of mass studies, this project develops different color-based algorithms to map office, entertainment, parks and residential areas within an urban field. Depending on density, the building types range from single houses to multifunctional skyscrapers, if density fields overlap, they create unique and distinct combinations of buildings.

Legend (left map):
- Hospitals
- Shoppingcenters
- Sportparks
- Parks
- Entertainmentzones
- Brownfields
- Industrialareas

Legend (right map):
- Residentail
- Offices
- Entertainment
- Parks

Mesa City

Alexander Karaivanov, Philipp Ostermaier, Milan Suchanek

Looking into the logics of vector fields and their power to react to different border conditions and object correlations within a field, the experimental application of density information results in a highly differentiated field with four simple basic typologies: tower, block, housing and park. The results of the outcome is then used to refine the articulation of the different typologies.

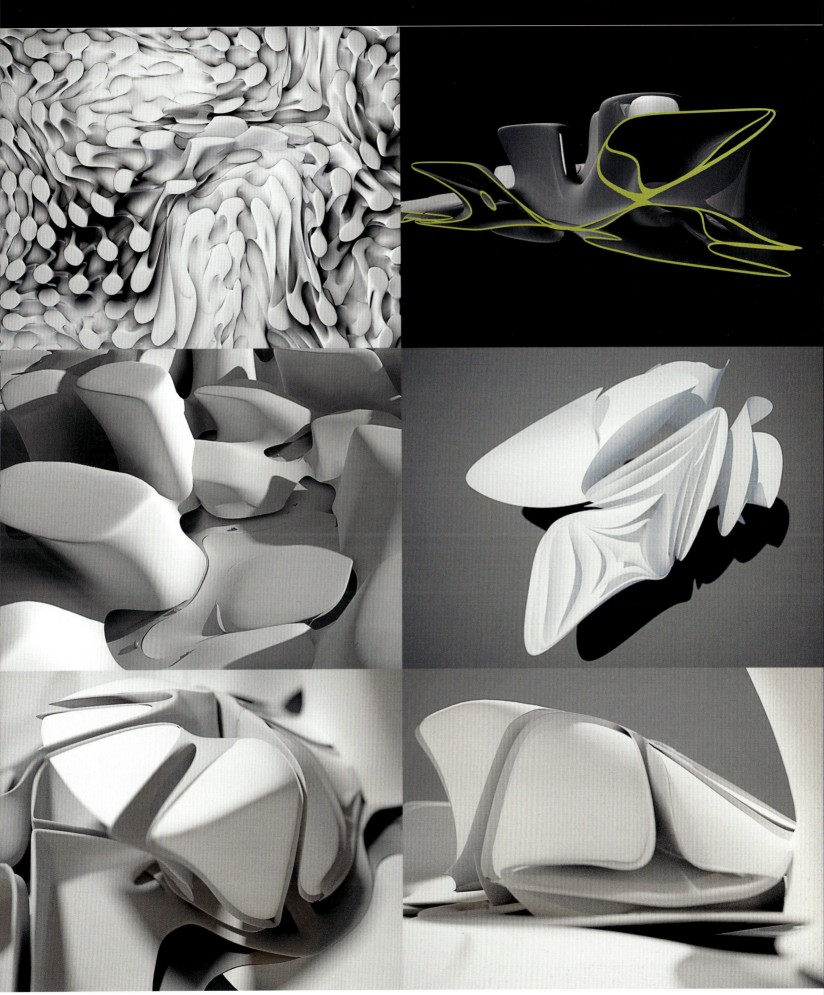

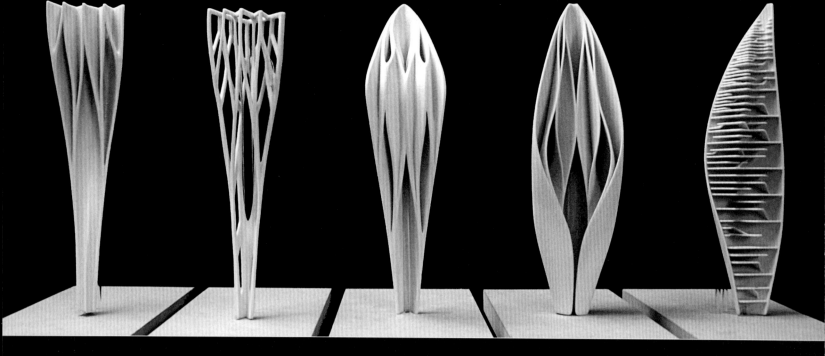

Infinitree

Manuel Fröschl, Sebastian Gallnbrunner, Sabrina Miletich, Philipp Weisz

The project is inspired by the branching systems found in nature, which are translated into a geometrical system for a 3-dimensional building structure. During the design process, additional leaf-like structures are introduced to achieve additional spatial hierarchy. The geometry of the facade is reflected in the interior organization.

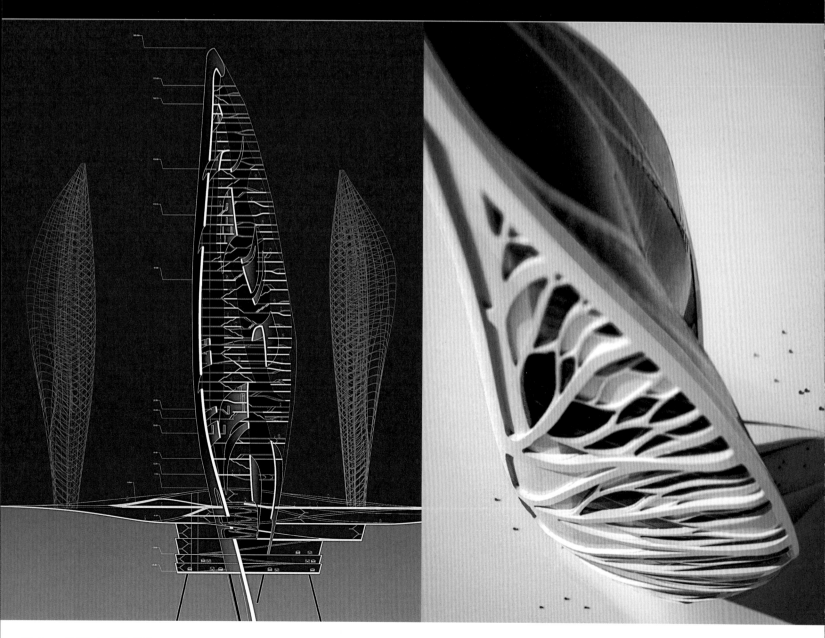

▲ **The Naked City –**
a Generative Situationist Theory
Manuel Lopez (UCLA), Martine Nicolay, Birgit Schmidt

▼ **Compacellicity**
Martin Blum-Jansen, Marius Cernica,
Krisztián Csémy, Jakub Klaska

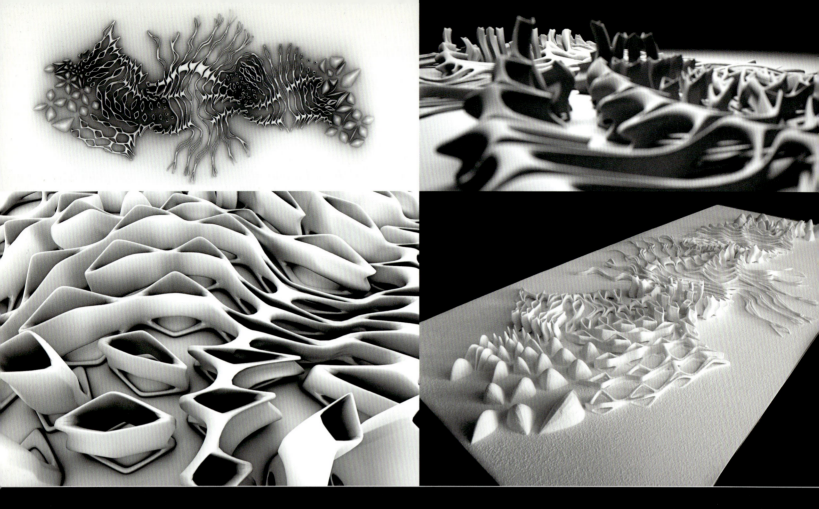

▲ Internal Connection
Niran Büyükköz, Nikolay Ivanov

▼ S.T.I.T.C.H
Konrad Hofmann, Wolfgang Windt

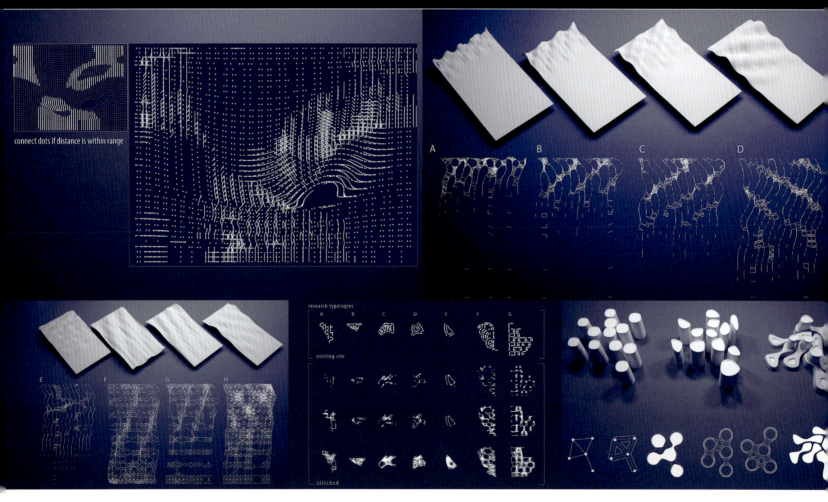

connect dots if distance is within range

A   B   C   D

E   F   G   H

research typologies

A   B   C   D   E   F   G

existing site

s.t.i.t.c.h.e.d.

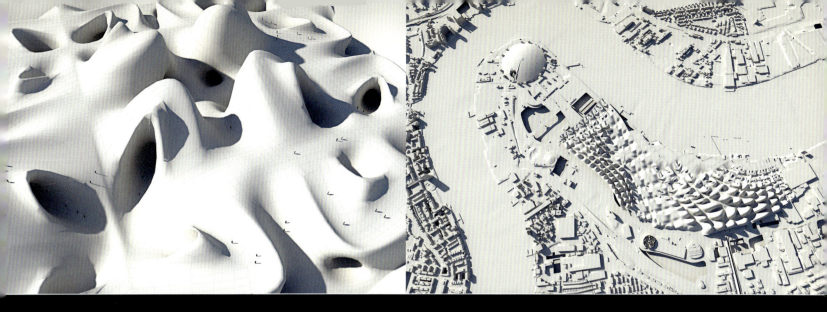

▲ **Wicked Ways**

Mirta Bilos, Jasmina Frincic, Nino Tugushi

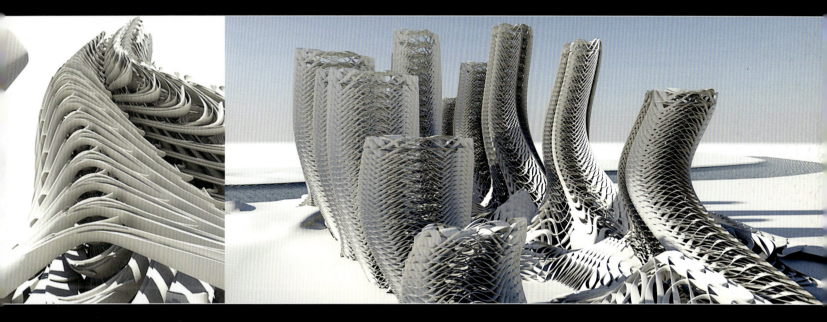

▲ **Minimal Skeleton**

Roxelane Güllmeister, Daniel Reist

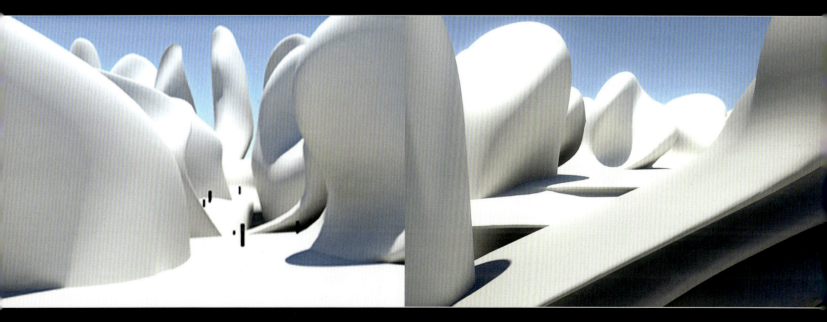

▲ **Geno / Fields**

Roxelane Güllmeister, Andrea König, Daniel Reist

FROM DIGITAL TECHNIQUE TO ELEGANCE

Ali Rahim

Cultural and technological innovations establish new status quos and updated platforms from which to operate and launch further innovations to stay ahead of cultural developments. Design research practices continually reinvent themselves and the techniques they use, and guide these innovations to stay ahead of such developments.

Reinvention can come through techniques that have already been set in motion, such as dynamic systems and other open source software programs that are mined for all their potential, through the development of new plug-ins that are able to change attributes within dynamic systems, or through changing existing or writing new expressions in the form of scripts in computer language – in effect changing the capacity of the operation of the software to develop new techniques for the design and manufacture of architecture. These techniques are important to design research to inform the form, space and material conditions of architecture. All will continue to be developed and alter the way architectural practices operate in the near and long term. Practices can also develop new techniques by investigating new technologies on the horizon of other fields. The necessary characteristics of the technologies selected are that they contain feedback, are inter-relational and have the potential to destabilize their current contexts. Techniques borrowed from other spheres can assist architectural practices to become more synthetic, seamlessly integrating the design, testing and manufacture of material formations.

BEYOND TECHNIQUES TO ELEGANCE

The development of techniques is essential for innovation in design. However, the mastering of techniques, whether in design, production or both, does not necessarily yield great architecture. In Studio Hadid, there is an attempt to move beyond techniques by mastering them to achieve nuances within a formal development of projects that exude an elegant aesthetic sensibility.

Architects who have been able to add such a layer of aesthetic sophistication to their designs share several characteristics that are key to current digital design discourse. All of their projects operate within emerging paradigms of generative techniques, and move past methods completely dependent on the rigorous application of scientific standards. Each exhibits a systemic logic of thought that eschews mapping a specific process, or revealing the process of an algorithm being generated, as strategies to generate a project's form. Instead, mastery of the techniques used allows each designer to assume a more sophisticated relationship with the creation of form – using malleable forms differentiated at varied rates that are correlated systemically – a position made possible only through the use of an aesthetic sensibility concomitant with a highly developed design ability.

WHY ELEGANCE?

Beyond the austerities of digital technique, elegance concerns refinement, precision and formal opulence. Elegance integrates an aesthetic desire, unleashing a visual intelligence pertinent for all design fields at all scales.

The concept of elegance has the ability to push the discourse of contemporary architecture forward, by accepting that complex architectural compositions require an accompanying visual aesthetic as sophisticated as the current techniques used to generate form.

Elegance mediates and enables complexity. A tightly controlled, precise refinement in technique is required to mold transformative surfaces that incorporate distinctly different topological features. The results are potentially chaotic. Negotiating and restraining the visual opulence of these compositions is an operation that entails elegance.

The works and works-in-progress presented in this issue probe the concept of elegance. They display a simultaneous maturation of digital and material practice: but beyond this refined mastery of technique, these architects move towards an integration of an aesthetic desire, that we believe yields elegant results.

DIGITAL TOOLS, ELEGANT FORMS

Studio Hadid is very interested in elegance that has arisen from the use of relational equations and scripting mediated by digital techniques. This includes subdivision surfaces and NURBS modeling, tools that incorporate the most advanced results of experimentation in digital design.

As a premise for Studio Hadid's investigation, they believe that progressive digital techniques are pivotal to moving forward in the field of architecture. But often taken for granted are the design research, mastery of techniques and sheer talent required to produce the most sophisticated of contemporary projects enabled by digital techniques. Elegance confronts this shortcoming in critical discourse by arguing that the mastery of techniques, whether in design, production or both, does not necessarily yield great architecture. As we all know – or can easily see by surveying institutions teaching digital technology – the most advanced techniques can still yield average, or even terrible, designs! Only certain projects achieve elegance. Some of the instances in which designers are able to move *beyond* technique, by mastering them to such a degree that they are able to achieve nuances within the formal development of their projects that exude elegance.

Architects who have been able to add that layer of aesthetic sophistication to their designs share several characteristics pivotal to the digital design discourse today. All of the featured designers operate within emerging paradigms of generative techniques, and have moved past methods completely dependent on the rigorous application of scientific standards. Each exhibits a systemic logic of thought that eschews mapping a specific process, or revealing the process of an algorithm being generated, as strategies to generate a project's form. Instead, mastery of technique allows them to assume a more sophisticated relation to the creation of form – a position only made possible through the use of an aesthetic sensibility concomitant with a highly developed design ability.

Design ability enables these architects to incorporate the myriad conditions for architectural creation – including, but not limited to, constraints associated with zoning, building codes, organization, space, program, circulation, fabrication, assembly, and cost – in a process facilitated by the digital algorithm and enabled by scripting. In the most elegant of designs, scripting is used to develop new types of interrelational schemes that integrate all of the design and manufacturing intentions in one seamless model. Ultimately, the architect's challenge is to control the modulation of these relations, in order to endow each project with the desired affect.

THE PURSUIT OF ELEGANCE

A beginning to the achievement of elegance in architecture is the use and mastery of the digital techniques afforded to us by customizable software. A reliance on scripting procedures rarely yields an elegant project, but manipulation of code through the mediation of digital technique is essential to yielding elegance. Working through the process of mastering techniques is internally driven, and is a necessary underpinning to developing a sensibility for the formal features achieved through the course of design.

Frei Otto used one parameter to generate all of his landmark research on tensile structures: that of gravity's relationship to the coefficient of material elasticity. Driven by an interest in the minimal use of materials, his research employed analog computing methods to yield results constituted of singular features: for example, a catatonic curve, or a derived surface that repeated itself to produce larger formal organizations. These analog methods did not have the capacity to produce two competing relational criteria as a means of generating form.

As architecture's multiple complexities are difficult to condense into a single formal criterion, it becomes apparent that a more interrelational set of criteria is needed to develop architecture through algorithmic methods. As more parameters are incorporated, the ability for a greater number of formal features to emerge becomes possible. The presence of several relational criteria allow for a family of interrelated features and forms to be constituted in the work; however, these arise only with specific intentions or goals for the project. When multiple criteria are employed, the formal design development is subsumed within the techniques used: the final design does not necessarily reveal the process of its creation. Hence, the process of production cannot be conceptually read in the final form that results from the design act.

The act of design is, therefore, ultimately framed not by a singular aesthetic end, but by the multiple constraints and ambitions of each project, as negotiated by the architect. To develop elegant work, layered levels of design intelligence are required, effortlessly incorporating *organizational and spatial* aspects.

Organizationally, the traditional concept of program is re-defined through the visible relationships produced by precisely controlled use-potential. In this definition, use-potential may yield relationships that emerge through the ongoing interactions between the user and the spaces.

Spatial configuration and organization act as criteria relational to the form of the project. The interior reveals its internal organization through the gradually transforming relationships it forms to the human body moving through the space. In addition, this internal organization is adapted to site constraints and the environment that it operates within. Elegance is achieved when, rather than allowing external constraints to alter and compromise the internal organization, the internal organization is manipulated and transformed to adapt to external constraints. Again, this requires a developed design and aesthetic sensibility: reliance on technique alone yields average buildings.

During the process of learning and mastering technique, a fineness of manner and expression develops through the cultivation of a refinement, exactness and precision that incorporates form, space and movement of the body. The projects that result are highly customized.

Once repertoire and technique are controlled through coordination, formal features allow for gracefulness and movement to reveal the precision and mastery achieved with specific techniques. Through its graceful aspect, the external appearance of the form allows the internal organization and its sophistication, experienced in movement through the space, to be perceived. There is a seamless transformation between internal and external organization, that puts the internal techniques and their mastery on display externally.

Elegant structures possess formal features and material articulation sufficiently rich so as to emphasize the realm of bodily sensation. This is also developed through the techniques and procedures used in the design. Buildings that achieve the possibility of producing elegant sensations have particular characteristics formally, including *presence, formal balance, refinement of features and surface, and restrained opulence.*

An elegant building needs to have a framework against which its presence is read, and at the same time, must participate as an extension of the field in which it operates.

Formal balance is achieved when the refinement of transformational spatial configurations achieves forms that seemingly defy gravity. An exceptionally sophisticated integration of structure, systems and new materials may allow for the form to appear suspended, or possessed of a particular lightness. In terms of formal appearance, this lightness includes qualities of fineness and daintiness, determined within the multiple individual elements that constitute the building design. The scale of the part to the whole needs to be attenuated, adjusted with precision and refinement, in order to produce the desired affect. If the scale of the part is too diminutive in relation to the whole, or if the whole is constituted of too many smaller pieces, then the viewer may be overwhelmed, and the potential of producing elegance is lost. When the relation of part to whole is attuned, elegant sensations – rather than chaotic ones – may be achieved at the point of transformation.

Crucial to the production of elegant sensations, the architect must design the project with the intention of elaborating refined surfaces to develop transformations between different formal features. The formal opulence of a building is comprised through creating a family of formal features that are each distinctive, yet remain inter-related as they transform from one to another. In an elegant composition, each feature is endowed with differences, and the transformation between features is attenuated and gradual. Transformations between features are mediated by a surface modulated in accordance with the transformation. These areas of change are constructed as deviations from a rule-generated surface, embedding geometrical characteristics within the perceptual and material circumstances of building.

The surface itself is key, as it provides a background for the features to be made legible – ultimately providing the perspective necessary for the features to yield affect.

THE PRESENCE – AND FUTURE – OF ELEGANCE

Relational equations and scripting mediated by digital techniques are powerful allies in producing, manufacturing, and assembling architectural projects that yield elegant sensations. An increasingly prevalent trend is the development of digital models that, in addition to incorporating formal constraints, integrate aspects of material and cost in one seamless model. Here, design intelligence moves beyond effective use of the CNC mill or laser cutter, towards a highly integrated model that can compute costs dependent on factors such as material curvature and joinery. The customization of these parts and their modulation, fabrication and assembly provides a bespoke quality to the architecture. Thus, the formal attributes of architecture developed during the design process may integrate nuances of negotiation with fabrication industries, directly reducing the cost of mass customization.

The pursuit of elegance, in Studio Hadid, ultimately incorporates a wider range of technologies in its quest to create elegant aesthetics manifest in built architecture. Mastery of technique remains important, and underpins the use of digital technologies in the design and manufacturing of elegant buildings. But ultimately, a highly sophisticated formal language – including the driving force of aesthetic pleasure – propels elegance.

Project: "Barotic Interiorities"

ALI RAHIM is an architect, Director of Contemporary Architecture Practice and member of the permanent architecture design faculty at the University of Pennsylvania where he directs Design Research Studios and co-ordinates the final year of the Master of Architecture Design Program. Mr. Rahim has recently served as the Zaha Hadid Visiting Professor at the University of Applied Arts [di Angewandte] in Vienna, Austria and has served as the Louis I Kahn Visiting Architecture Professor at Yale University and Visiting Architecture Professor at Harvard University. Mr. Rahim's books include Catalytic Formations: Architecture and Digital Design, December 2006 and three Architecture Design volumes published by Academy Editions. John Wiley and Sons: Contemporary Processes in Architecture, 2000, Contemporary Techniques in Architecture, 2002 and Elegance, Co-edited with Hina Jamelle in 2007.

Rahim has delivered public lectures extensively on his work nationally and internationally at Harvard, Yale, Penn, SCI Arc, Georgia Tech, University of Toronto, Architectural Association and the Bartlett, London, TU Delft, Netherlands, Universitat Internacional Catalunya, Barcelona, Aristotle University of Thessaloniki, Greece, and the American University Sharjah, UAE to name a few.

Contemporary Architecture Practice [www.c-a-p.net] was founded in 1999 and is located in SoHo, New York City. Contemporary Architecture Practice has established an award winning profile in futuristic work using cutting edge digital design and production techniques. Their work includes masterplans, residential, commercial and product design projects. A book on Contemporary Architecture Practice titled Catalytic Formations is now in its second edition.

Contemporary Architecture Practice has published extensively in the press – most recently featured in the Nikkei, Frame, Monitor, Vogue Japan, Elle Japan, Casa Brutus, Mainichi Shimbun, Harvard Design Magazine and A+U. and. Past publications include Architectural Record, Architectural Design London, Yale Constructs, Arkiteketen Denmark, Domus, Slate, Space China, Architettura Milan, Der Spiegel and the New York Times to name a few. CAP has been nominated for the Ordos Prize and was awarded the Outstanding Award for FEIDAD 2006 and Architectural Record Product of the Month for their lighting fixture titled 'Opale' in 2007. They were also selected for Phaidon Press's 10x10_2, 2005 curated by "10 internationally prominent critics, architects and curators," and Architectural Record's Design Vanguard 2004, as one of eleven architectural practices worldwide "building the future of architecture".

Contemporary Architecture Practices projects have been most recently exhibited at the Museum of Modern Art, New York, Tel Aviv Museum of Art, Serpentine Museum, London and Entry 2006 Expo in Essen, Germany. Past exhibition venues include Artists Space, New York, Royal Institute of British Architects [RIBA], London and the Beijing and Shanghai Architectural Biennale's in 2004, 2005 and 2006 respectively.

The notion of interiority suggests the elaboration of tectonic systems that unfold and differentiate within the terms of their own internal logic.

We are interested in developing complex, layered and highly differentiated tectonic systems that can start to compete with the best historical examples in terms of their richness, coherency and precision of formal organisation. We are aiming to reach the level of designed luxury we find for instance in the most filigreed gothic spaces or the most excessive baroque or rococo interiors, to go beyond all known historical precedents in terms of qualitative differentiation and the intensity of part-to-part and part-to-whole relationships.

We are striving to build up multi-layered complexity with a high degree of lawful differentiation within each involved system as well as a high level of correlation between these various systems that constitute the overall tectonics. Each modification of a given subsystem is associated with corresponding or complementary differentiations within the other subsystems. For example, structural differentiation is correlated with material/textural differentiation, etc. As each interior must feature such a multi-layer (multi-subsystem) build-up, one strategy of integration might be that certain subsystems (e.g. structure, lighting, furniture layer, etc.) might operate across several spaces – each time entering a new symbiosis and each time being modulated in specific ways due to the specific correlation in each specific interior.

These ambitions are shared within the contemporary architectural avant-garde and constitute a clearly identifiable style: Parametricism. Like all avant-garde styles, parametricism can be characterised by its dogmas (positive heuristics) and taboos (negative heuristics) that give a clear a priori direction to the design research:
Negative heuristics: avoid simple repetition of elements, avoid collage of unrelated elements.

Positive heuristics: consider all forms to be parametrically malleable, differentiate gradually (at variant rates), correlate systematically.

As means to facilitate the design research we propose the design of an urban club in New York. Within this concrete framework we are focusing our design effort on a cluster of primary social rooms: A lounge, a dining room, a library, a conference room and a ballroom. Once those spaces have been established with a clear individual internal logic, their interior logics can be subjected to various influences: From one interior to another as well as from the exterior environment.

At this stage the respective interior logics have to demonstrate their potential as adaptive logics in order to form a convincing series of spaces which are distinct, yet formally related.

The design should synthesize all of the following registers or aspects that contribute to a full-blown architectural experience: Form, structure, material, texture, ornament, colour, transparency/opacity and light/shadow.

The first task is to build up three 'architectural surfaces' that are – each in their own way – characterized by a great range of internal differentiation. Each surface should then be differentiated according to a qualitative opposition like hard/soft, light/heavy etc. The next step is the development of each surface into a full enclosure before we bring in the programmatic concerns of the brief.

At this stage we are elaborating a system of performance-related morphological characters. We then can start to establish a spatial order between the different spaces, and articulate connections and transitions. Then we work from the inside out in order to produce the external expression of the cluster. Finally, the whole complex is worked into and made to respond within an environment.

It is a significant property of all architecture that it can never be brought into view within a single unifying vista. The experience of architecture is therefore always stretched out across time. This concerns the front versus the back of a building, but more importantly it concerns the exterior versus the interior of the building. This lack of visual simultaneity continues within the interior as we have to use time and sequence when we move from room to room. This poses the problem of experiential synthesis.

This problem is posed both with respect to the distinction of exterior and interior as well as with respect to the complex multiplicity of different interiors within the building. Instead of for example providing for deep visual penetration to alleviate this problem, we need to create an architectural order that achieves unity without literal spatial continuity. This can neither be achieved with pure difference, nor with pure sameness. Both are disorienting.

The unity of experience can only be achieved via the combination of variation and redundancy. Sequencing might be important so that a particular sequence by which the rooms are traversed is providing more unity (or a different unity) than any other (or another) sequence. In the end we have a network of rooms organized via laws of transformation that might include inversions and contrasts as much as modulations and continuities.

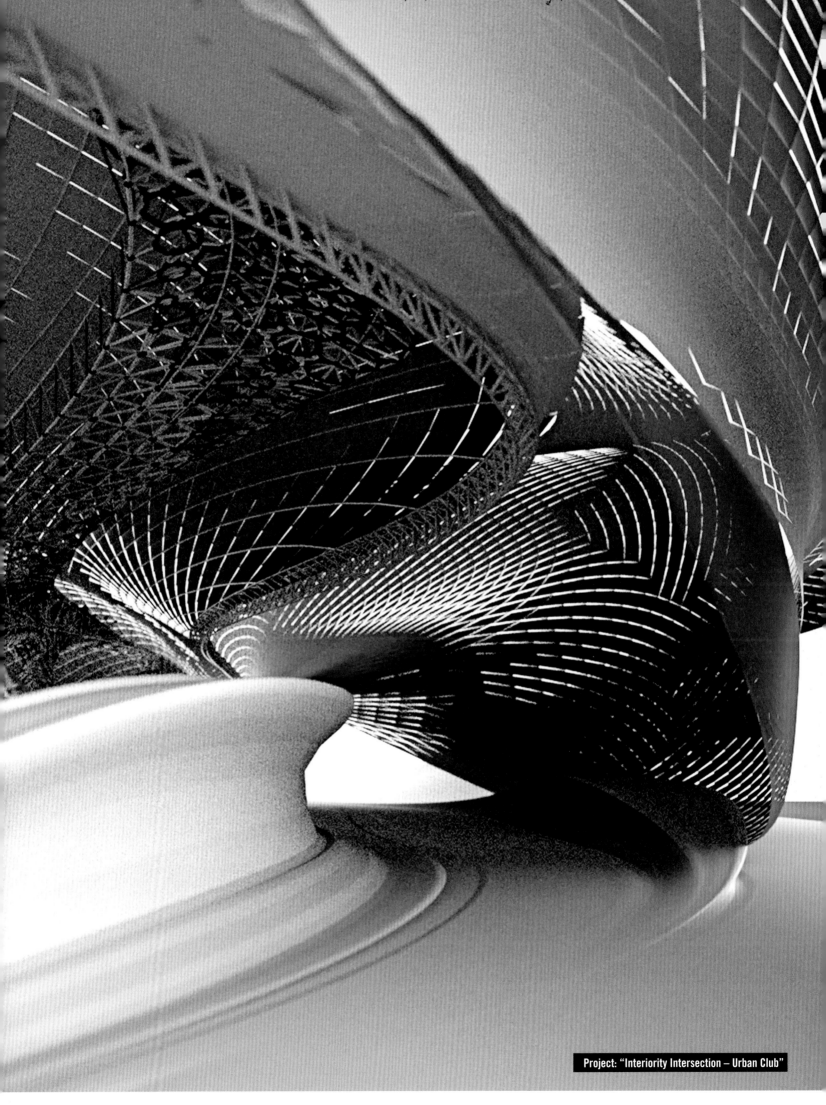

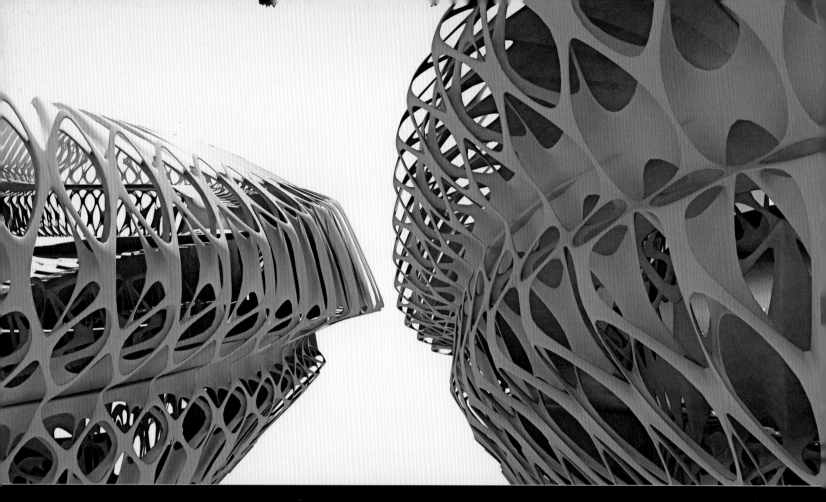

Surface Modulations

Manuel Fröschl, Thomas Milly, Maya Pindeus

The experimental focus of this project was to create a shift between a planar surface and a 3D-mesh, that change and adapt parametrically in relation to the highly differentiated structural, functional and programmatic requirements of various interior spaces.

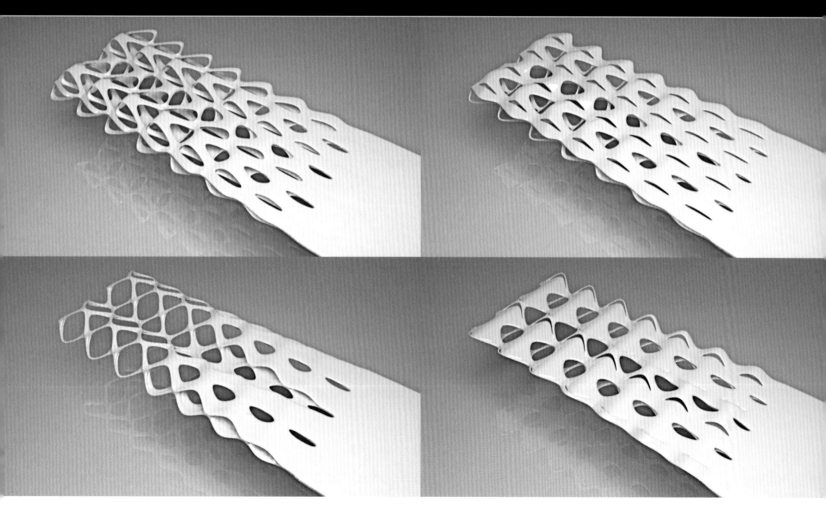

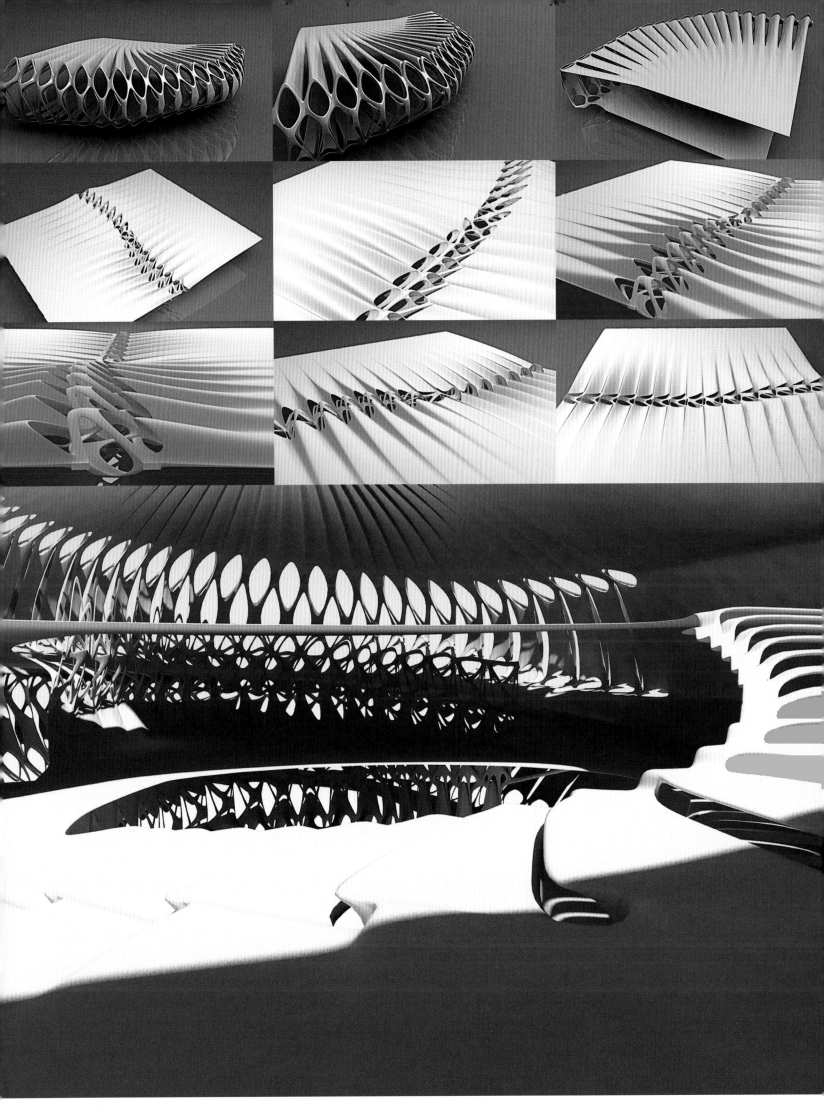

Compo.ment.ics

Gilles Greis, Nikolay Ivanov, Irina-Elena Preda

Emanating from the coherency and precision of historical patterns (Gothic, Baroque and Rococo), this project reunifies the elements of classical tectonic systems into one computational set up, open to variation and change, shifting from the circular to the hard-edged, from small to big thresholds, operating on multiple scales and shifting from a tectonic connections, to performance-related attributes.

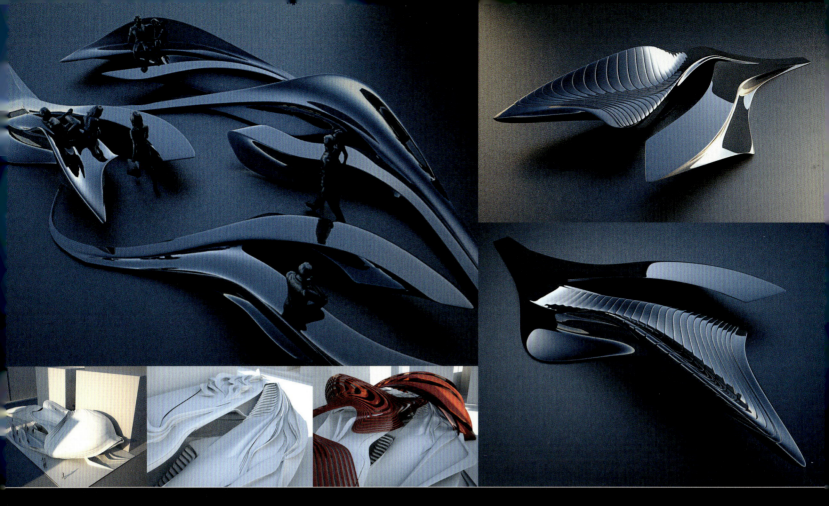

▲ **Delicious Collective**
Seongheon Kim, Sergiu-Radu Pop, Dimitri Tsiakas

▼ **Urban Club New York**
Manuel Fröschl, Sabrina Miletich

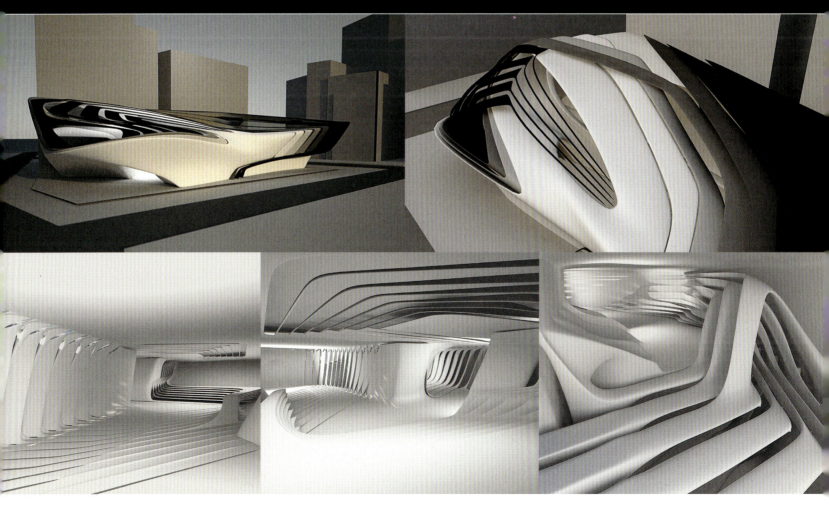

Adaptive Grid

Philipp Hornung, Dimitri Tsiakas

The project's focus is to investigate adaptive surface behavior under specific quality conditions. On top of a parametrically defined primary system (wall), an interconnected secondary system (components) is introduced, immediately affecting its organization and scaling. To test the performative aspects of the ornamental system, it is applied to two different types of spaces, an introversive and an extroversive environment.

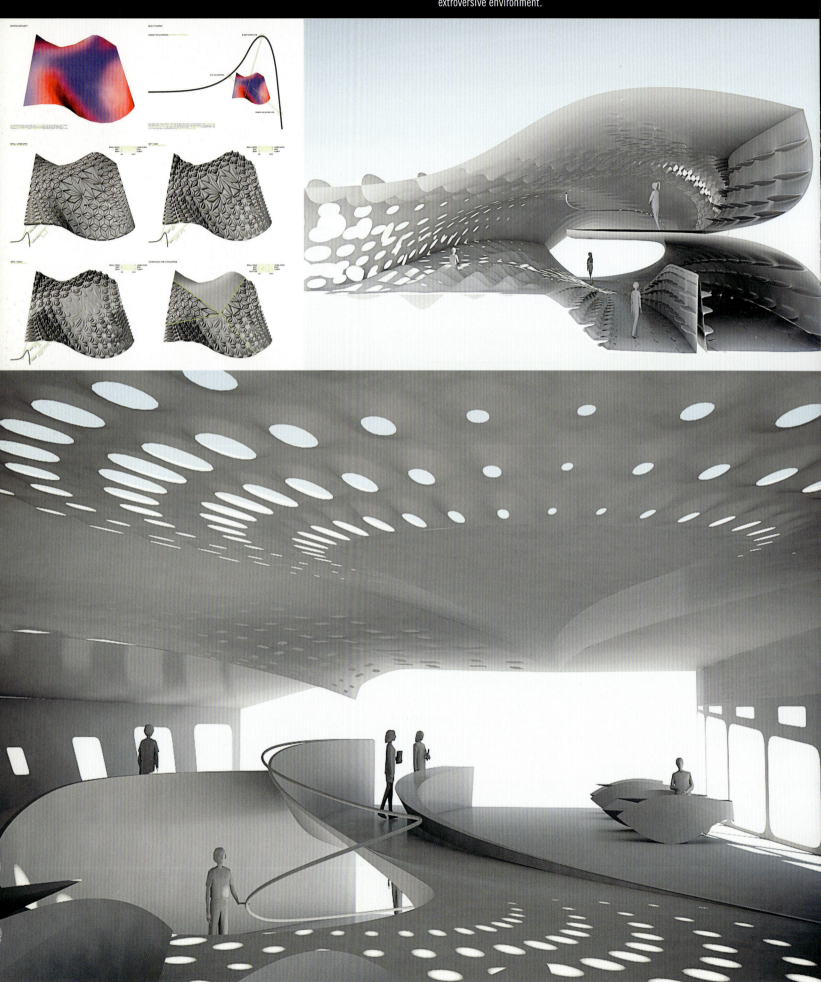

Interiority Intersection

Mi Na Bae, Romina Hafner, Monir Karimi,
Seongheon Kim, Sergiu-Radu Pop

Starting with simple line diagrams, a system of layered surfaces is developed, which interlock to form structurally sound spatial organizations and envelopes. At the same time, different delicate color effects are devised, correlating with the complex structural and spatial articulations at varying scales.

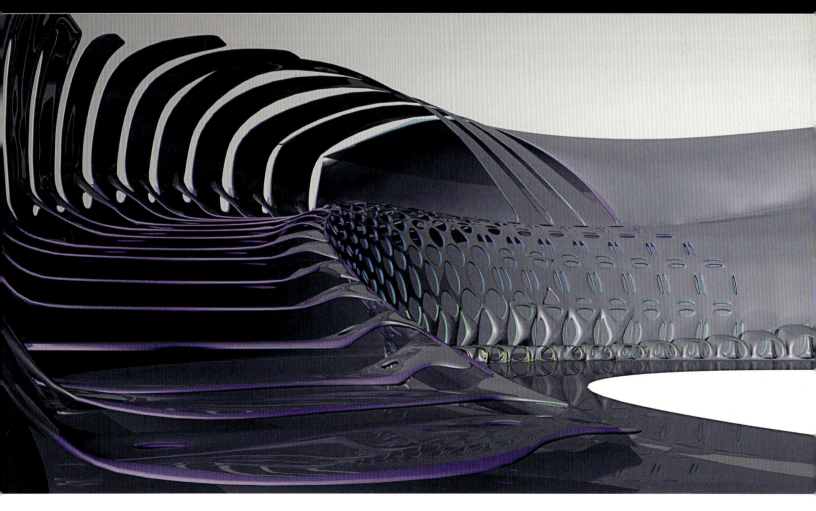

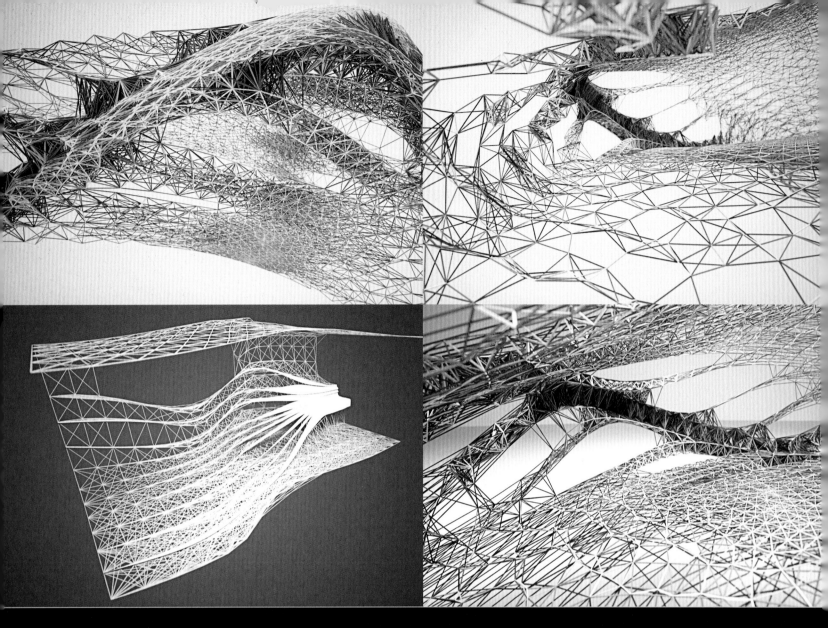

In-form

Krisztián Csémy, Jasmina Frincic, Jakub Klaska

'In-Form' develops the interior spaces of a club in New York as an intricately orchestrated and deeply correlated setup of three subsystems (envelope, structure and furnishing). Their relation is set up so that it allows for adaptations in one subsystem to trigger meaningful reactions in the others, creating an architecturally expedient and formally coherent spatial model.

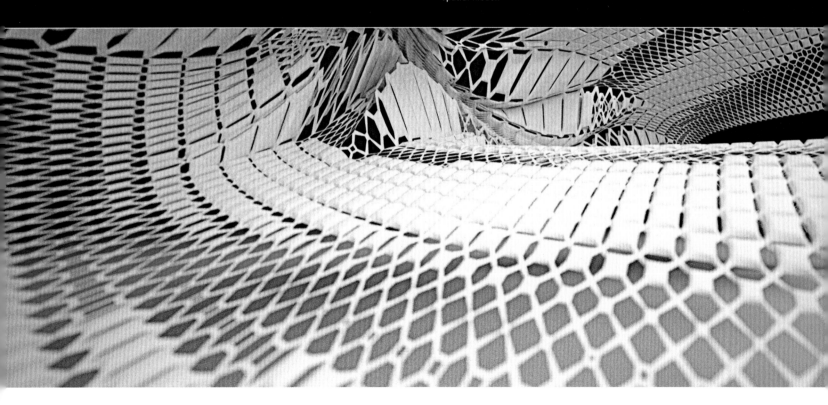

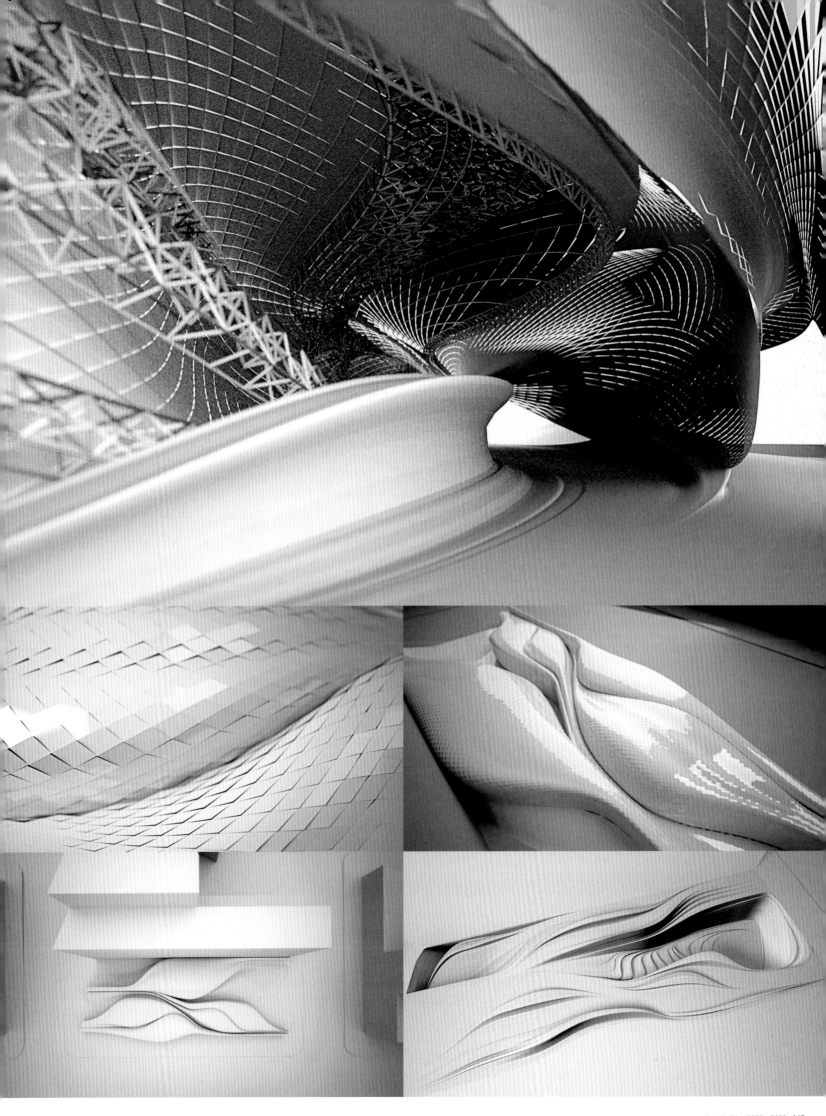

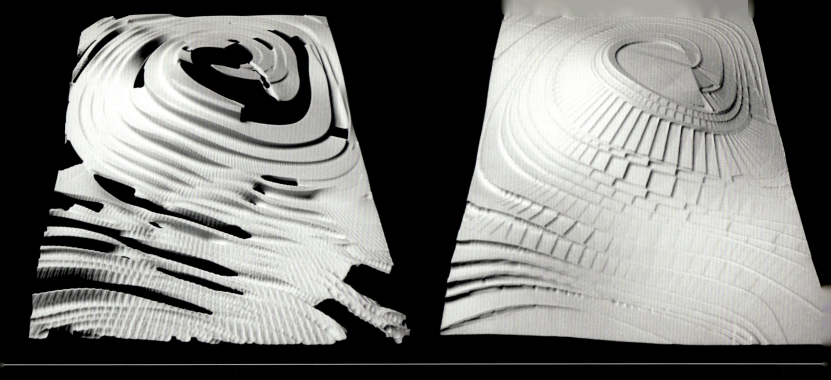

Barotic Interiorities

Roxelane Güllmeister, Christoph Hermann,
Alexander Karaivanov, Daniel Reist

The 'barotic' project explores the potential of vector fields as a generative design tool. As the name suggests it seeks to mimic and surpass historic examples of intricate and highly differentiated interior spaces from the Baroque, Rococo and Gothic epochs. The tool allows the design to embed a quasi-infinite amount of interior diversity, detail and opulence without losing the overall coherency.

Strandification

Niran Büyükköz, Martin Kleindienst, Raffael Petrovic

The project revolves around the parametric principle of achieving architectural complexity through the deliberate inter-articulation and co-development of related subsystems. Of particular interest are interior interstitial spaces in which one pure atmosphere transitions to another without impairing the overall coherency of the design.

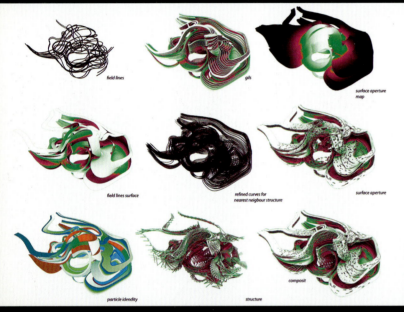

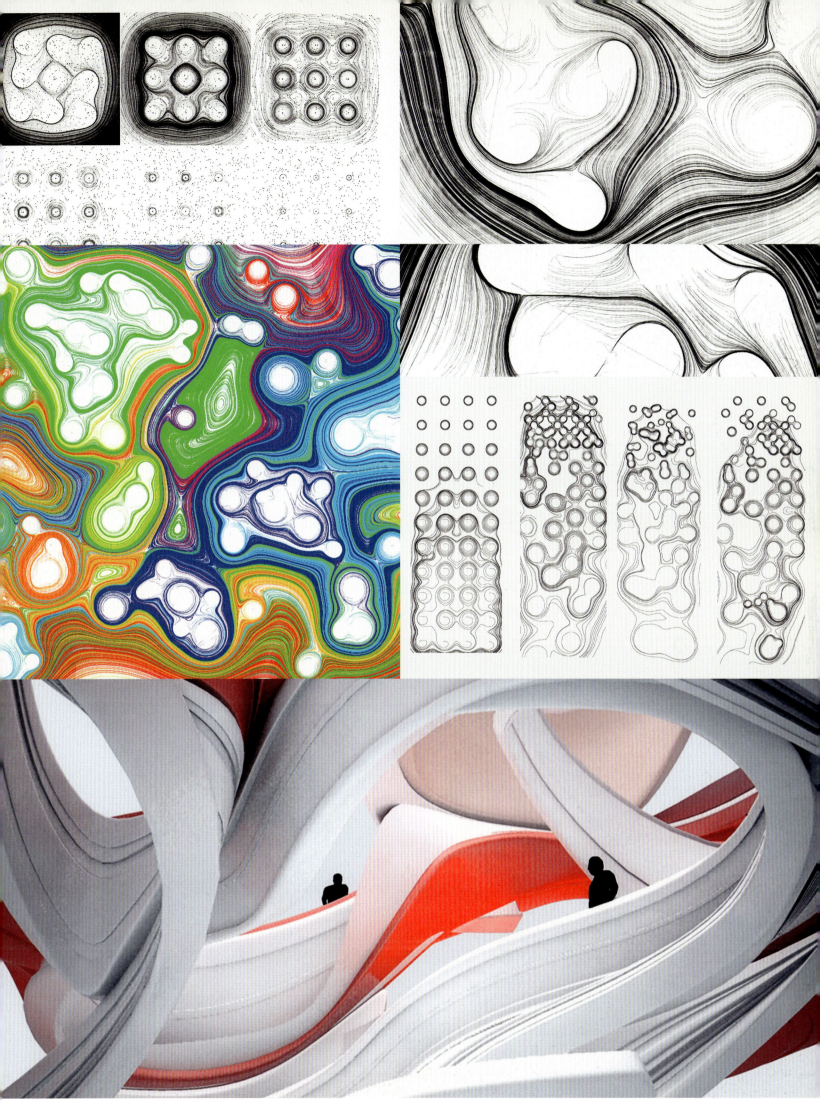

▲ **Interiorities**
Katharina Hieger, Galo Moncayo-Asan, Maya Pindeus

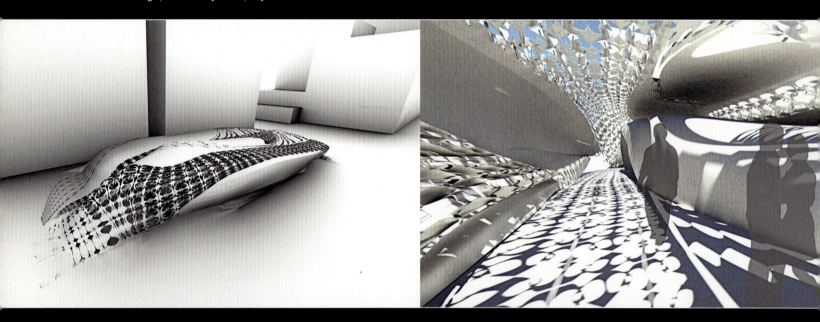

▲ **Element of Crime**
Agnieszka Grochowska, Cornelia Klien, Magda Smolinska

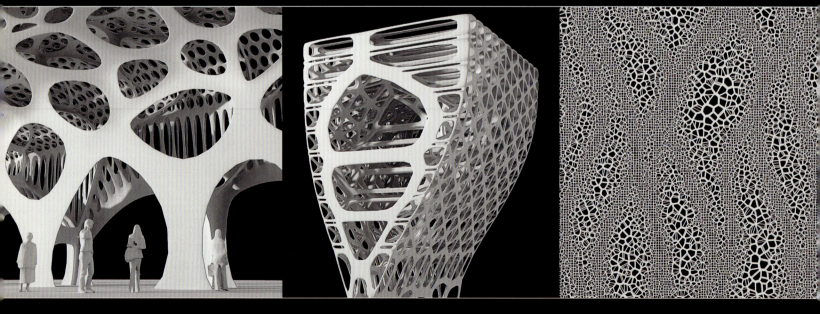

▲ **Porosity**
Nicola Beck, Christoph Zimmel

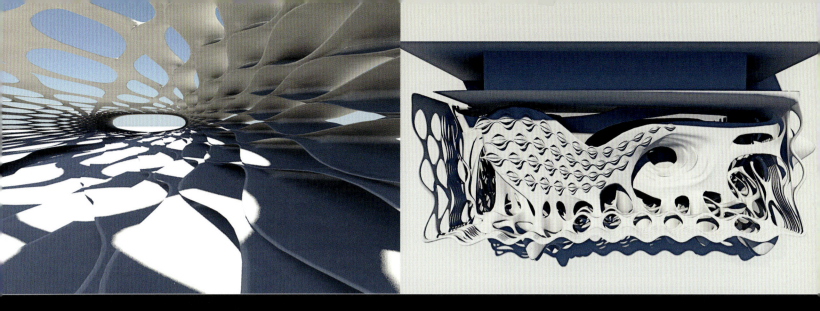

▲ Transforming Happiness

Kerem Akin (SCI-Arc), Hila Shomrat, Pavel Zeldovich

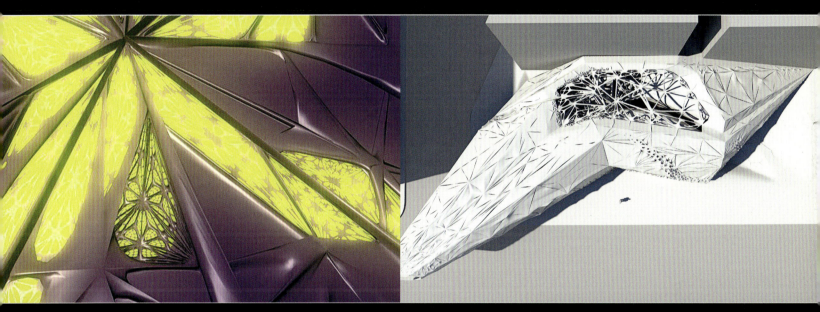

▲ Tridensity

Simon Aglas, Romina Hafner, Philipp Hornung, Jakob Wilhelmstätter

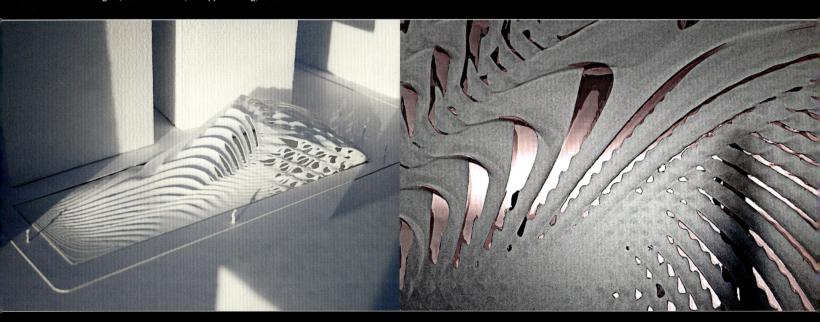

▲ Differelations

Kourosh Asgar-Irani, Josip Bajcer, Johannes Michael Bak, Marius Cernica

4(X + Y)=WORLD

2009- 2010

In 2009/2010 studies at the Studio Zaha Hadid Vienna focused on developing space and structure-generating processes whose architectural potential was implemented, tested and further developed in various design tasks in different increasing dimensions. Two thematically complementary objects were combined and developed in keeping with the found design logic.

In developing and processing architectural concepts for subsequent pairs of tasks ("shoe-bag", "sitting furniture-laptop", "car-garage" and "villa-boat") already developed work processes and the resulting material systems were adopted and adapted to the changing circumstances of internal and external parameters, refined and further developed, giving way to genotypically, species-related world of forms based on a contemporary repertory of formally and structurally related objects that are differentiated in various ways in terms of size and complexity.

Project: "Systematic Morphologies"

Customotation

Vladimir Ivanov, Robert Löffler, Bin Lu (SCI-Arc)

As they adapt to volumes of different sizes, textile structures change their skin texture and visual appearance when they are stretched over building volumes of different sizes. These mutations facilitate certain degrees of individualization corresponding to a specific usage and are further utilized to generate adaptive behavior and to account for an optimized environmental performance in architectural dimensions.

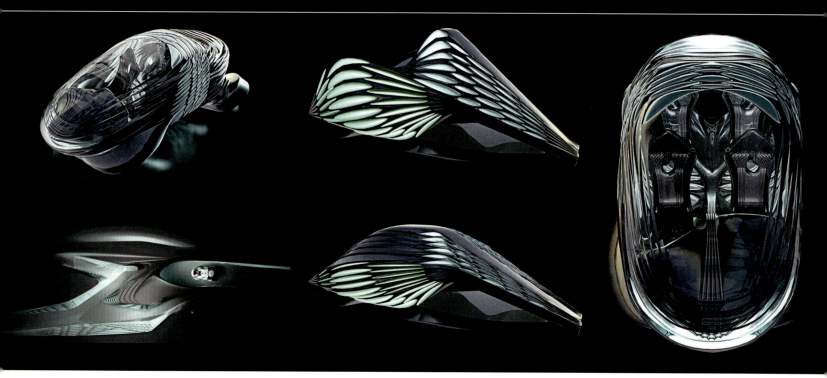

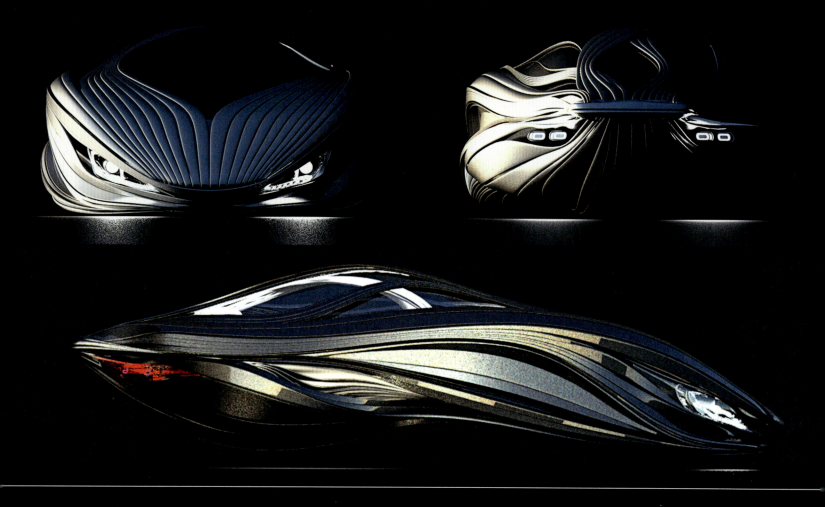

Systematic Morphologies

Moritz Dörstelmann, Sergiu-Radu Pop,
Ryan Russell (UCLA), Marc Wieneke

The properties of fiber bundles such as muscles originate in a system that is capable of creating a series of coherent design species. However, each case study expresses explicit functional, aesthetic and ergonomic criteria. Fibers consisting of rigid materials form stiff and structural elements while interwoven stretchable and soft material provides for flexible and cushioned characteristics.

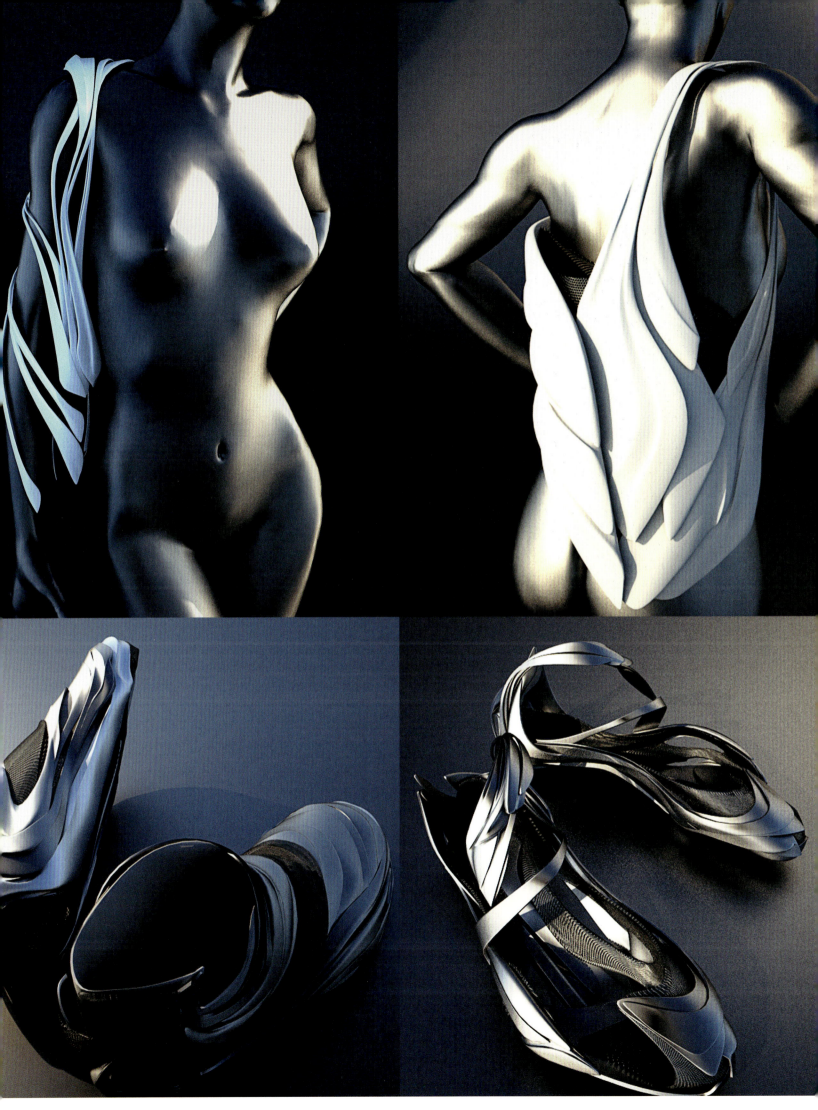

(A)Live

Moritz Dörstelmann

The potential of constantly self-regulating systems is explored and adapted in order to provide optimized climatic conditions in correlation to user-activated spatial configurations and atmospheric qualities. Bent rods and membranes consisting of smart materials build up a structure that combines functions of sensor controllers and/or actuators.

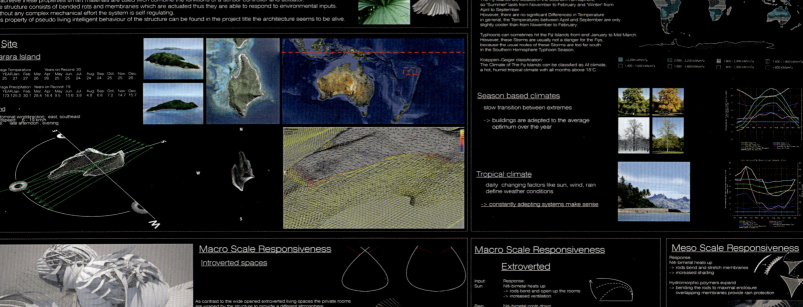

Concept

...y project (A)live deals with intelligent self regulating systems wich reconfigure the interior climate, programm,
...nd spacial qualities according to users demands and environmental inputs.
...he main aim is to provide best possible ventilation with wide opened rooms instead of insulating and cooling the interior.
...he climate in tropical regions is mainly influenced by fast changing daily factors,
...us a constantly adepting system makes sense.
...o achieve these properties smart materials are used wich combine the funktions of a sensor controller and actuator.
...he structure consists of bended rods and membranes which are actuated thus they are able to respond to environmental inputs.
...ithout any complex mechanical effort the system is self regulating.
...is property of pseudo living intelligent behaviour of the structure can be found in the project title the architecture seems to be alive.

Climate Fiji Islands

Fiji enjoys an ideal South Sea tropical climate and can get hot
in the summer but seldom reaches above 35°C
Trade winds from the east southeast bring year long cooling breezes
late afternoon and early evening.

The season for our tropical rains is from December throughFebruary
coinciding with the warmest summer months.
The Fiji Islands are situated in the southern Hemisphere,
so "Summer" lasts from November to February and "Winter" from
April to September.
However, there are no significant Differences in Temperature
in general, the Temperatures between April and September are only
slightly cooler than from November to February.

Typhoons can sometimes hit the Fiji Islands from end January to Mid March.
However, these Storms are usually not a danger for the Fijis,
because the usual routes of these Storms are too far south
in the Southern Hemisphere Typhoon Season.

Koeppen-Geiger classification:
The Climate of The Fiji Islands can be classified as Af climate,
a hot, humid tropical climate with all months above 18°C.

Season based climates

slow transition between extremes

-> buildings are adepted to the average
   optimum over the year

Tropical climate

daily changing factors like sun, wind, rain
define weather conditions

-> constantly adepting systems make sense

Site

Jarara Island

average Temperature   Years on Record: 30
 YEAR Jan. Feb. Mar. Apr. May Jun. Jul. Aug. Sep. Oct. Nov. Dec.
 25   27   27   26   26   25   24   24   24   25   25   26

average Precipitation   Years on Record: 19
 YEAR Jan. Feb. Mar. Apr. May Jun. Jul. Aug. Sep. Oct. Nov. Dec.
 173 125.3 30.1 28.4 16.4 9.5 10.6 3.8 4.8 6.8 7.2 14.7 15.7

Wind

predominat winddirection: east, southeast
time: late afternoon , evening
windspeed: 6 - 19 km/h

Macro Scale Responsiveness

Introverted spaces

As contrast to the wide opened extroverted living spaces the private rooms
are wraped by the structure to provide a different atmosphere

At night the private rooms open up thus sleeping under the night sky is provided
Over the day these rooms are enclosed providing a private sun protected atmosphere
(counter movement to the public rooms)

Input: Response:
Sun   Niti-bimetal heats up
           -> rods bend and wrap around the room enclosing it
Rain   Hydromorphic polymers expand
           -> bending the rods to maximal enclosure overlapping them

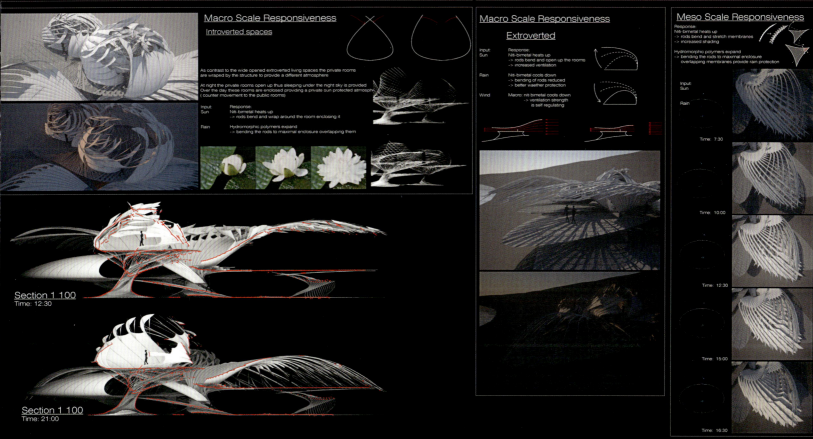

Section 1 100
Time: 12:30

Section 1 100
Time: 21:00

Macro Scale Responsiveness

Extroverted

Input: Response:
Sun   Niti-bimetal heats up
           -> rods bend and open up the rooms
           -> increased ventilation
Rain   Niti-bimetal cools down
           -> bending of rods reduced
           -> better weather protection
Wind   Macro: niti bimetal cools down
           -> ventilation strength
              is self regulating

Meso Scale Responsiveness

Response:
Niti-bimetal heats up
-> rods bend and stretch membranes
-> increased shading

Hydromorphic polymers expand
-> bending the rods to maximal enclosure
   overlapping membranes provide rain protection

Input:
Sun

Rain

Time: 7:30
Time: 10:00
Time: 12:30
Time: 15:00
Time: 16:30

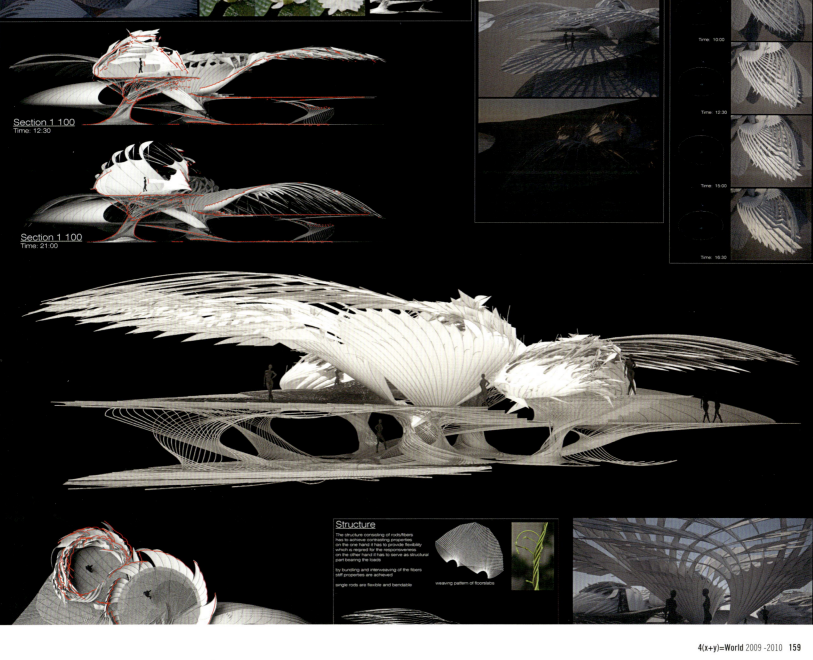

Structure

The structure consisting of rods/fibers
has to achieve contrasting properties
on the one hand it has to provide flexibility
which is regired for the responsiveness
on the other hand it has to serve as structural
part bearing the loads

by bundling and interweaving of the fibers
stiff properties are achieved

single rods are flexible and bendable

weaving pattern of floorslabs

$Int'dense/$addApting

Martin Kleindienst, Thomas Milly, Galo Moncayo-Asan

Figurative complexity and a formal indication of areas with high activities are attained by a varied and graduated intensification of lines and linear shapes on objects with different scales. The geometrical properties are harnessed in favor of an endeavor to create spatial scenarios that reduce the necessity of artificial climate control and create a variety of comfort levels throughout buildings.

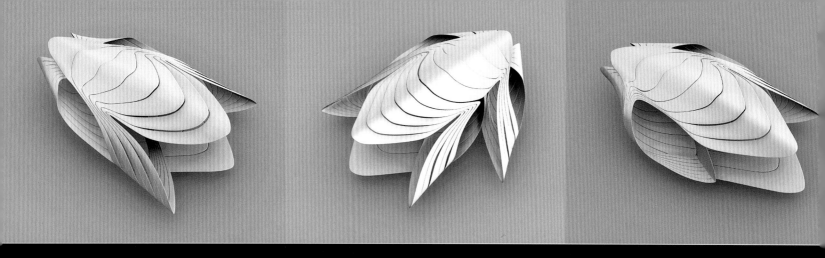

Beach Villa Fiji
Manuel Fröschl

An accumulation of strips forming closed loops and blades that work as wind-scoops makes use of the Venturi effect that occurs when wind blows through narrow passageways. The spatial arrangement is evaluated according to the conditions of a rather harsh environment in terms of humidity and temperature and maximizes cooling effects at desired times of the day.

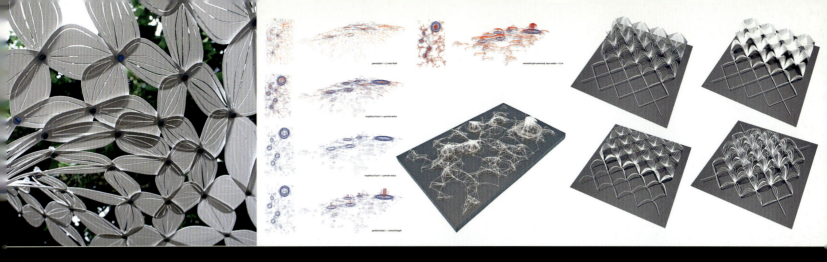

Biot(r)opics

Niran Büyükköz, Gilles Greis, Raffael Petrovic

The study of tropical vernacular architecture and their efficient strategies to deal with extreme habitats conducted a lightweight modulation of roofscapes and landscapes. They smoothly blend into the surroundings in terms of atmospheres and climates, facilitating transitions between different micro-climatic conditions that provide various zones of comfort for daily activities.

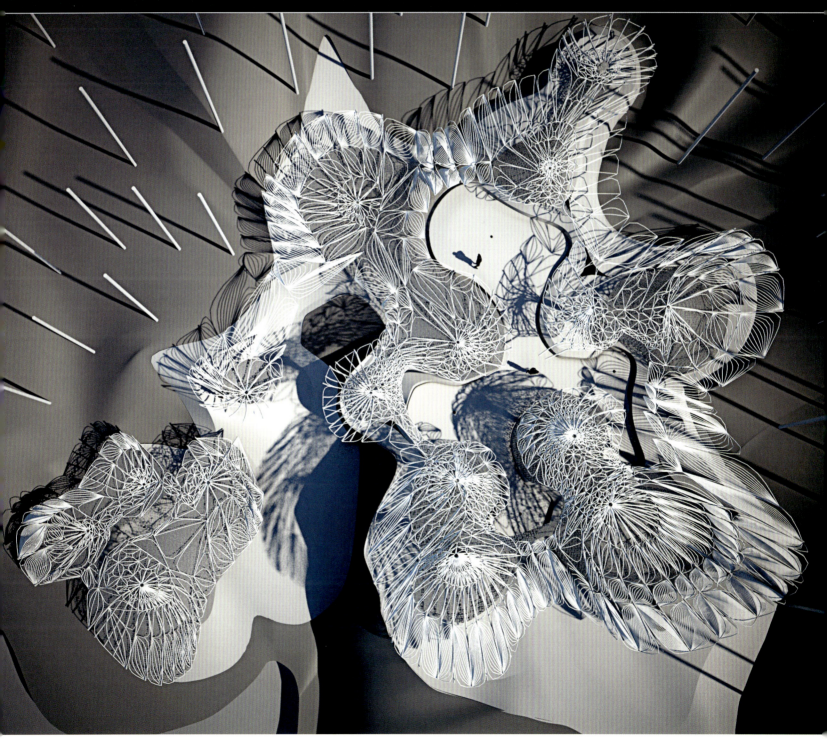

▲ **ExtraMateriality**
Mirta Bilos, Nikolay Ivanov, Rasa Navasaityte

▼ **Inside Out**
Yin Wu Shu, Ming Yin, Jing Jing Zhou

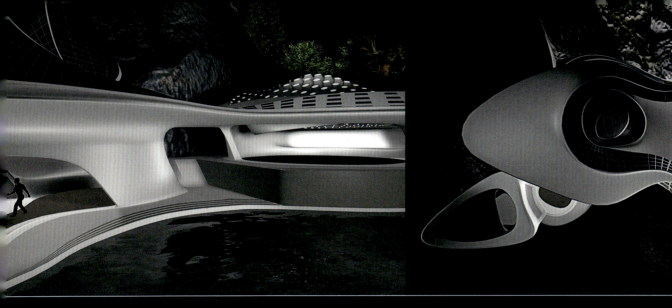

▲ Villa St. Lucia

Saara-Leena Koljonen, Barnabas Kovács-Dobák

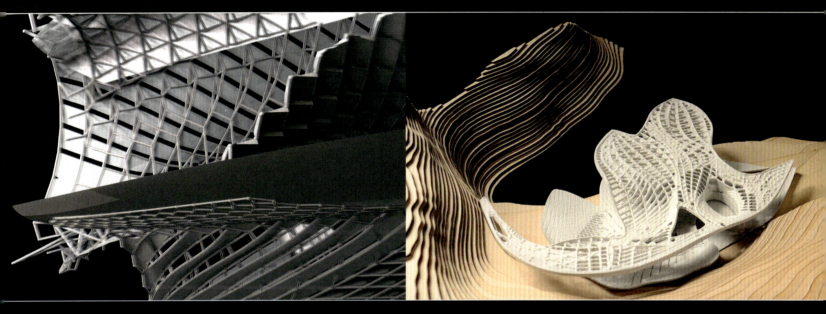

▲ X+Y=Boat+Villa

Alexander Karaivanov, Daniel Reist

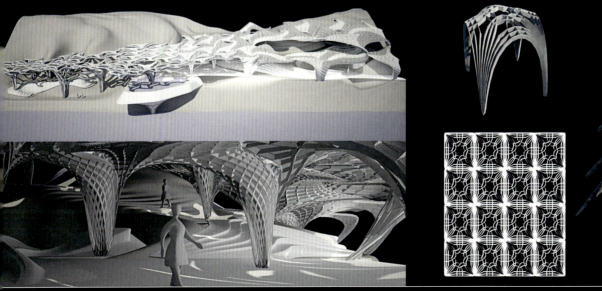

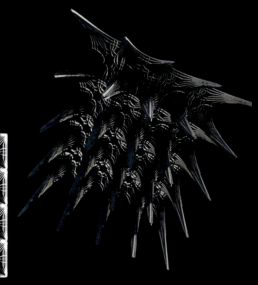

▲ Gothicfication

Uli Schifferdecker, Marc Wieneke, Jing Jing Zhou

▲ **Collectherenz**

Simon Aglas, Maya Pindeus, Madeleine Plass, Jakob Wilhelmstätter

▲ **Reptile Behavior**

Antonio Monserrat, Uli Schifferdecker, Pavel Zeldovich

▲ **The Pendulous-Mansion**

Simon Aglas, Jakob Wilhelmstätter

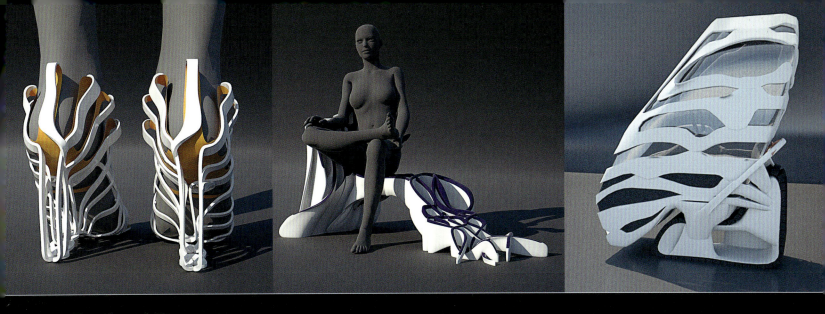

◣ Torsional Moment
Sarah Knize (UCLA), Saara-Leena Koljonen, Lorenz Krisai

◣ Cloth
Marcela Chyliková, Seongheon Kim, Stephan Ritzer

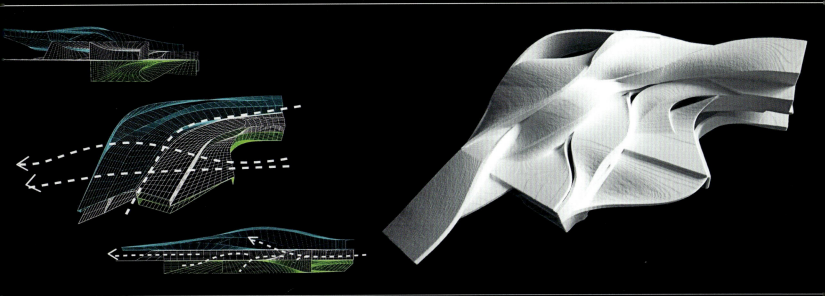

◣ Sin-Cos-Villa
Mi Na Bae, Romina Hafner, Monir Karimi

10 EXALTATIONS FOR AN EXCITABLE PLANET

Evan Douglis

As we move forward through a turbulent millennium burdened with economic strife, tribal warfare, unstable ecologies, growing energy demands, and the continuous rise and fall of totalitarian regimes across our planet earth, the ineffable role of the visionary and futurist becomes increasingly more attractive as a necessary seer for the sustenance of humankind.

Operating according to a model of productive resistance, their common pursuit of *radical innovation* represents an alternative pathway for a world often paralyzed by conformity and the inability to manage change. Their modus operandi favors the immeasurable value of an elastic mind, the purposeful ambiguity between the real and the imaginary, and the inexplicable merits of continually reassessing the conceptual, methodological and material underpinnings of any critical practice.

Within the discipline of architecture lies an exclusive yet influential core of global research communities that abide by this unique paradigm of productive radicality. *Studio Zaha Hadid*, which has been operating for over a decade within the venerable academic setting of the University of Applied Arts in Vienna, represents one such beacon of speculative inquiry that has forged an international reputation for producing some of the most brilliant and creatively experimental graduates entering the architecture profession in recent years.

Recognized as a leader in architectural education, *Studio Zaha Hadid* can be credited with establishing a nimble and innovative pedagogical curriculum notorious for its unique morphogenetic strategies and their increasingly evolving and opportunistic effects in response to a changing planet. Developed in tandem with an acute appreciation for analogical models, parametric design, state-of-the-art building assembly systems, the politics of space, and the demand for a radical reconceptualization of the city through the eyes of the architect at the turn of the century, the collective research that has emerged over the last ten years from *Studio Zaha Hadid* represents a tour-de-force that has indirectly reconfigured the future design priorities of our profession for years to come.

As a tribute to the studio's visionary approach and the ambition to which they charge architecture with a miraculous capacity to revolutionize the world, I submit the following *10 Exaltations for an Excitable Planet*;

01 IN SEARCH OF SYNTHETIC IMMORALITY

With the rise of interest surrounding emergent systems as the new organizational model for a planet undergoing continuous change, the opportunities to develop a more robust bio-mimetic approach in architecture are becoming increasingly more attractive. The once exotic and ineffable metamorphosis of the chameleon octopus, the otherworldly bioluminescence of the sea cucumber, and the strange gelatinous and reconfigurable anatomy of a comb jelly creature are no longer unobtainable effects underlying nature for the futurist at the turn of the century. The dazzling life of invertebrates is just one example of a complex system of behavior innate to a family of living organisms that is currently being reassessed on a computational level in order to extract out the base code inherent to these uniquely divine creatures.

Reconceptualizing the bridge between organic and inorganic systems as a transfer of essential genetic information is not an entirely a new proposition in the history of the world if one considers the exhaustive legacy of ancient and contemporary alchemists in a variety of fields throughout time that sought to create a parallel animistic universe through the transmutation of matter. Conceived as an extension of our timeless desire to bring inanimate material to life, this continuous chase for synthetic immortality has preoccupied our imagination for centuries.

Given our predisposition for even greater control today over an ever-increasingly complex universe, the next generation of animate assemblies within the discipline of architecture will inevitably be comprised of a more complex amalgamation of scripted equations capable of reenacting the most spectacular effects. Harnessing the unlimited power of programming as a vast hereditary engine for emergent design we will see an unimaginable increase in surface and behavioral variation on a level of intricacy and control unparalleled in the history of digital design.

In the dream of recombinant technology and biologically mimetic surfaces, *autogenic structures* represent an alternative model of production seamlessly obedient to the process of modern strategy. Situated somewhere between an indeterminate topology and a strange vehicle of desire, this seemingly life-like fleet of new building components will represent an entirely new synthetic ecology.

Project: "Compo.ment.ics"

Conceptualized as a new era of manufactured flesh, the architecture of the future will serve to highlight the endless algorithms of difference found in the indeterminacy of everyday life.

02 THE INFRA-THIN

The *Infra-Thin* at the turn of the century, represents the 'new' scale at which all-emergent behavior, as we know it will be reconceptualized and in turn be unleashed back in to the world with the aim of a perfect future. Whether we're referring to the smallest increment of matter on a genomic level or the underlying code regulating the building blocks in nanotechnology; this is the new battleground within which the future 'game of life' will be played. Given this radical leap in to a 'deep interiority', as a means to reassess the underlying structure in all things, the project of the Infra-thin proposes a kaleidoscopic explosion of surface development and material behavior for the next generation of architectural building components that is unprecedented in the history of the world.

03 DIGITAL ALCHEMY

In an 'era of information' where the dexterity of visual branding extends so effortlessly throughout the public domain reaffirming the 'messages of persuasion' of a capitalist agenda, *Digital Alchemy* represents 'a project of resistance' where the computational power of the computer is skillfully mined and strategically aligned in favor of reaffirming the sustenance and memory of people and places, the claim for authenticity as an ethical imperative, novel effects, and sentient surprise.

Mindful of an impressive legacy throughout the history of the world beholden to a more spiritual and mystical conception of life, our current technological regime faces an extraordinary opportunity with its ever-expanding digital design and manufacturing prowess to reassess the proper recombinatory relationship between structure and ornament at the turn of the century. It's a compelling moment in architecture where the cultural imprint of a civilization can now slide seamlessly between meaning, memory and matter.

04 DAZZLE TOPOLOGY

In celebration of the value of the 'haptic' in architecture, *Dazzle Topology* represents an invaluable source of insight underlying the retinal effects of intricacy and surface complexity. Seeking to elevate the status of the 'surface in architecture' today as the new site of projected desire, understanding the relational correspondence between 'surface' and 'seeing' is a critical area of inquiry for all those committed to maximizing the full effects offered in this new era of topological expression. For example, in the spirit of Hans Holbein's legendary anamorphosis painting, 'The Ambassadors', one might reassess with our ever-increasing engine of computational power, the role of illusory

techniques today as an opportunity to achieve greater control over the conceptual and cinematic effects in architecture.

05 EXCITABLE MATTER

Greek and Judaic mythology, early science fiction novels and the writings found in Magic Realism at the turn of the century all share a compelling desire to bring inanimate matter to life. Preoccupying the imagination of countless civilizations is the dream of synthetic immortality where the material world surrounding us obtains an air of excitability, self-determinism and a range of performative attributes that radically challenges our enduring sense of all living things as divine and absolute.

Given our current efforts in the disciplines of material science, bio-engineering, nanotechnology and robotics, the next generation of material behavior in architecture will assume a level of intelligence and sentient superiority to rival the most spectacular fiction novels ever written.

06 PERPETUAL DESIRING MACHINES

At a time when the 'economy of desire' continues to assert pressure globally on the rapid distribution of goods based upon the promise of novelty and surprise, mass-customization in architecture continues to represent an ideal response that reaffirms heterogeneity for a multicultural planet at the turn of century.

Analogous to a *Perpetual Desiring Machine* the promise of infinite variation for a distributed model of interchangeable modular construction represents the perfect counterpoint to the slow yet determined eradication of difference often discovered in the wake of globalization.

Although fundamentally different in terms of their unique cultural practices, M.C. Escher and Hans Bellmer, for example, curiously share a similar vision of the world based upon an anagrammatic assembly. Here the continuous rearrangements of similar parts serve to perpetuate the illusion of infinity and erotic surprise.

07 BIOLOGICAL MIMESIS

Often the most extraordinary secrets concerning the laws of nature and our very existence as a species among many can be found by looking more closely at the underlying behavior of the natural world as a complex ecology of seemingly indeterminate orbits of activity. At a time where we aspire to truly manifest emergent behavior in order to respond more effectively to the cultural and environmental aspirations of the 21st century, learning more about the elegantly designed life-forms that share our planet represents an invaluable opportunity for the next generation of architects and bio-engineers. Offered as an infinite archive of analogical models, bio-mimicry represents a major paradigm shift that has the capacity to revolutionize the history of architecture, as we know it.

08_INTRICACY

Complex macramé, ornate scrolls, full-body tattoos, Persian tiling and calligraphic manuscripts, Russian nesting dolls, old Italian wood inlay music boxes, the pointillism paintings of Seurat, Damien Hirst's Diamond Skull, M.C. Escher's drawings, Louis Sullivan's ornamental embellishments, and the strange and beautifully eerie portraits of 'alternate realities' by Max Ernst, are all timeless examples of a shared obsession with surface exuberance at the most intimate scale. Seeking to imbue another level of chromatic and topological variation within the surfaces of real or imagined places represents a timeless project and one that has particular relevance for architecture in an era of digital and manufacturing control.

09 CONJOINED IDEATION

Given the increasing demands of our profession to manage an extensive number of interests impacting the design, environmental, economic and technological considerations facing architecture today, the 'autonomous model' of architectural education is no longer adequate to successfully prepare our students to assume a future leadership role in a complex and highly competitive market.

The daunting challenges we face at the turn of the century require an interdisciplinary response where a multiplicity of knowledge and expertise drawn from a variety of research streams beyond architecture is brought together as 'conjoined ideation' in favor of new and innovative proposals. The distinct boundaries traditionally delineated within architectural programs must be reconceptualized as an elastic constellation of collaborative arrangements mining the natural affinities within and beyond every academic institution.

10 ETHICS + AESTHETICS

Architecture is situated at a unique moment in history where a convergence of global interests demands that our discipline responds in a critical and innovative manner. Faced with an ever-increasing focus on creating new forms of renewable energy, smart grids and coastal city solutions, sustainable and zero-carbon technology, and environmentally responsive buildings for the 21st century, we need to simultaneously reaffirm the ethical imperative to respond to these serious environmental priorities while at the same time aggressively advocating 'the invaluable role of design'.

Given the recent surge to politicize the debate over Green building as one exclusively bias to quantifiable data as the sole criteria of a successfully designed building, it is of enormous importance that our community of architects participate on the most proactive level

to reassert the inextricable bond between ethics and aesthetics. 'Sustainability' as a slogan and a detached focus of architectural production threatens to oversimplify the larger challenge facing all of us at the turn of the century.

The real project calls for 'radical innovation' which emerges so effortlessly from the *Studio Zaha Hadid*: where the buildings of the future exemplify the full breadth of human creativity and ideation in order to celebrate on the most benevolent level the ethos of our diverse culture and community around the world in relation to a planet undergoing continuous change.

EVAN DOUGLIS Evan Douglis is the principal of Evan Douglis Studio LLC, an internationally renowned architecture and interdisciplinary design firm committed to the practice of digital alchemy. The firm's unique cutting edge research into computer-aided digital design and fabrication technology, new materials and multi-media installations as applied to a range of diverse gallery installations, commercial projects, and more recently a series of prefabricated modular building assembly systems has elicited international acclaim.

Prior to his appointment as Dean of the of the School of Architecture at Rensselaer Polytechnic Institute he was the Chair of the undergraduate department at Pratt Institute, an Associate Assistant Professor and the Director of the Architecture Galleries at Columbia University, and a Visiting Instructor at The Irwin S. Chanin School of Architecture at the Cooper Union.

Recognized for his innovative approach to design Douglis' awards include: a NYFA fellowship, a Design Vanguard profile by Architectural Record, an I.D. Magazine Honorable Mention, a FEIDAD Design Merit Award, finalist nominations for the North American James Beard Foundation Restaurant Design Awards, a selected fellow in the EKWC European Ceramic Work Center's Brick Project Residency Program, an ACADIA Award for Emerging Digital Practice and more recently a Presidential Citation from The Cooper Union and an AIA/LA People's Restaurant Choice Award.

His work has been exhibited at the SAM Swiss Architecture Museum, ARCHILAB in Orléans, France, the MOCA Museum at the Pacific Design Center in Los Angeles, Artist Space in New York and the Rotterdam and London Biennales. His Helioscope project is in the permanent architecture collection at the FRAC Centre in Orleans, France.

His publications include; Sign as Surface, INDEX Architecture, The State of Architecture at the Beginning of the 21st c, the Phaidon publication titled 10 x10_2, Distinguishing Digital Architecture, the SAM catalog Re-Sampling Ornament, the AD issues; Protoarchitecture: Analogue and Digital Hybrids and Programming Cultures: Design, Science and Software, FURNISH: Furniture and Interior Design for the 21st Century, Architecture Now 5 by Taschen Publishers and Digital Architecture Now: a Global Survey of Emerging Talent. His book Autogenic Structures was published by Taylor & Francis.

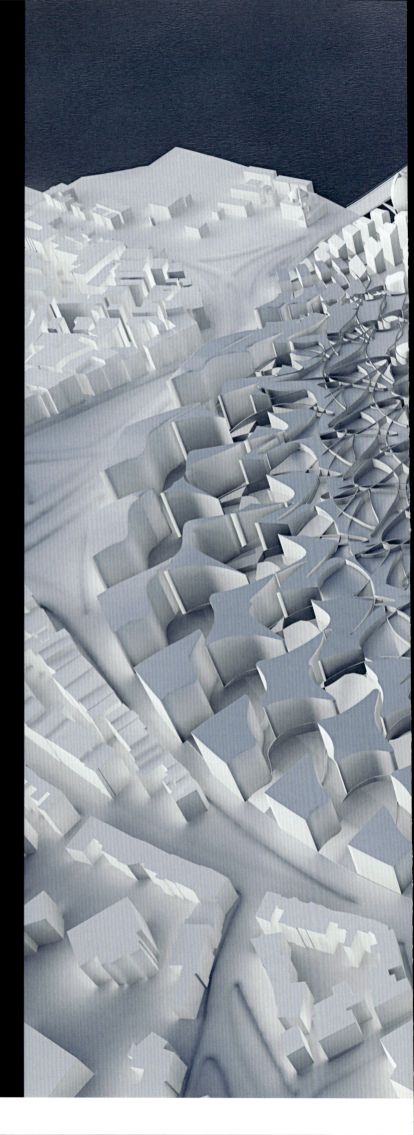

DIPLOMA PROJECTS
2000 - 2010

The diploma projects, compiled in a separate chapter, showcase in a compressed way the progression the studio was going through the last ten years. Though all projects present specific interests of the authors and are developed as individual approaches to the task nevertheless they refer to the pool of notions within the studio's ideology and participate in the ongoing debate in a contextual way. The diploma projects demonstrate the abilities and skills of the students as a condensed result of the prior education but at the same time demonstrate the competence that is accumulated in an extraordinary way through the challenging teaching method of the studio.

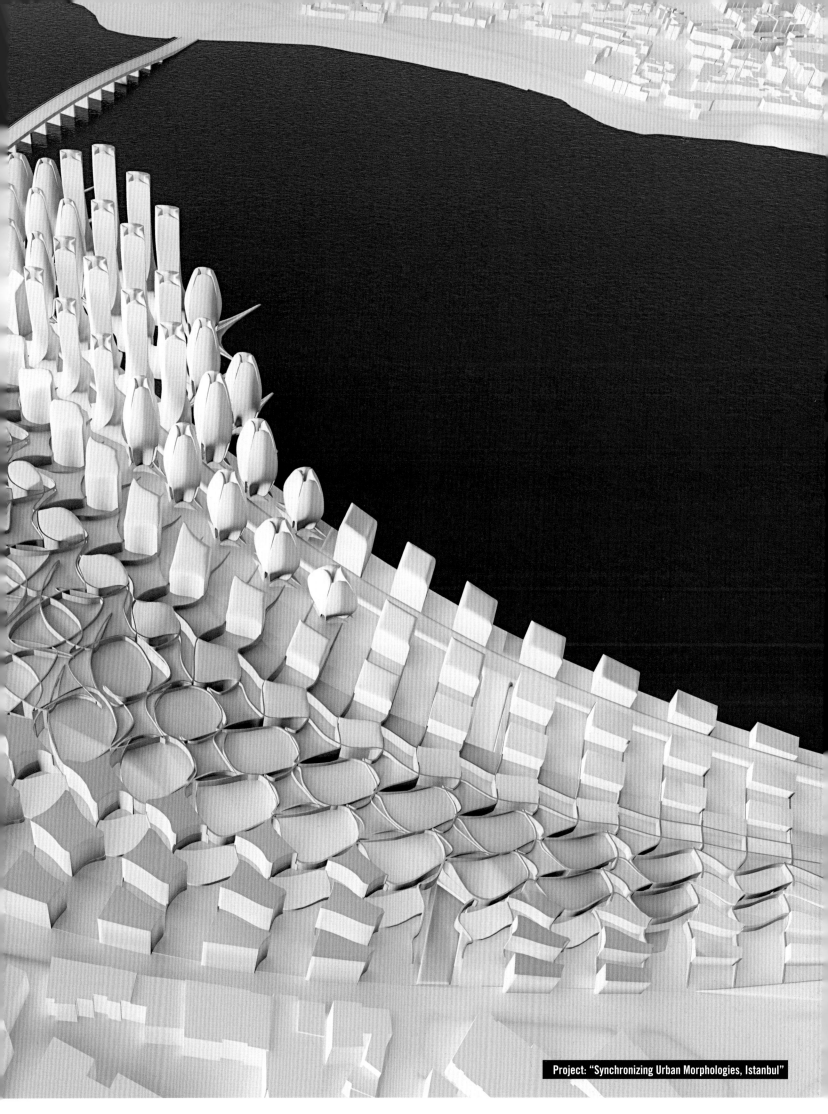

Project: "Synchronizing Urban Morphologies, Istanbul"

Proto Towers 2010

Christoph Hermann

By articulating a tower along its axis according to specific properties (e.g., structural, functional and performative), prototypical arrangements are developed which demonstrate a morphological range of meaningful correlations between all relevant subsystems. Some of nature's most fascinating features are explored: complex inter-articulation of systems and subsystems, individual adaptivity and versatile functionality.

Area Fusion, Berlin 2009/10

Jakub Klaska

'Area Fusion' prototypically demonstrates the capacity of parametric design tools with regard to setting up meaningful and deeply correlated part-to-part and part-to-whole relationships across all scales. It seeks to integrate the site's context, building morphology and detailed interior organization into one parametrically malleable and formally cohesive unity.

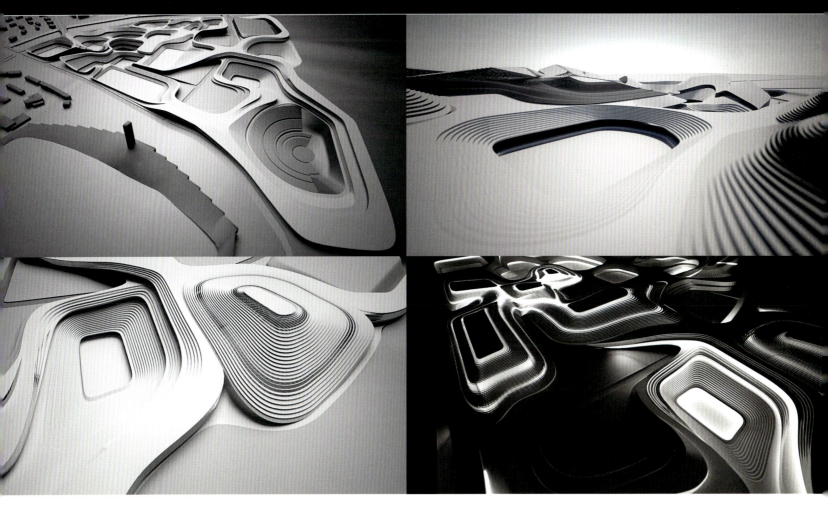

Performing PopMusic, Taipei 2010

Sabrina Miletich

24-hour accessibility has led to a change of the significance of music in everyday culture and a restricted mode of perceiving it. The reevaluation of physical experience becomes an architectural task and the mode of interaction between actors and audience move to the foreground. Differentiated typologies generate a field of stages that orchestrate all kinds of musical genres and spectacles.

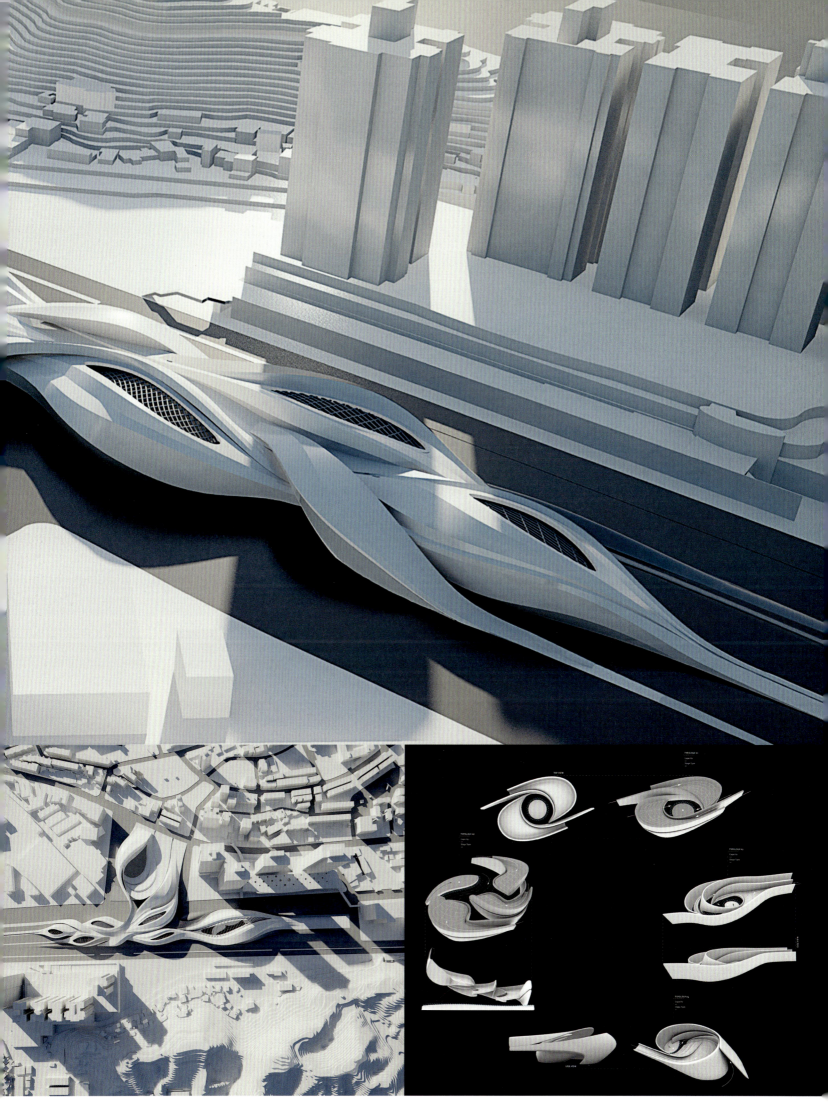

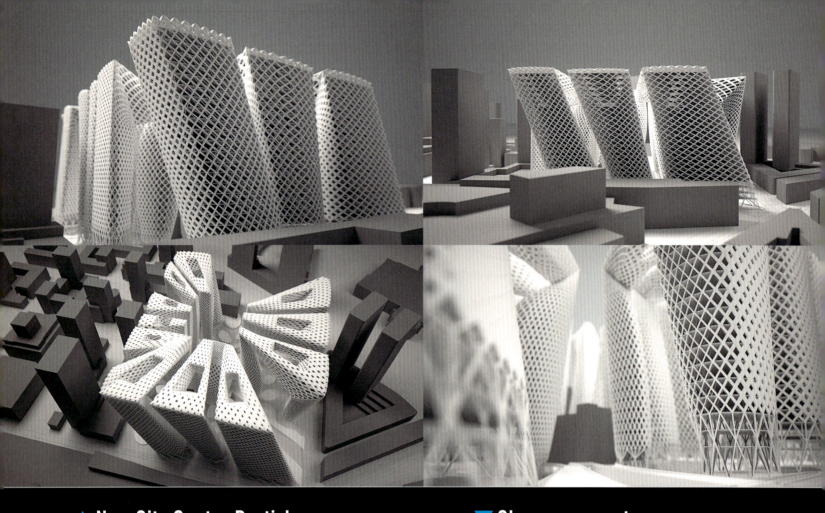

▲ New City Center Bratislava 2010
Krisztián Csémy

▼ Choreograments 2010
Rasa Navasaityte

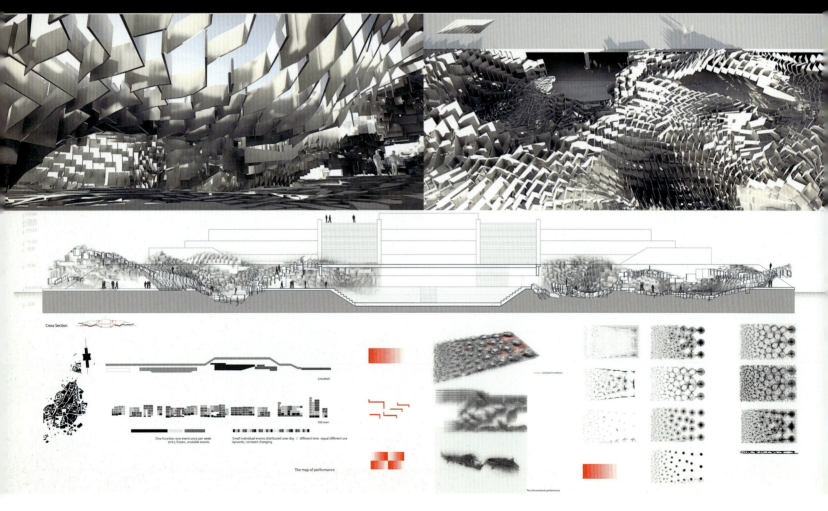

Cross Section

Linzahall

Old town

One function-one event once per weak
strict, frozen, unstable events

Small individual events distributed over day / different time -equal different use
dynamic, constant changing

The map of performance

courtyard conditions

The 3dimentional performance

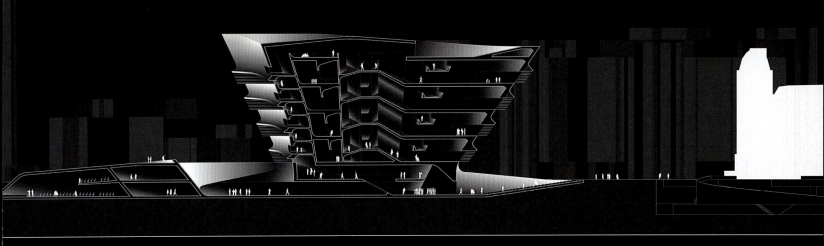

Exhibiting The Other /
House Of Cultures Vienna 2009/10

Georg Wizany

The permanent collection is organized as simultaneous narratives.
Three chronological, geographic routes spiral down, relations within
a fixed timeframe can be experienced on the different horizontal levels,
and theme-specific relations in the collection can be established
with horizontal and vertical shortcuts in the core of the building.
The conic shape of the museum reflects the increase of content from
past to present.

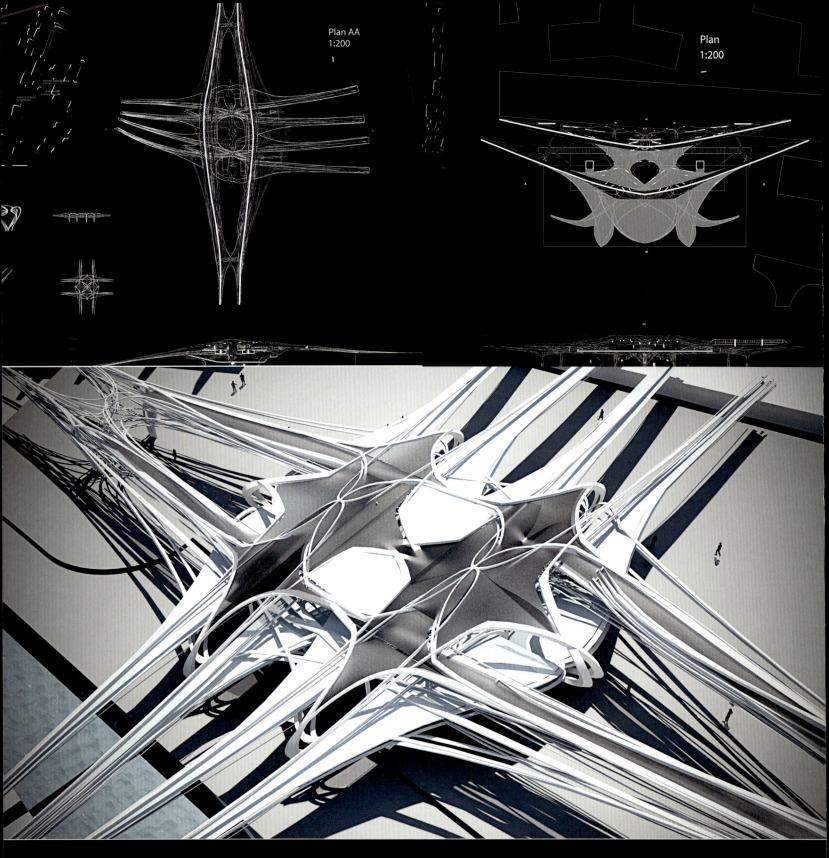

Plan AA
1:200

Plan
1:200

Prishtina Infrastructural City 2010

Clemens Nocker

Prishtina as a young European capital aims at achieving identity and recognition with different projects manifesting architecture. Besides expressing this ambition through the strong formal aspect of articulated streamlines the proposal showcases the adaptive character of a monorail transport system in its parametric reference to the adjacent urban site conditions and different functional requirements.

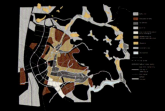

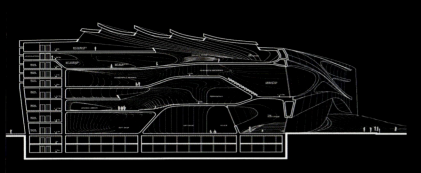

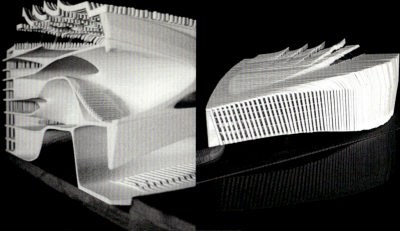

Aarhus Library / House of Knowledge 2009/10

Johannes Elias

The project's goal is to propose an architectural design that combines the potential of digital archives with that found in traditional libraries. It seeks to re-think the typology of the latter beyond that of the mediathèque, combining the advantages of the digital with those of the analogue, thus overcoming each one's deficiencies.

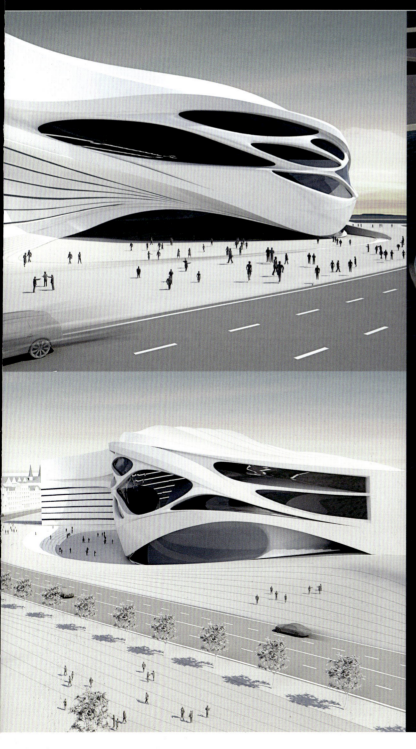

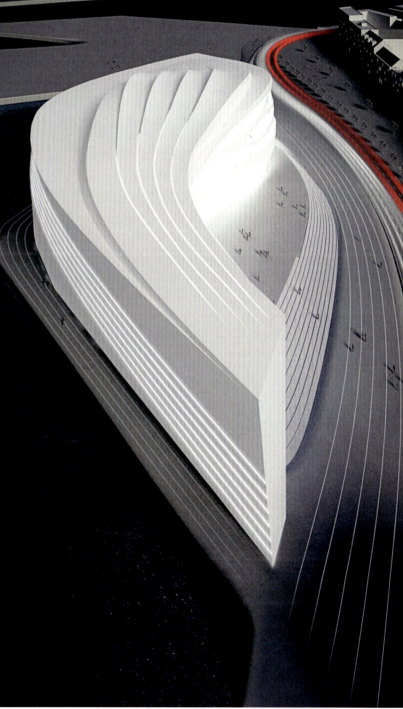

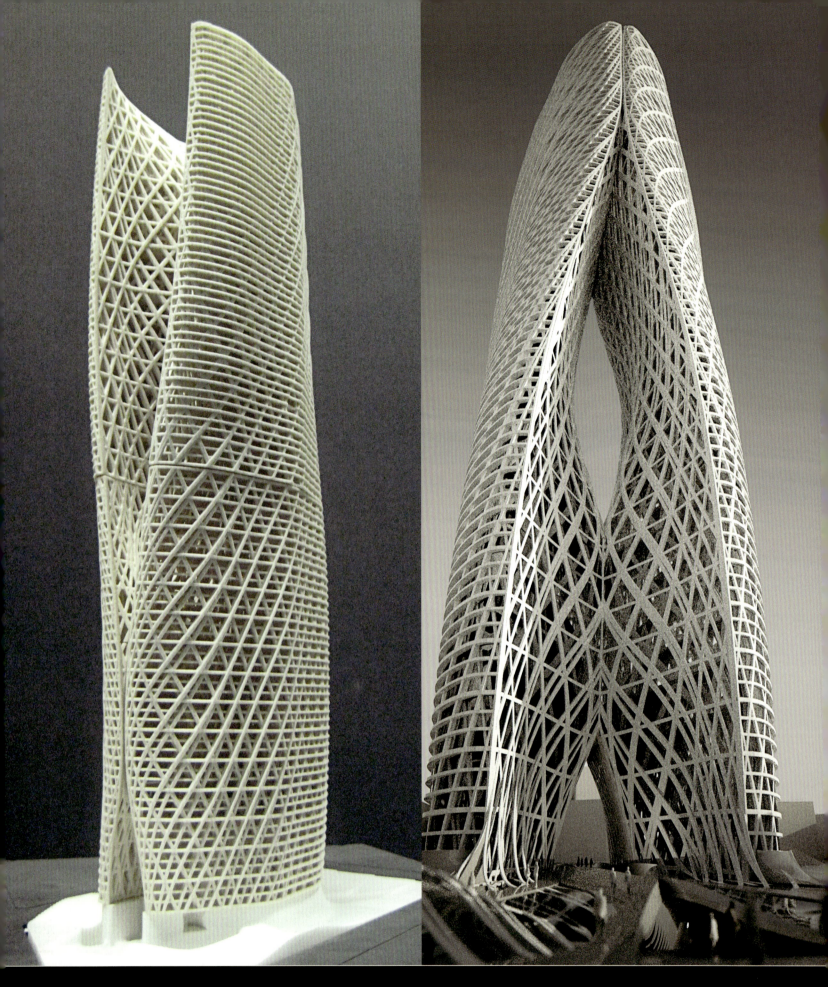

Brooklyn Arts Tower 2009

Philipp Weisz

The project proposal offers a strategy to flip mixed-use urban programs into a compressed complex verticality. By using structural and programmatic slices the tower provides massive voids and views in the inside, and so reflects its mixed-use program in a strikingly vertical Broadway.

810° Theater Taipei 2009

Philipp Ostermaier

The diploma project is based on a competition brief for a performing arts venue in Taipei, Taiwan. The brief asks for a cohesive overall design, which encompasses three theaters in a single building. As means of cohering the different typologies into the required single envelope, the project proposal exploits the parametric malleability of delaminating shell surfaces as primary design tool, allowing them to be read as individual units but also making them recognizable as part of a whole.

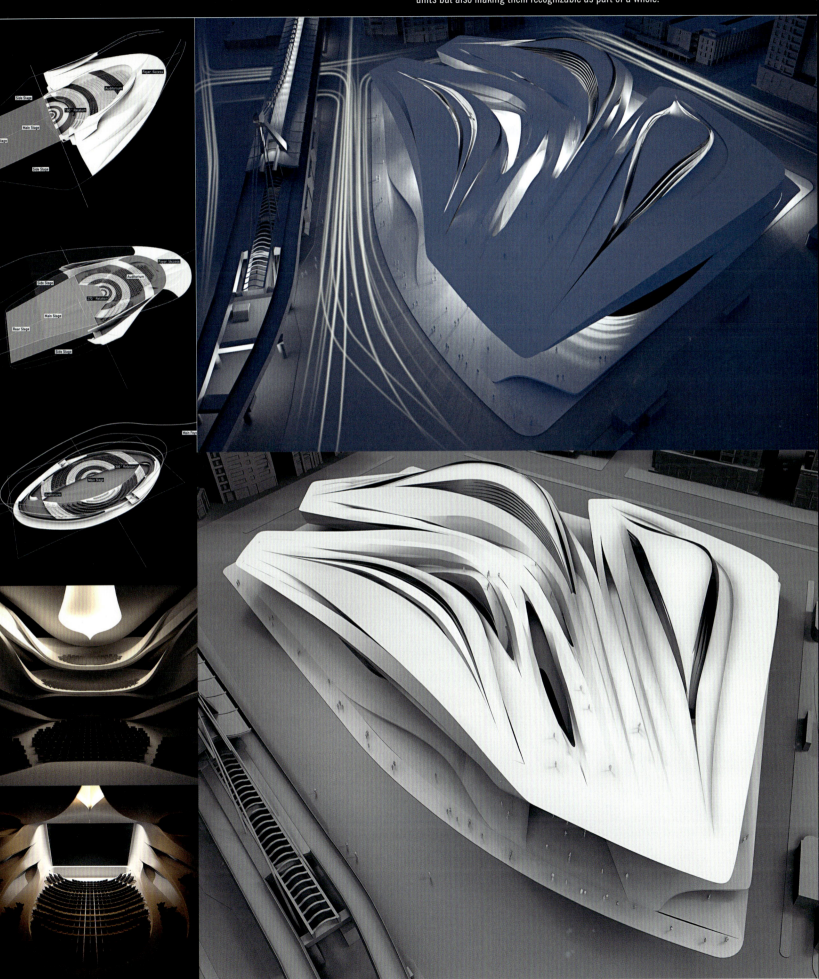

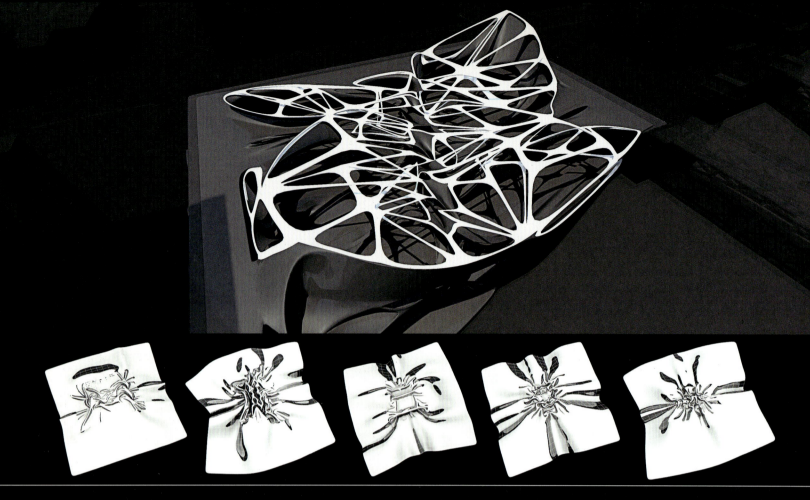

▲ **Chicago Train Station 2020** 2009
Saman Saffarian

▼ **Public Library Oslo** 2008/09
Milan Suchanek

New Bouwkunde Delft 2008/09

Peter Mitterer

The diploma 'New Bouwkunde Delft' proposes a replacement for the burnt down faculty of architecture building. It is situated between Delft's historic city centre and the campus of the Technical University. The project substitutes the binary circulation logic of educational buildings for a highly differentiated network logic, short-circuiting content and architectural form into one cohesive entity.

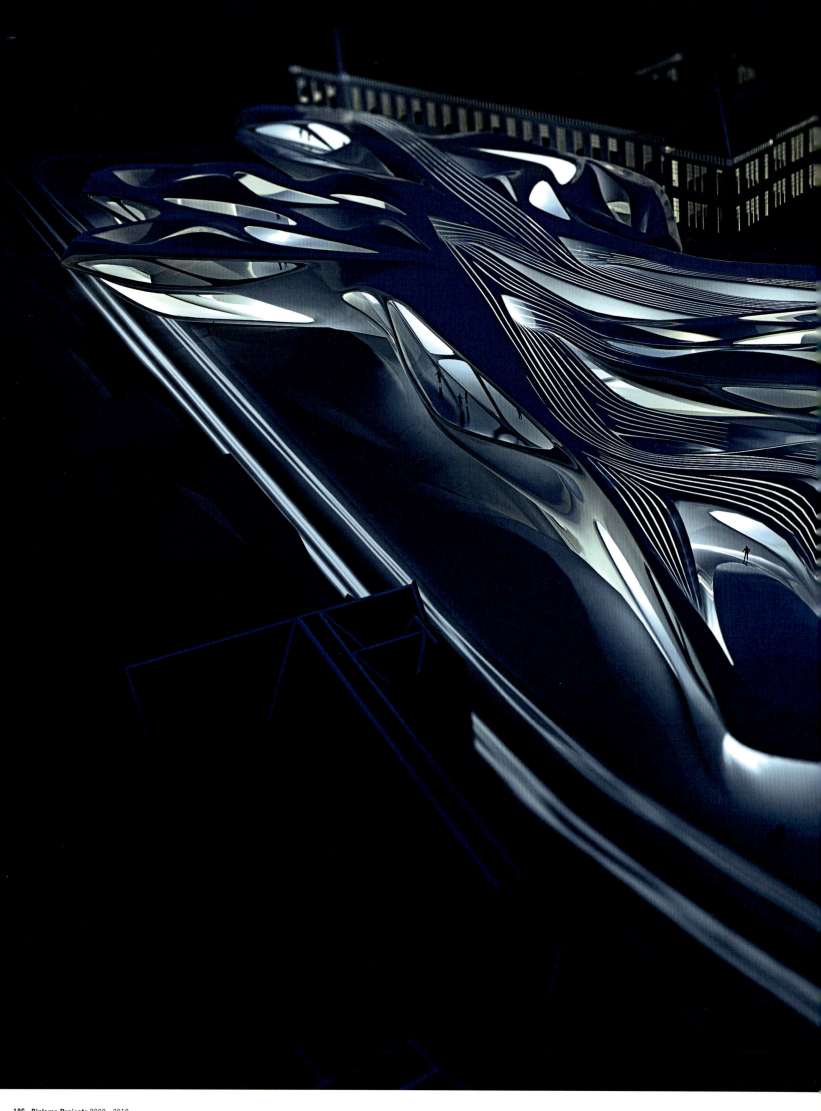

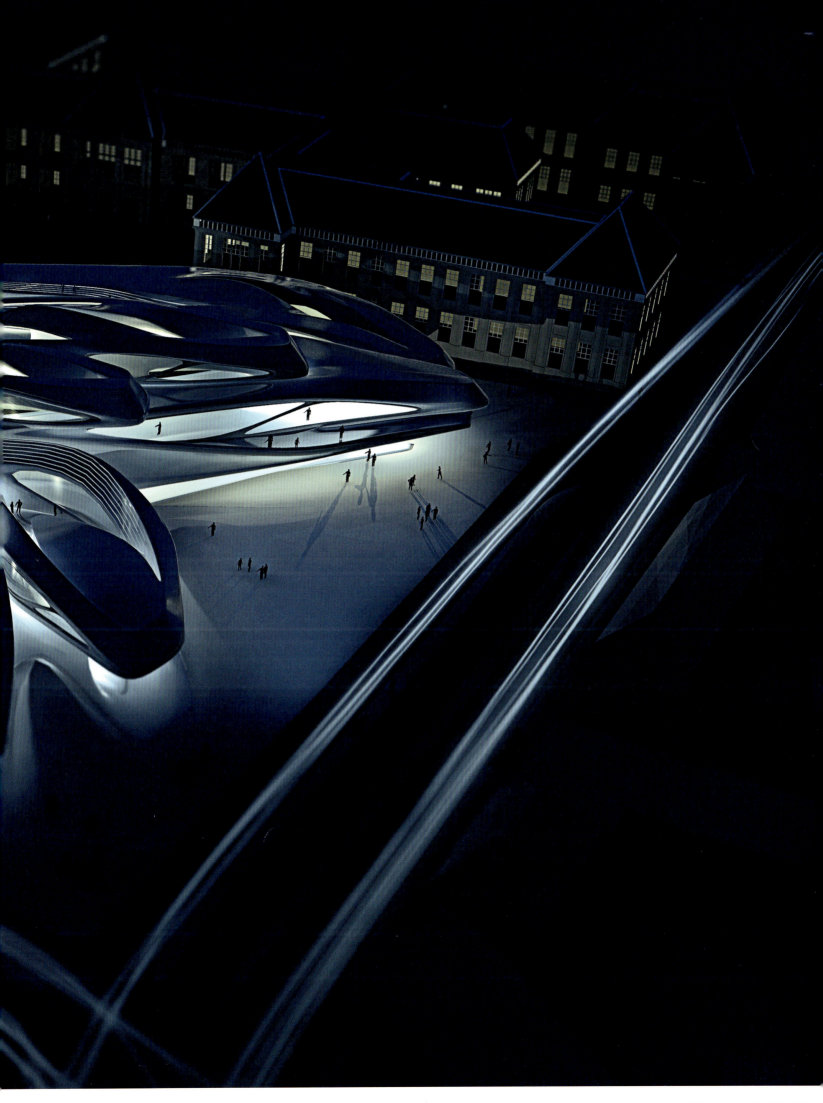

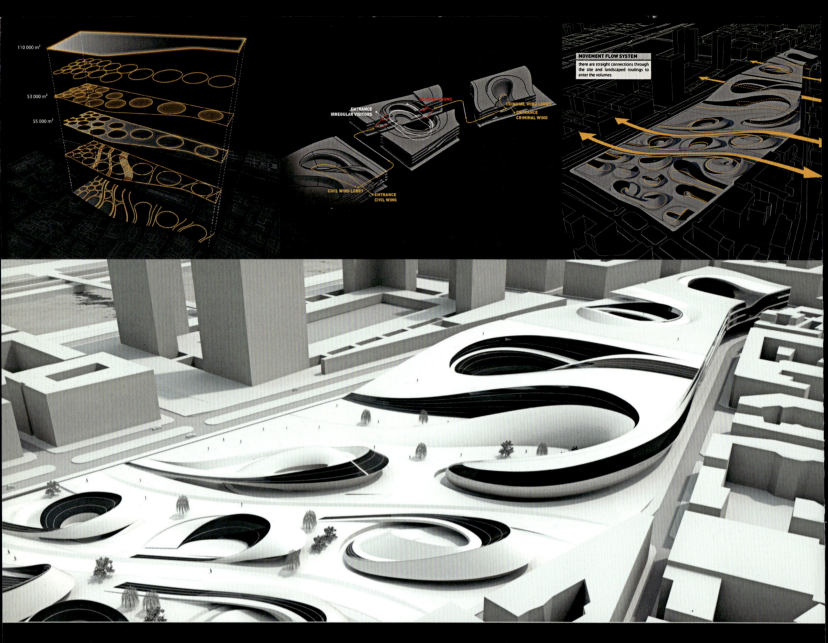

Paris Court Housing 2008/09

Markus Innauer, Felix Lohrmann

The project develops the Paris Court and its environment on a site nearby Bibliothèque de France. The proposal uses circle packing to distribute the urban mass and applies a sophisticated geometry to create spectacular volumes and complex interior spaces: a square is moved along a torus by continuously turning around. Extroverted and introverted zones emerge while spiral-like paths evolve from this system providing access to the buildings for different users.

University Campus Vienna 2008

Konrad Hofmann

The diploma project demonstrates an alternative to the established educational campuses and dispersed faculty networks in Vienna.
Its spatial configuration incorporates the positive aspects of single monolithic educational buildings and traditional campus morphologies alike, proposing a university typology which is intricately woven into the surrounding city as a single porous system.

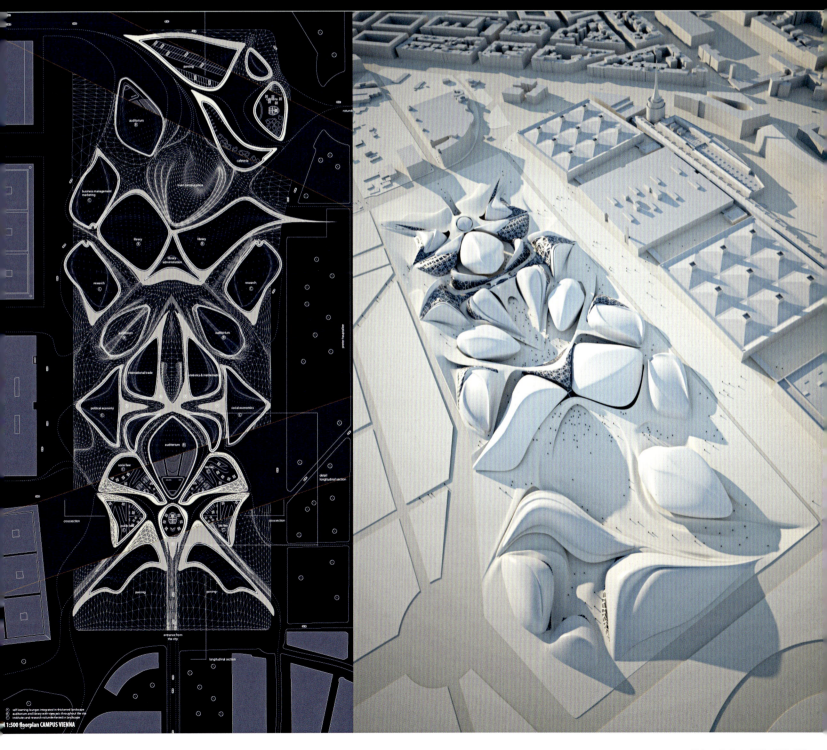

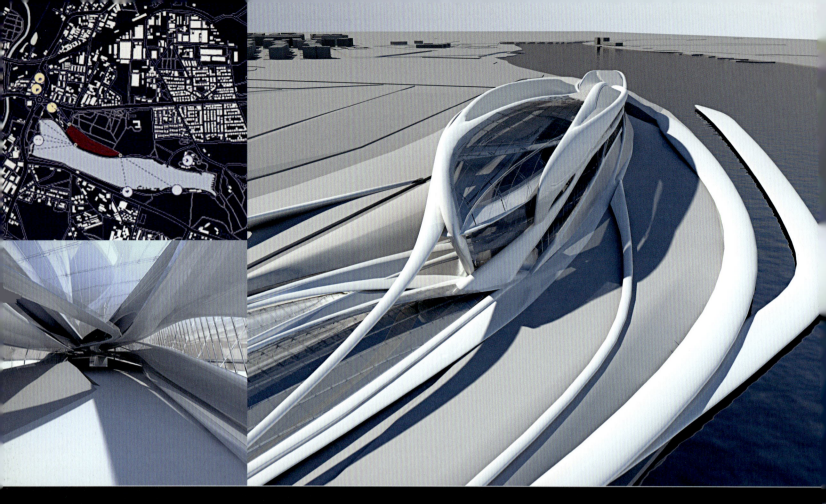

▲ Wyborowa Factory & Event Center, Posen 2007/08
Sofia Maria Hagen

▼ Pier 45° N 8° O, Lake Garda 2007/08
Daniela Overbeck

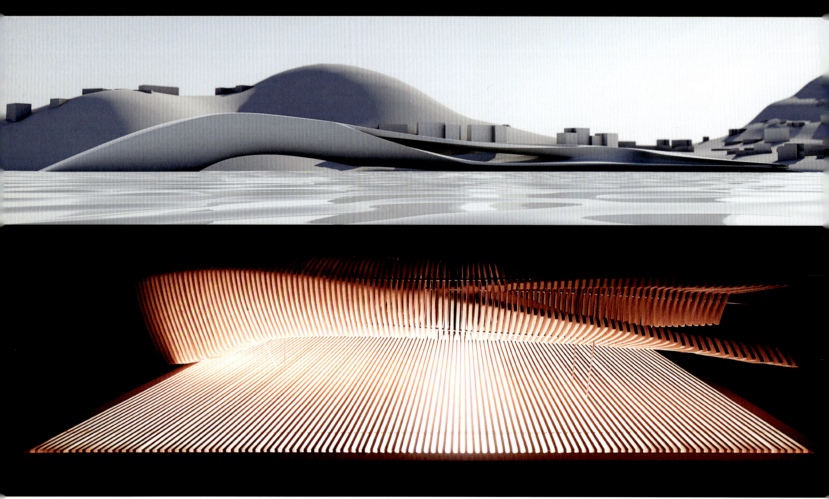

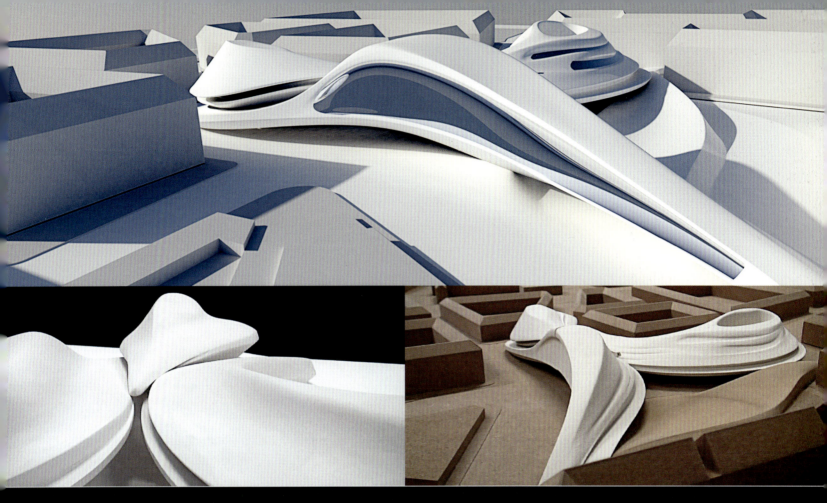

▲ **Arctic Arts Center Copenhagen** 2008
Anna Weilhartner

▼ **C Dense / Controlled Urban Densification, Monaco** 2008
Peter Pichler

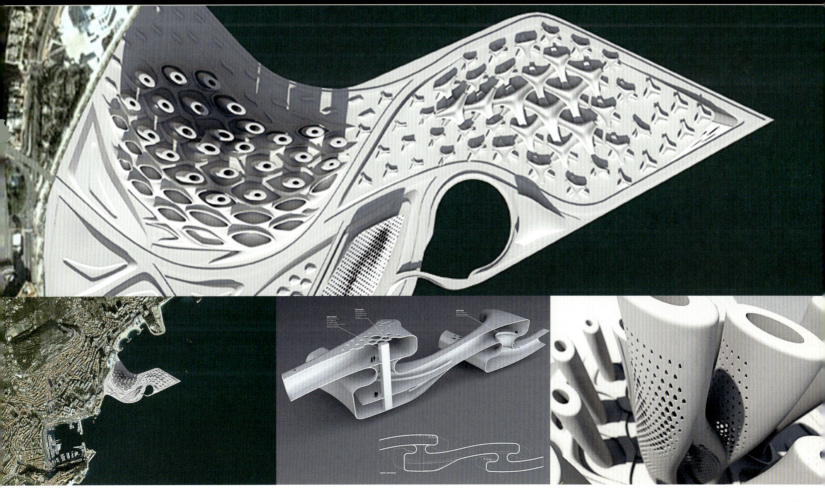

▲ **Edaphication, Essen** 2008
Daniel Köhler

▼ **Shanghai Offspring** 2008
Martine Nicolay

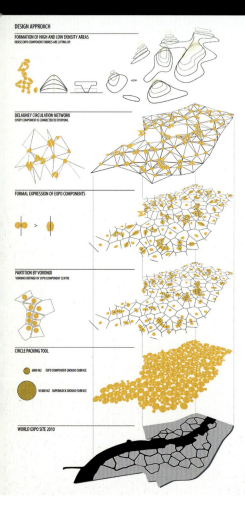

DESIGN APPROACH

FORMATION OF HIGH AND LOW DENSITY AREAS
DENSE EXPO COMPONENT FABRICS ARE LIFTING UP.

DELAUNEY CIRCULATION NETWORK
EVERY COMPONENT IS CONNECTED TO EVERYONE.

FORMAL EXPRESSION OF EXPO COMPONENTS

PARTITION BY VORONOI
VORONOI DEFINED BY EXPO COMPONENT CENTRE

CIRCLE PACKING TOOL

WORLD EXPO SITE 2010

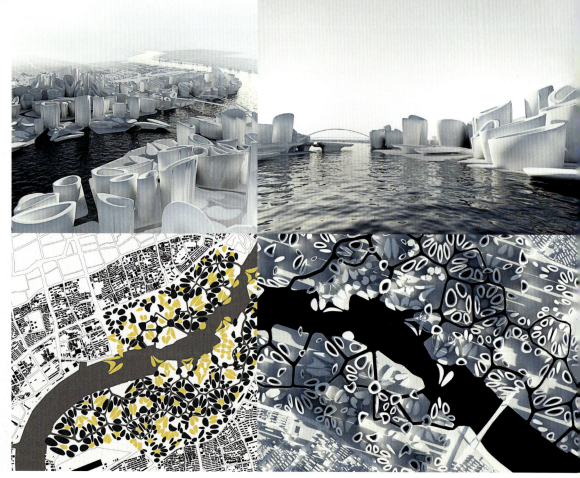

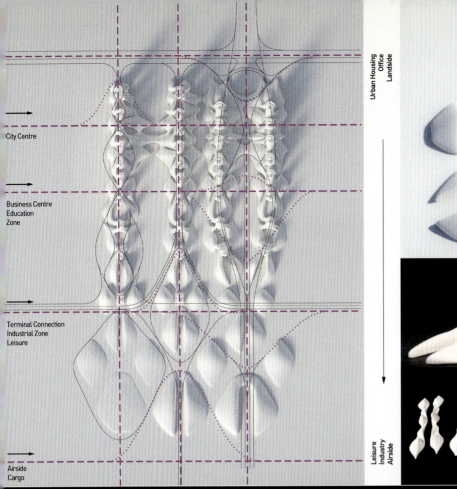

City Centre

Business Centre
Education
Zone

Terminal Connection
Industrial Zone
Leisure

Airside
Cargo

Urban Housing
Office
Landside

Leisure
Industry
Airside

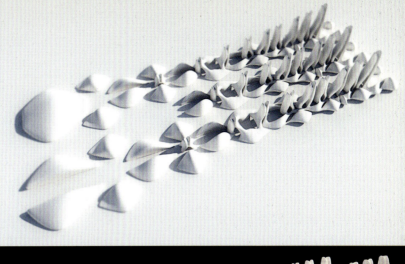

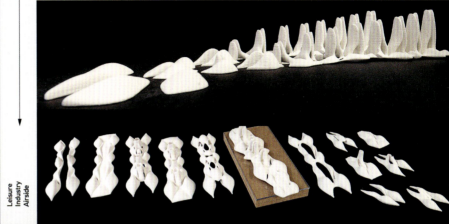

▲ **Airport Urbanism, San Diego** 2008
Birgit Schmidt

▼ **Hybrid Demarcation, Venice** 2007/08
Tamara Friebel

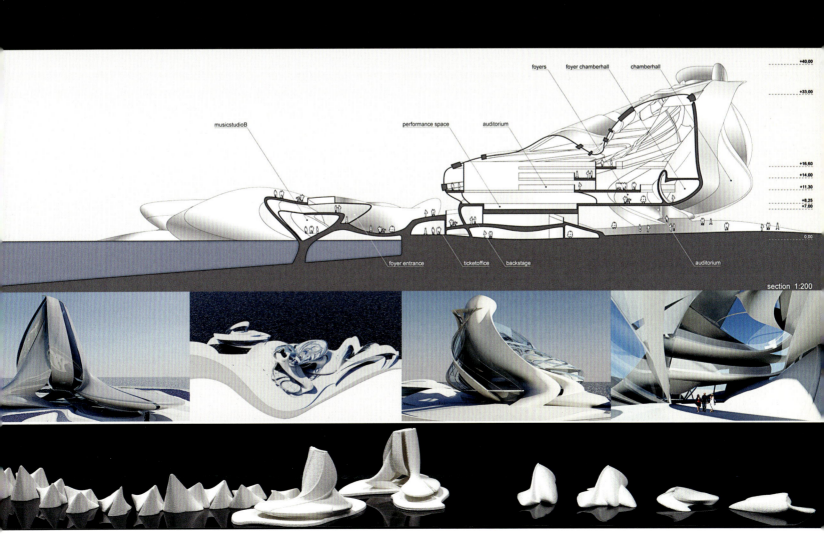

foyers   foyer chamberhall   chamberhall

musicstudioB

performance space   auditorium

+40,00

+33,00

+16,60
+14,00
+11,30
+8,25
+7,00

0.00

foyer entrance   ticketoffice   backstage   auditorium

section 1:200

Gen.ITE.Rating 2007/08

Maren Klasing, Martin Krcha

The diploma project seeks to explore the potential of parametric design tools in a two-fold process. After an extensive repertoire of algorithmic routines is developed on a purely experimental level the project further assesses the capacities of the developed toolset through the concrete development of an architectonic prototype.

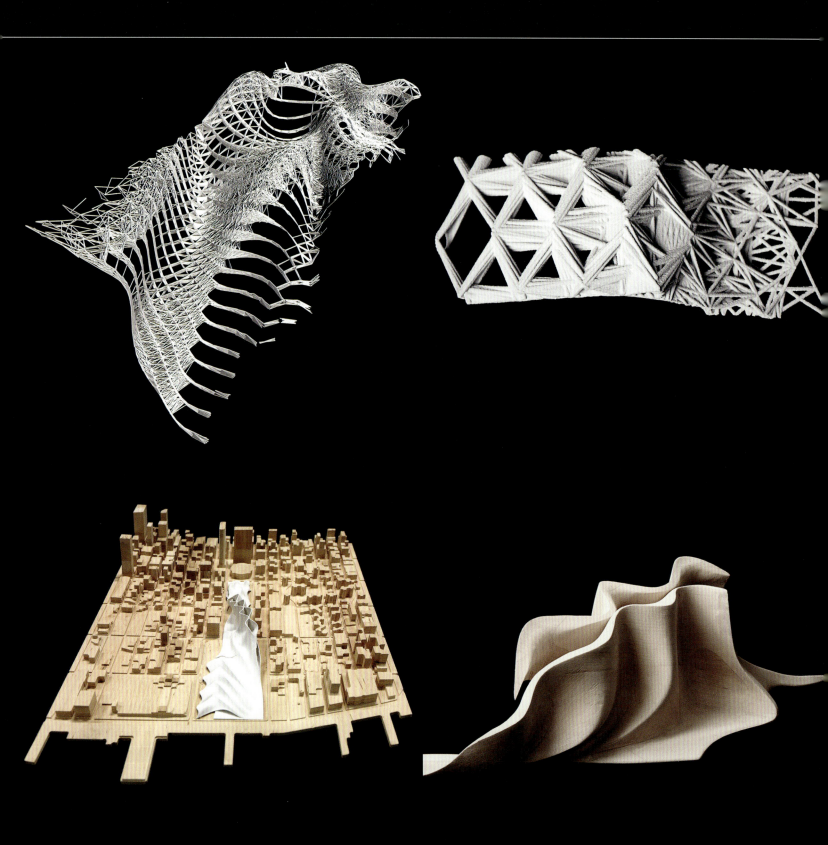

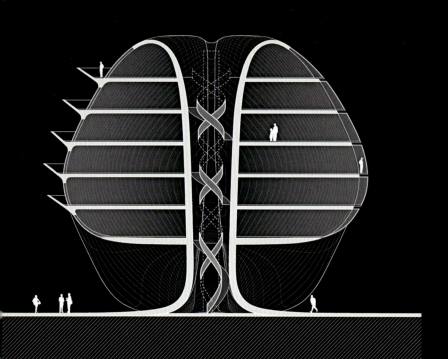

Sync – Synchronizing Urban Morphologies, Istanbul 2007/08

Mario Gasser

SYNC deals with existing characteristics of urban life in Istanbul, the permanent shift between inside, outside, covered situations, the transition between public and private spaces, especially because the city is equipped with a network of retail spaces. When urban space is considered as three-dimensional elements, urban space becomes figure as a positive element, and buildings become its ground.

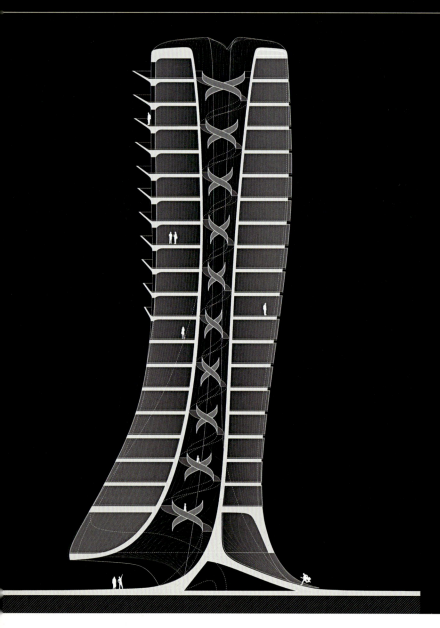

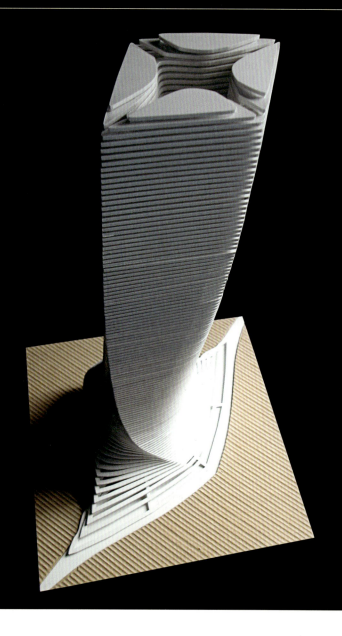

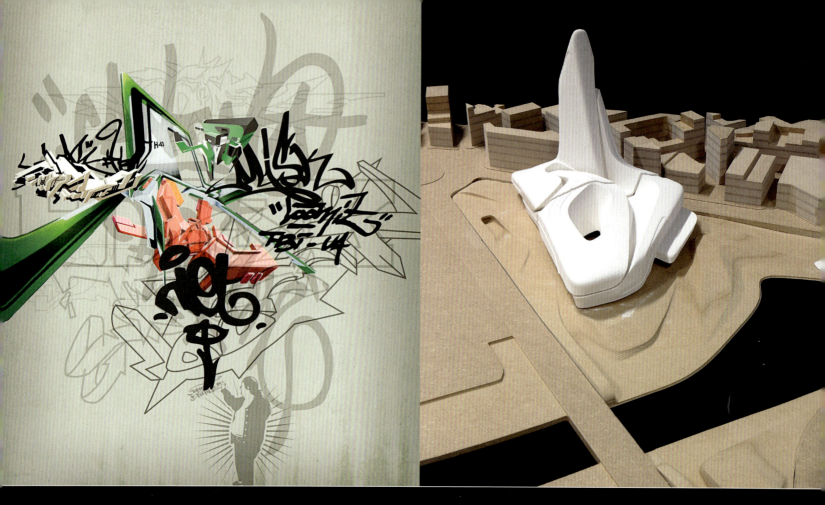

3D Calligraphy, Madrid 2007/08

Andrés Schenker

The diploma project focuses on the structuring principles of calligraphy as well as the basic concepts of gestalt theory and draws analogies to the architectural domain. The hypothesis put forward in the project is that the intricate part-to-whole relationships, gestalt grouping principles and inherent formal aesthetics of graffiti art can be meaningfully discussed as part of an architectural toolset.

Center for Biodiversity, Barcelona 2007

Judith Schafelner

Museums of natural history usually feature a very limited set of spatial ordering systems, such as linear sequences of rooms to reflect chronographic developments or axial symmetries to depict distinctions between certain species. The diploma project seeks to expand this limited repertoire of spatial articulation in favor of a deep and complex representation of what the museum exhibits.

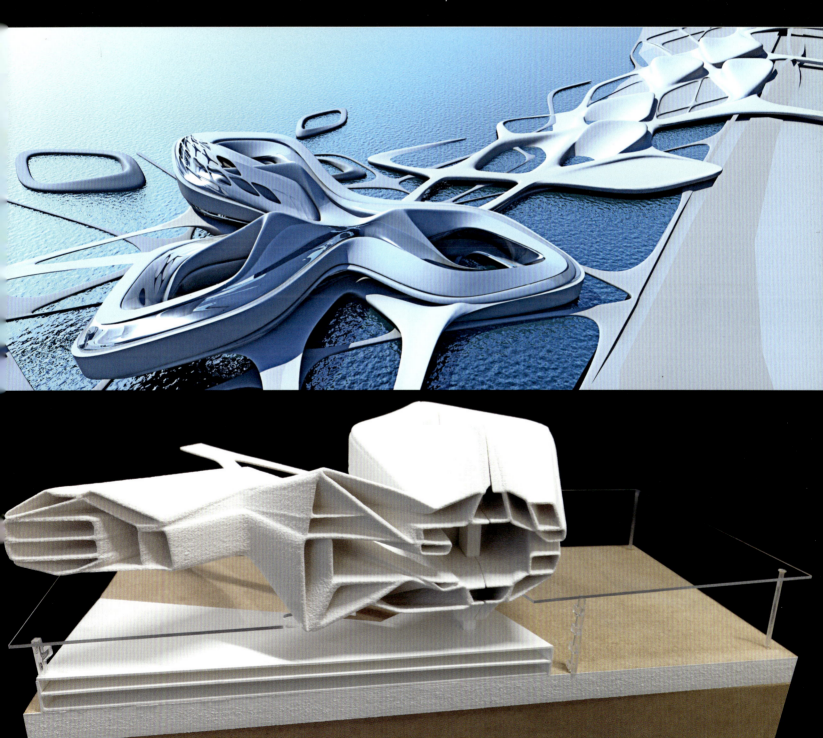

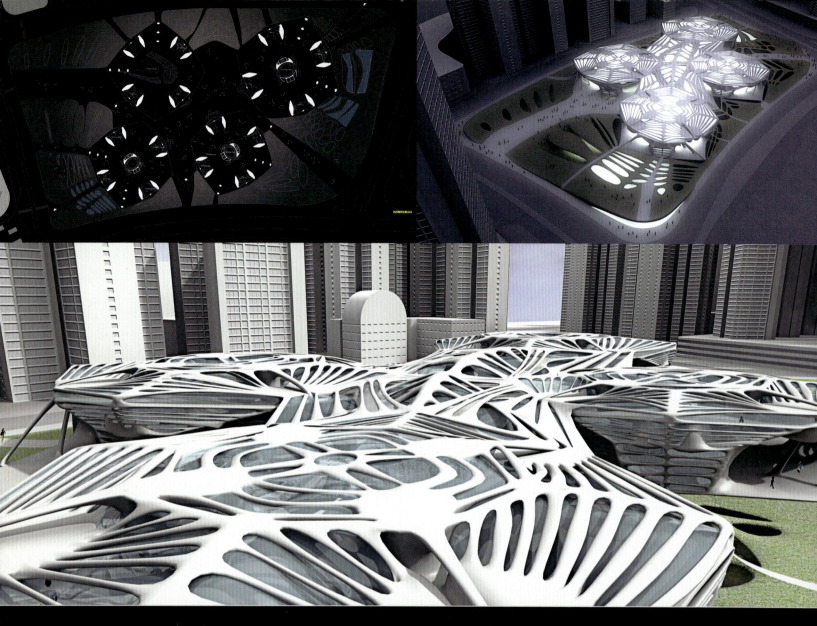

HKDI Hongkong Design Institute 2006/07

Ariane Stracke

According to the program of a high standard design university the project comprises four main buildings (design departments), which are connected. Each department possesses a central public attractor (presentation) around which seminar spaces (teaching) and work spaces (production) are organized. The proposed learning landscape provides an open structure that allows a high level of communication and interaction.

Berlin's Densest 2006/07

Cornelis van Almsick

The design strategy for this project is based on a Voronoi geometry to maximize the urban density of the site. The proposal for the urban master plan for the area located near the center of Berlin refers to the traditional Berliner Block allowing differentiation according to urban and programmatic requirements of each block. The interdependence of the underlying cell structure of the Voronoi provides a coherent urban structure with great variety and differentiation within itself.

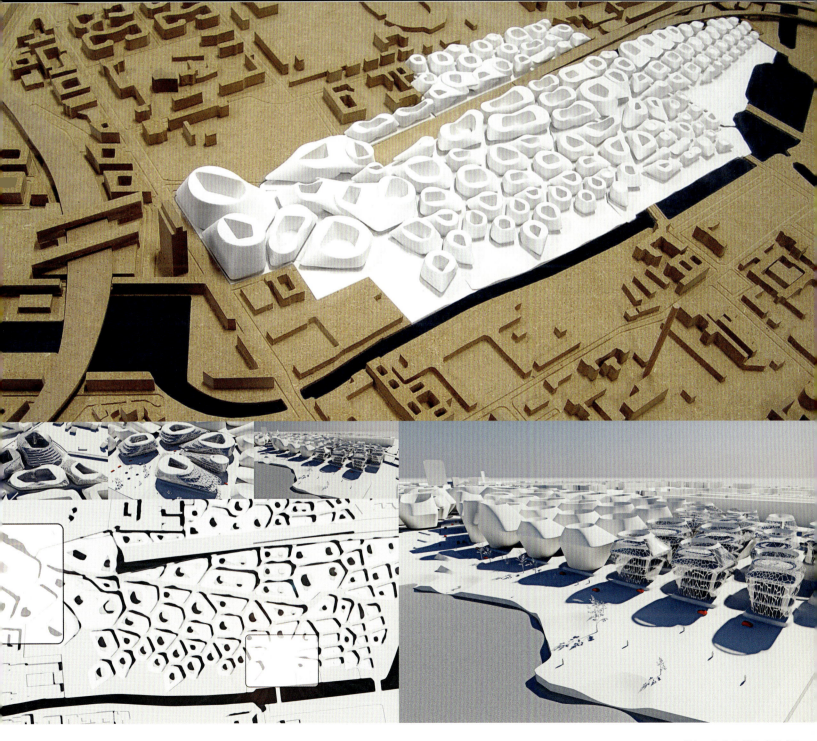

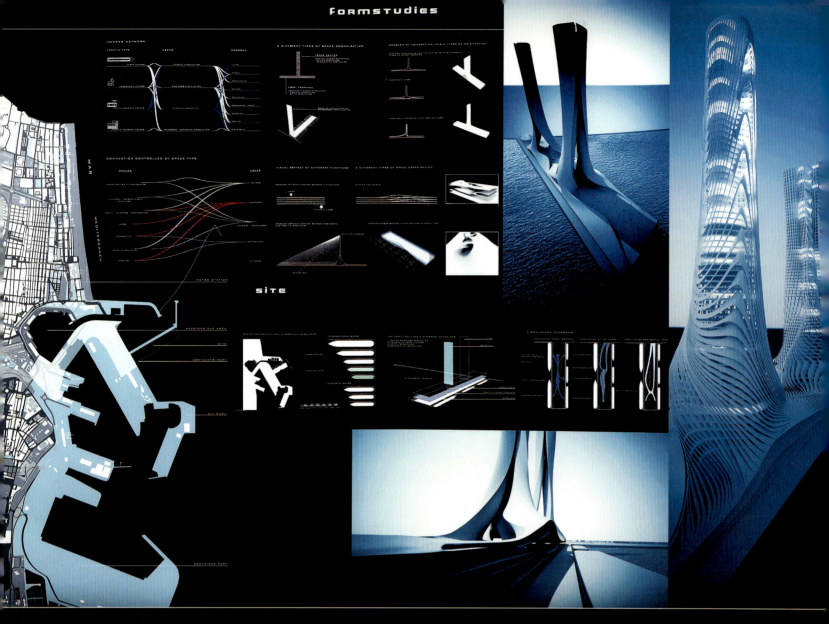

Valencia International Port Terminal 2007

Peter Schamberger

Controlled radiation of direct and indirect sunlight, thermal performance, program specific openings and self-shadowing are the parameters for a solar radiation analysis over the course of one year. The result becomes apparent as facade structure that is gradually transforming and adapting the specific exposure conditions on the respective location of the facade.

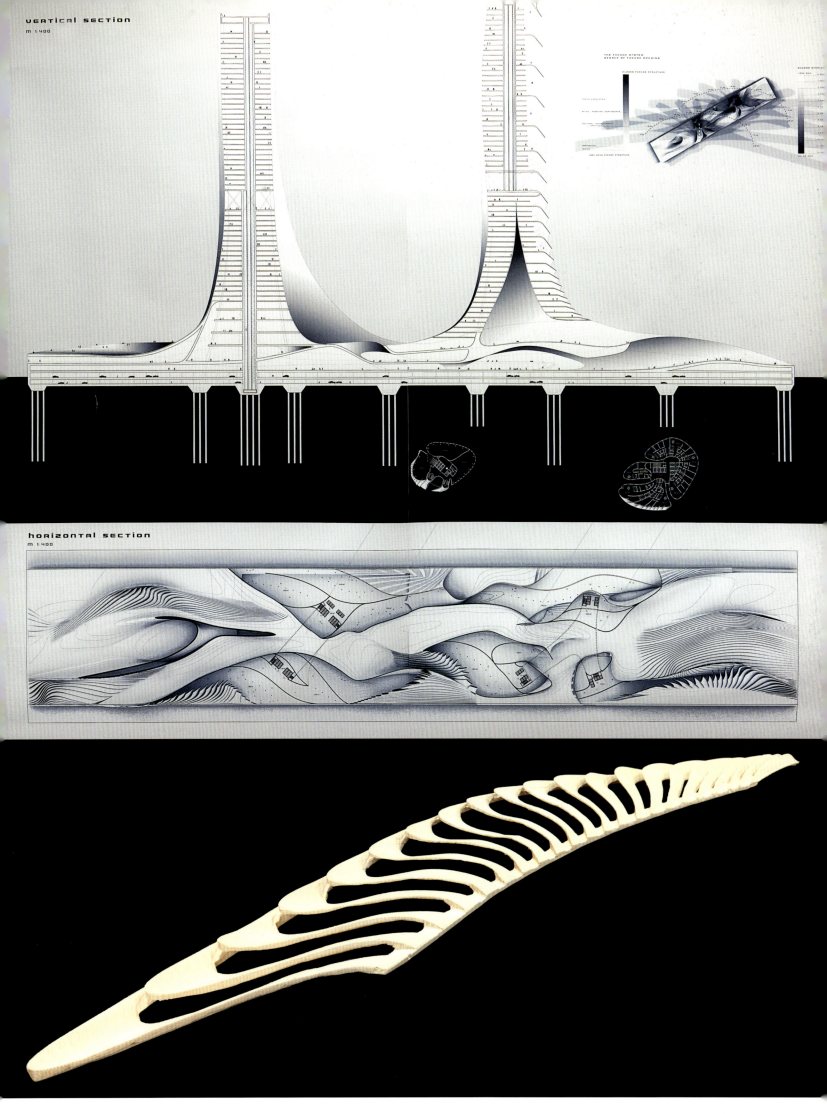

VERTICAL SECTION
m 1:400

THE FAÇADE SYSTEM
DEGREE OF FACADE OPENING

HORIZONTAL SECTION
m 1:400

Plastic Network – Zone B5, Sofia 2007

Kaloyan Erevinov

The project proposes a single three-dimensional network as architectural space, creating a homogenous, loosely differentiated 'field-space'. Alternation in the scale and thickness of the network's members results in finely differentiated local conditions, where gradient conditions replace those of polar opposites such as structure/volume, open/closed, public/office.

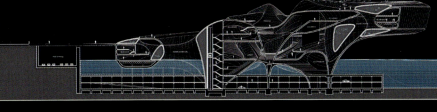

MIXITÉ – Multifunctional Subcenter Paris 2007

Eldine Heep, Gerhild Orthacker

Targeting an actual architectural competition in Paris, the project discusses new strategies of urban densification. Network typologies and radial growth patterns form the underlying principle of the design, allowing it to credibly fuse the extremely heterogeneous spaces of the competition site into a new whole. The project (re)establishes a visible and coherent unity across a differentiated scheme.

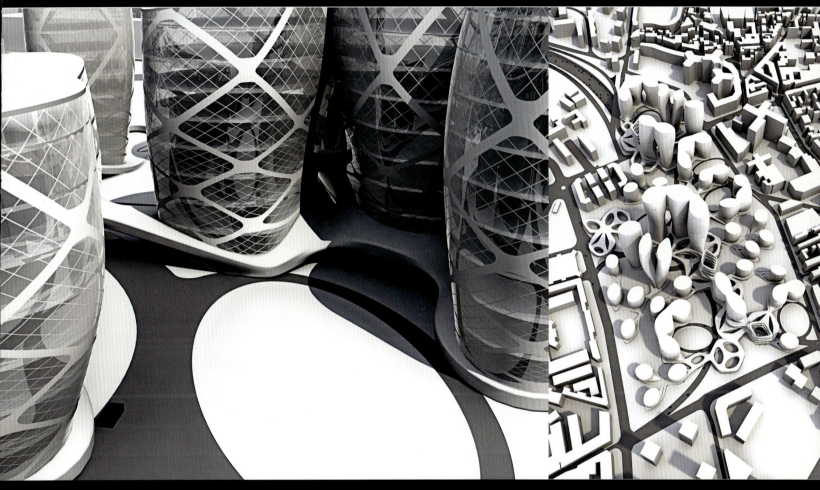

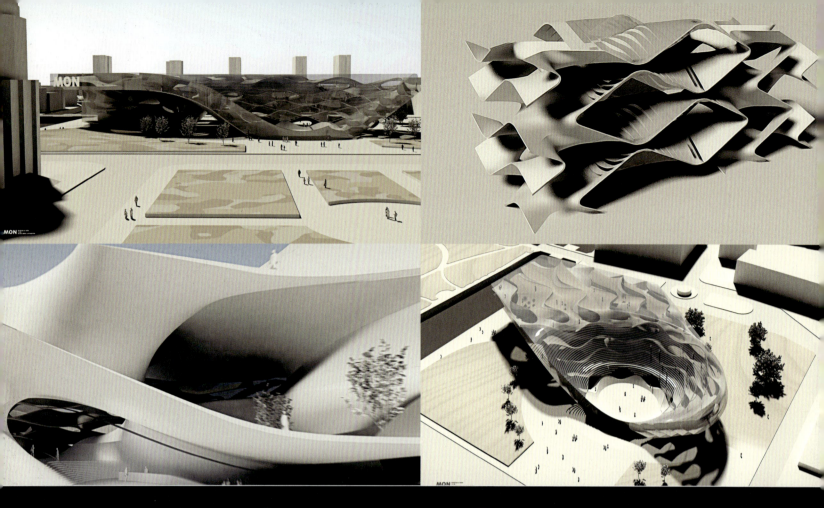

▲ **Museum of Now, Berlin** 2007
Julian Breinersdorfer

▼ **Public Library, Prague** 2006/07
Petra De Colle

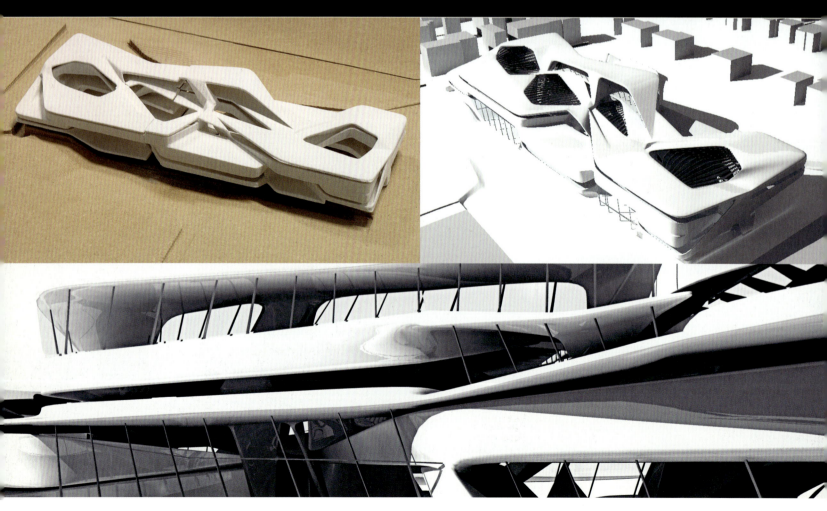

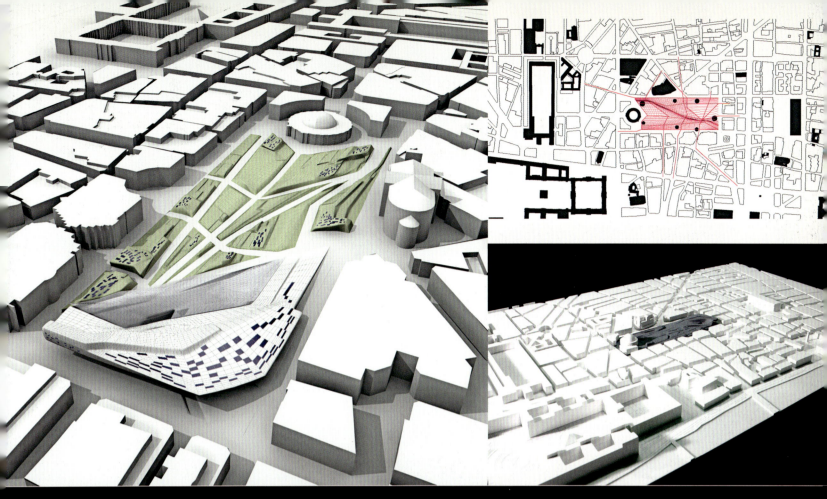

▲ Les Halles Paris 2006/07
Nicole Stöcklmayr

▼ Center for Performing Arts Istanbul 2006
Sophie Luger

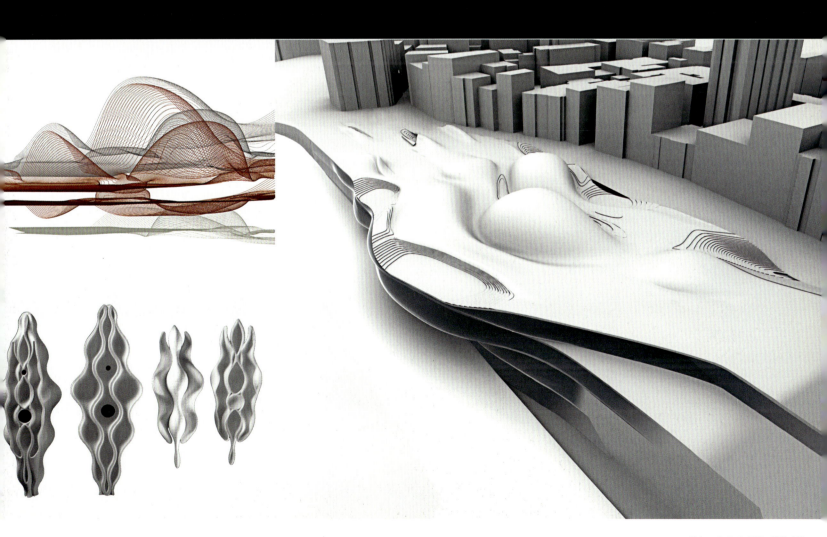

Bangkok Spine 2006
Florian Gypser

The project proposes an urban intervention for the area along Chao Phraya, the River of Kings in Bangkok, enhancing the neglected west bank of Thonburi. The Bangkok spine, a bundle of twelve inhabitable bridges, connects the western riverbanks with the eastern ones. As a large-scale multifunctional structure it is intended to become a new urban center of the historic city of Bangkok.

$$\sum_{i=1}^{n} \frac{\partial^2}{\partial x_i^2} \varphi(x) =$$

$$\nabla^2 \varphi = f$$

$$\Delta \varphi = f$$

Parametric Urban Fabric 2006

Felix Strasser

The diploma project's main goal is to thoroughly research the possibilities afforded by the architectural application of software originally developed to simulate electromagnetic fields. The process of writing, fine-tuning and adapting the actual code is thereby part of the thesis in order to maximize the software's potential as meaningful analogy for the discipline of architecture.

Film and Architecture Center,
Las Vegas 2005/06

Katharina Tanzberger

The concept of the film museum is based on the analysis of Peter Kubelka's film "Arnulf Rainer" and its harsh contrasts sound/no sound, black/white frames) and the rhythmic succession of those basic elements. These ideas of contrast and sequence reappear in the design of the film museum: the contrast of organic to rigid forms inform the duality of projected film and exhibited object in the building.

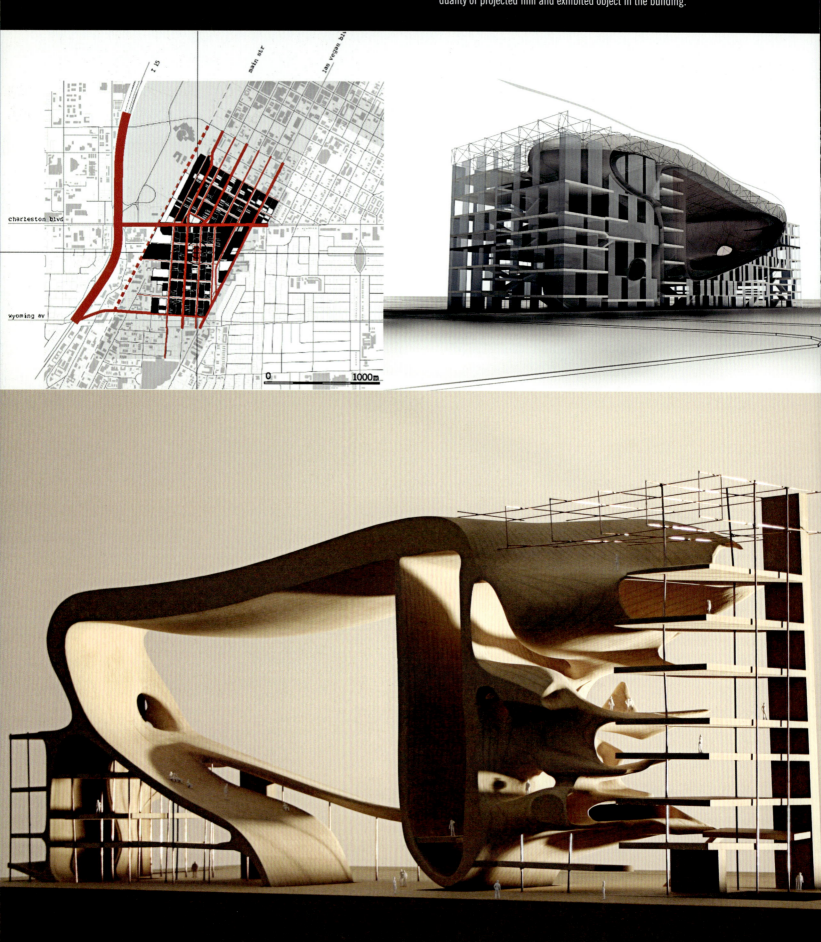

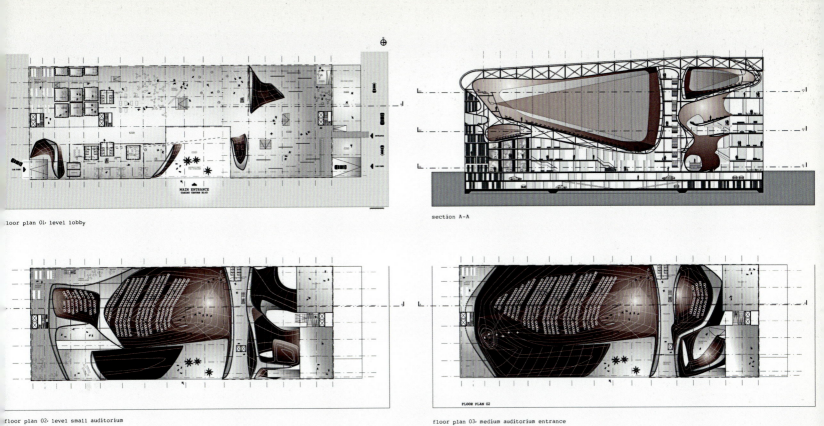

floor plan 01· level lobby

section A-A

floor plan 02· level small auditorium

floor plan 03· medium auditorium entrance

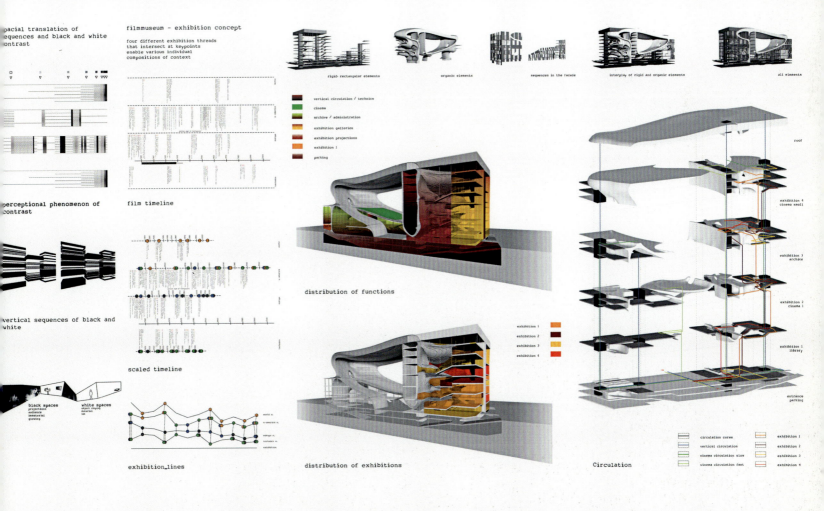

spacial translation of sequences and black and white contrast

perceptional phenomenon of contrast

vertical sequences of black and white

black spaces
projections
audience
immaterial
glowing

white spaces
object display
material
let

filmmuseum - exhibition concept

four different exhibition threads
that intersect at keypoints
enable various individual
compositions of context

film timeline

scaled timeline

exhibition_lines

rigid· rectangular elements   organic elements   sequences in the facade   interplay of rigid and organic elements   all elements

vertical circulation / technics
cinema
archive / administration
exhibition galleries
exhibition projections
exhibition 1
parking

distribution of functions

exhibition 1
exhibition 2
exhibition 3
exhibition 4

distribution of exhibitions

roof

exhibition 4
cinema small

exhibition 3
archive

exhibition 2
cinema 1

exhibition 1
library

entrance
parking

circulation cores   exhibition 1
vertical circulation   exhibition 2
cinema circulation slow   exhibition 3
cinema circulation fast   exhibition 4

Circulation

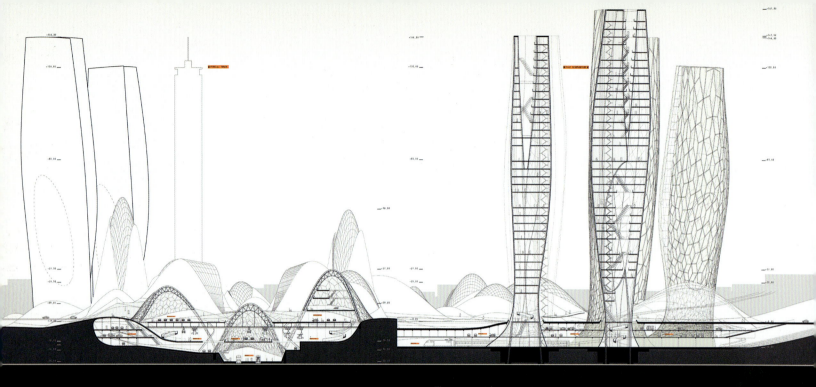

Milano R&D Design Center 2005/06

Simone Fuchs, Johannes Schafelner

The proposal for a new Automotive R&D Design Center is based on a new urban geometry as connective fabric for programmatic and infrastructural elements. A circular packing system as initial pattern was grafted onto the site of the vacant area of Milan Central Station. Out of this a multilayered 3d landscape evolved that interweaves the production of automobiles with the urban infrastructure.

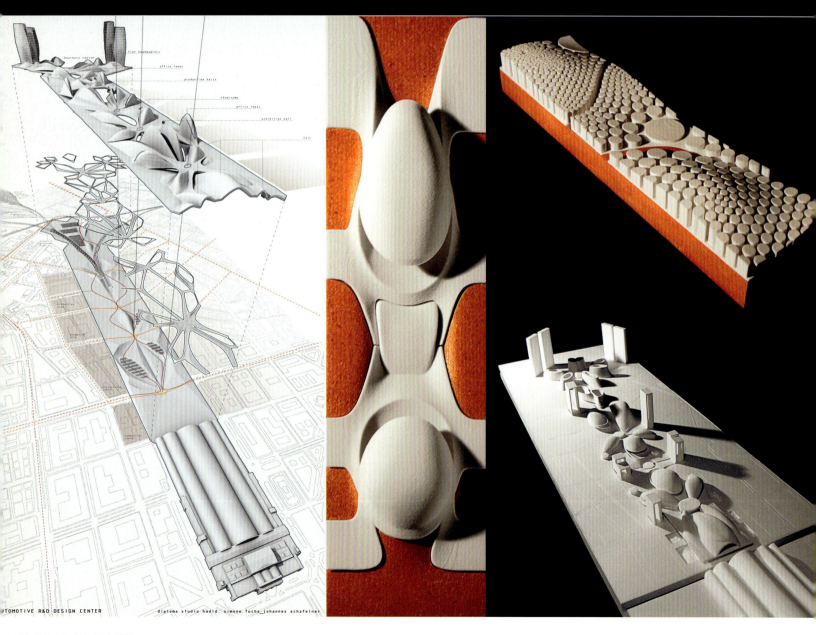

AUTOMOTIVE R&D DESIGN CENTER   diploma studio hadid. simone fuchs_johannes schafelner

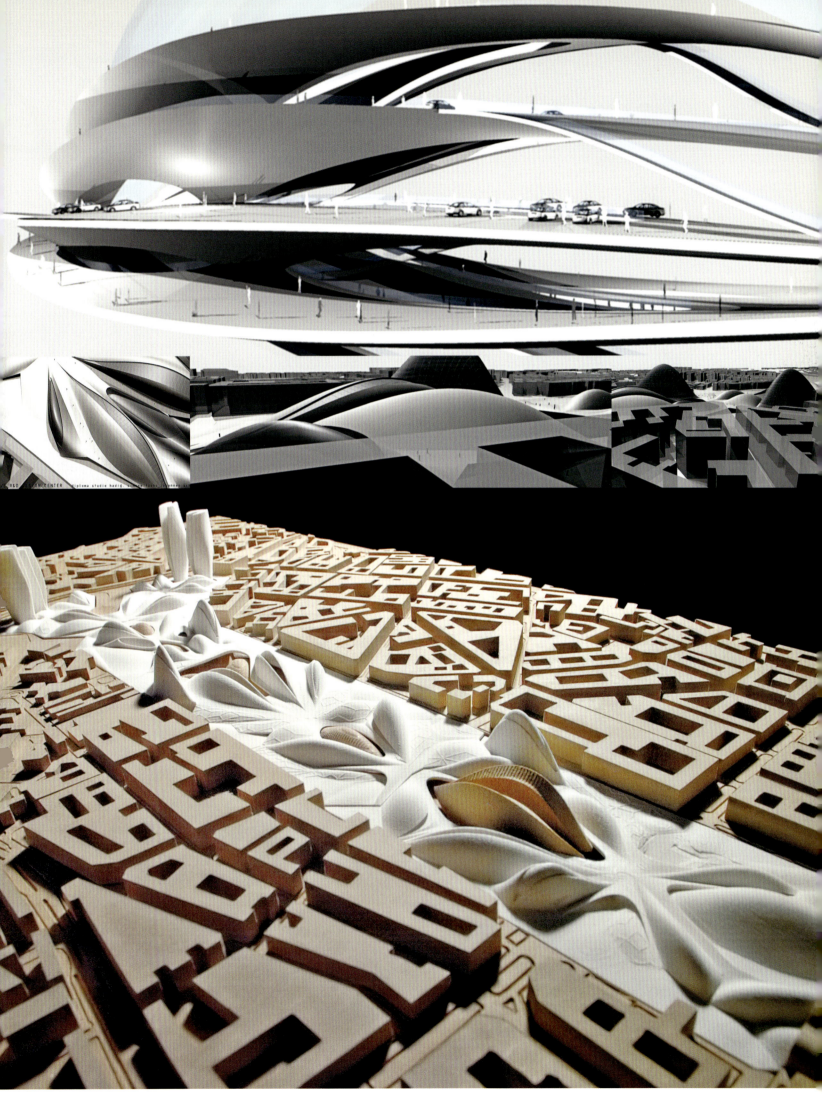

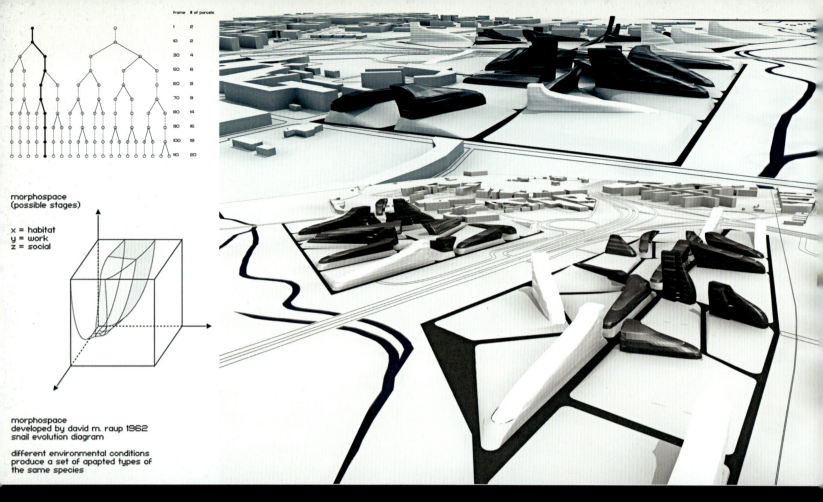

morphospace
(possible stages)

x = habitat
y = work
z = social

morphospace
developed by david m. raup 1962
snail evolution diagram

different environmental conditions
produce a set of apapted types of
the same species

▲ **UrbanPattern Re-written –**
An Adaptive City Code 2005
Paul Peyrer-Heimstätt

▼ **Missing Link – Crossing the**
Danube River 2005
Daniel Grünkranz

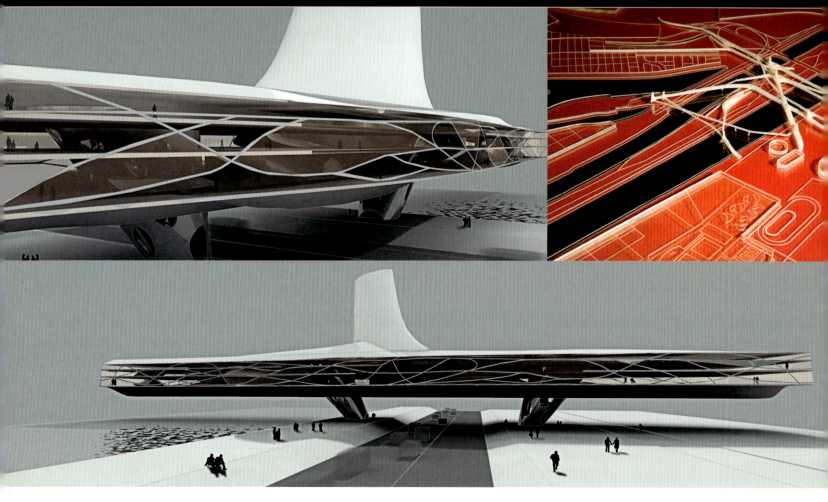

exhibition hall

▲ **B.Poetics – Policultural Interference** 2005
Katharina Mayr

▼ **Sibirian Resort** 2005
Marcin Gregorowicz

▲ **M.Knot – Tate Extention** 2005
Eva Scheucher

▼ **Parkstadium** 2004/05
Robert Grössinger

02 STADION PARK
Vösendorf bei Wien
Diplomarbeit, Wien
2005

01 BIOMIMETICS
Studienarbeit

2003

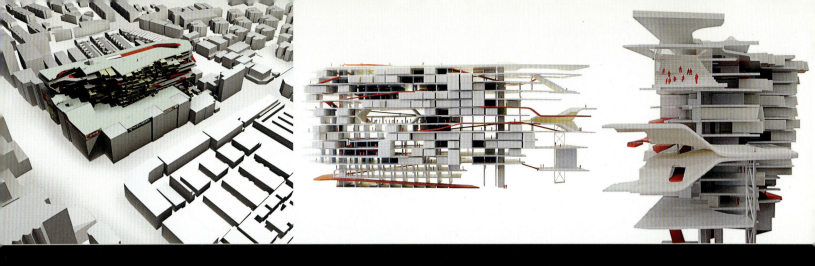

Lilong Development China 2004

Florian Pucher

The project deals with the typical Lilong building type and the historic city fabric of Shanghai. It tries to relocate the overpopulated compound in a single new building by preserving the surrounding historic buildings of the area. The proposed new urban city block further enhances the qualities of the quarter by adding missing parks and green areas as well as public and communal spaces.

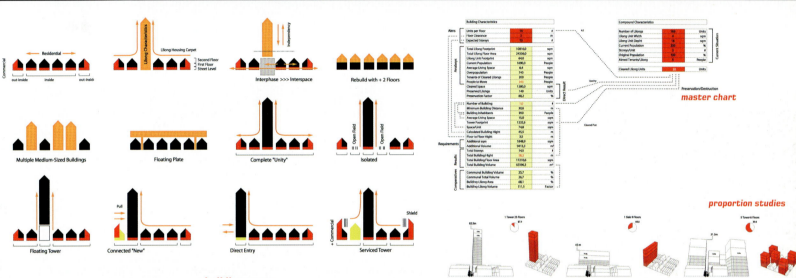

building types

integration proposals

master chart

proportion studies

Moscow Skyscrapers 2004/05

Matthias Bär

The project is based on the current urbanistic discussion in Moscow to erect a series of new skyscrapers within the city of Moscow. The proposal concentrates the skyscrapers on an axis that was projected in the 1935 Stalinist master plan. The urbanistic figure accentuates existing morphologies and historic sites. Each skyscraper responds to contextual and functional parameters and evolves as a highly specific new typology.

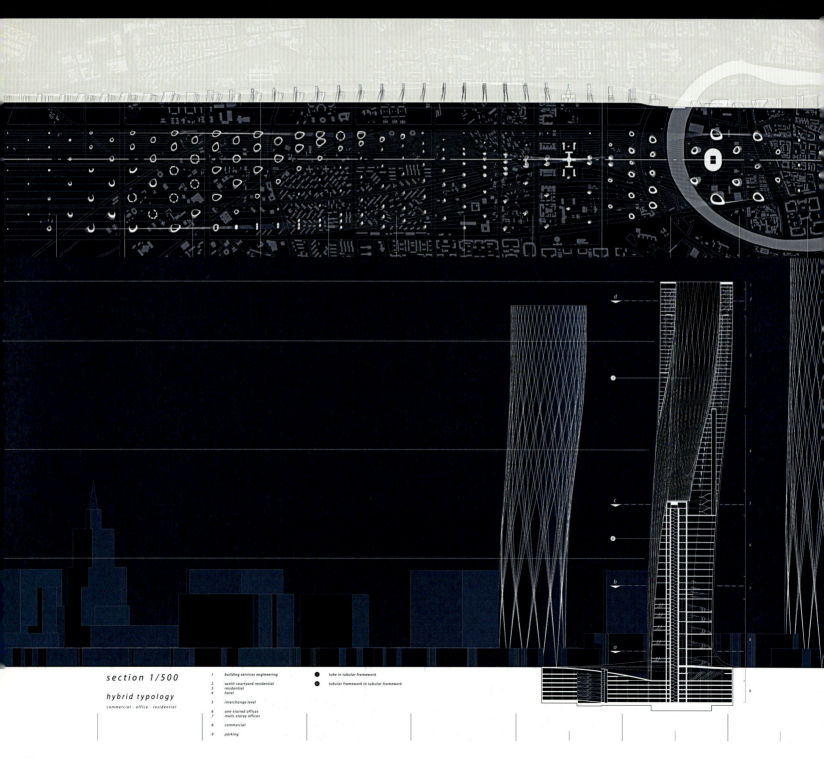

section 1/500

hybrid typology
commercial - office - residential

1. building services engineering
2. sunlit courtyard residential
3. residential
4. hotel
5. interchange level
6. one-storied offices
7. multi-storey offices
8. commercial
9. parking

● tube in tubular framework
● tubular framework in tubular framework

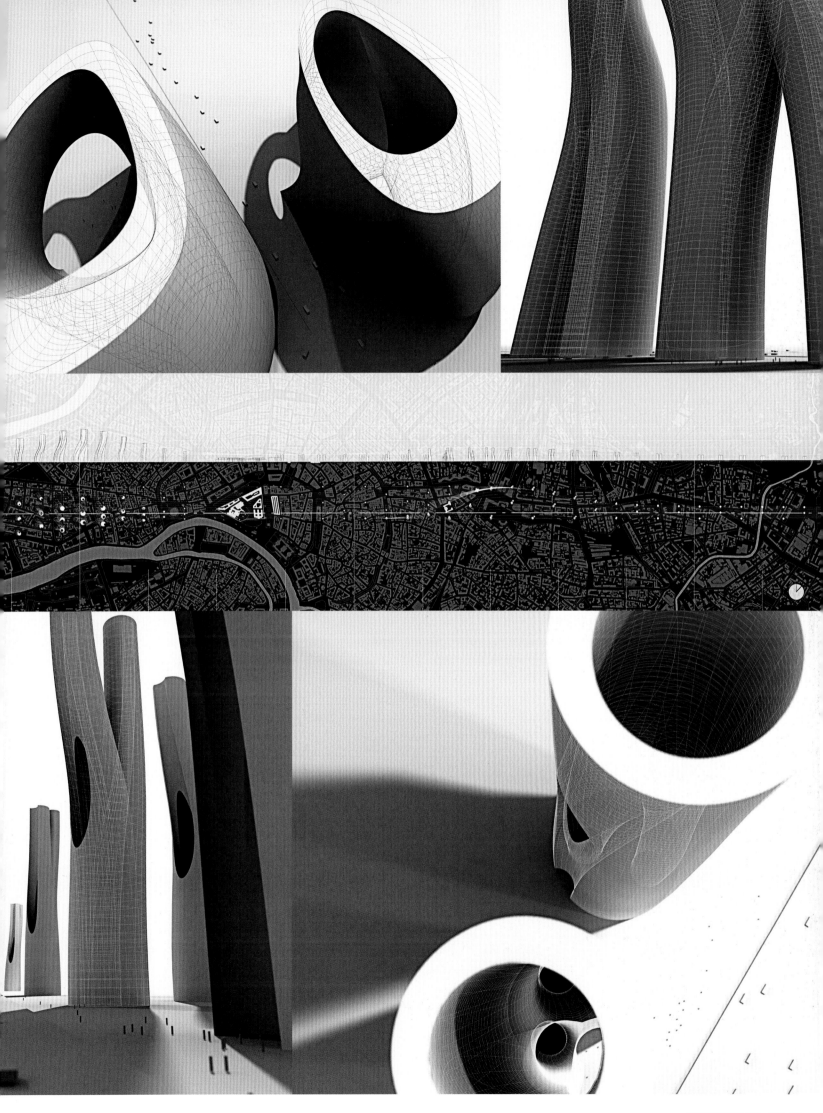

Osaka Station 2004

Jörg Hugo, Jens Mehlan

The diploma project aims at deriving a context-specific morphology for the highly specific urban conditions of dense transit spaces. While maintaining an equally efficient flux over current station typologies the project 'Osaka Urban Station' demonstrates space-making strategies, which enable the city to truly draw on the potential of such urban conditions.

Urban Jam Session, Boston 2003

Daniel Baerlecken, Judith Reitz

With reference to Giedion´s analysis of parkways around New York and his postulate for an architecture of movement the project proposes an urban structure, linking city and traffic and thus reinterpreting the unobstructed freedom of movement. The proposed structure is layered in five levels with different speeds and length of stay to accommodate different requirements.

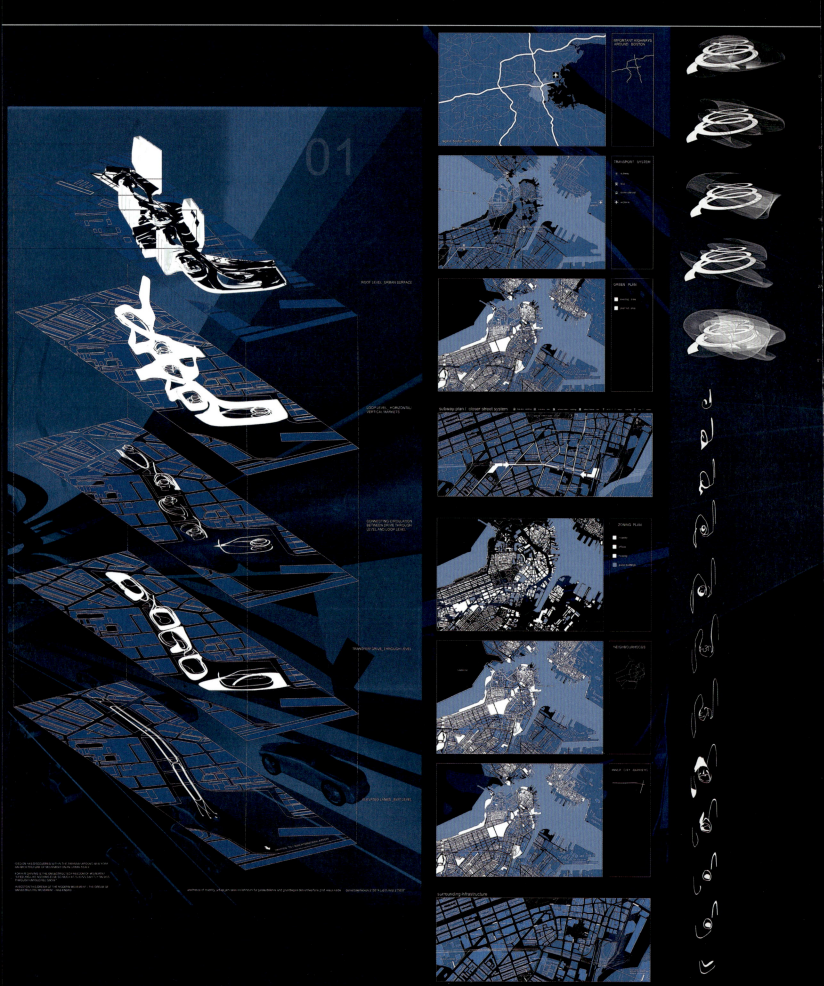

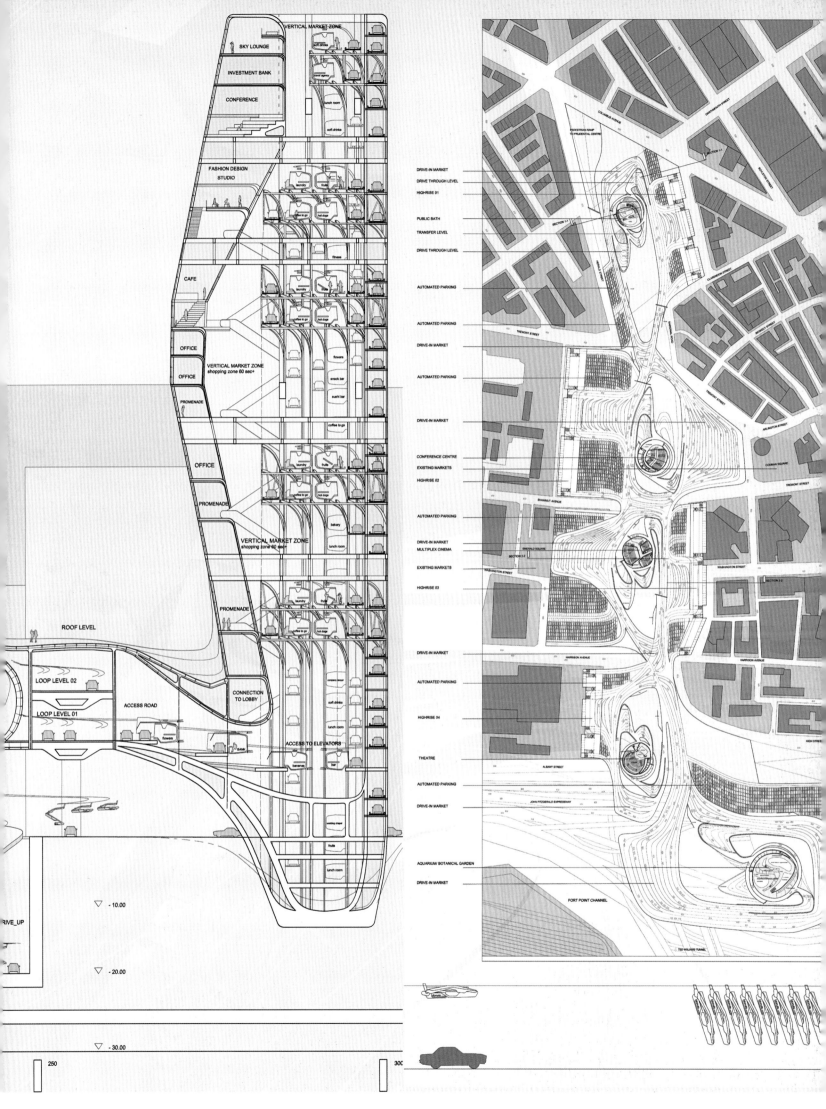

Berlin City Modulation 2003
Paul Fürst

The diploma project deals with the phenomenon of perception. Along rail tracks in Berlin, with the focus being the site of Bahnhof Friedrichstraße, specific geometric rules produce different arrays of urban blocks to establish continuously changing readings of the environment while passing by with the S-train. Similar to the stroboscope-effect, dynamic patterns produce additional information for the passengers.

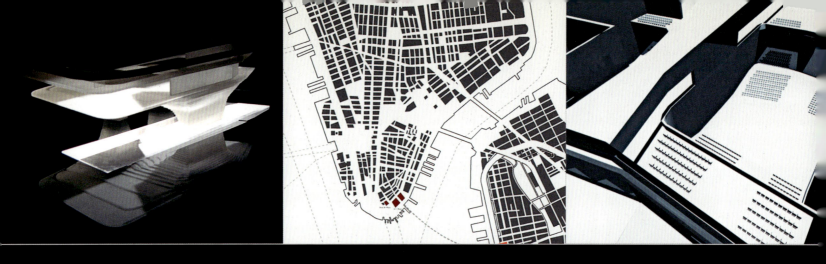

Congress and Knowledge Center, Brooklyn, New York 2002/03

Jörg Hofstätter

Accessibility is the subject explored in this diploma project. On-site implementation gives the public all kinds of access. The building unit provides the visitor of the centre with multiple connections to all internal functions. The analysis of knowledge management is the foundation for internal space distribution in an intricate 3-dimensional way, allowing a concurrent flow of information.

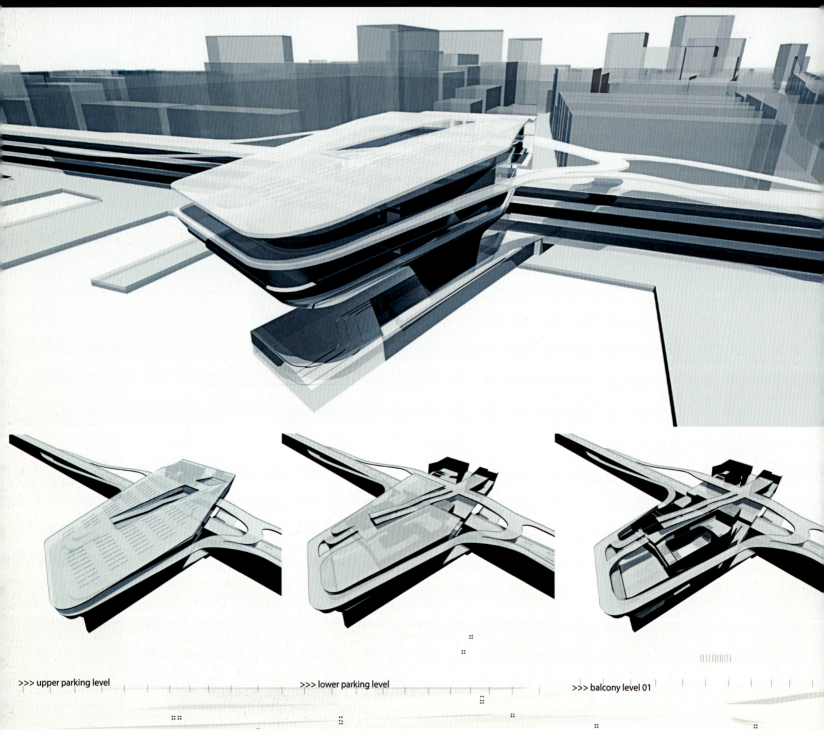

>>> upper parking level

>>> lower parking level

>>> balcony level 01

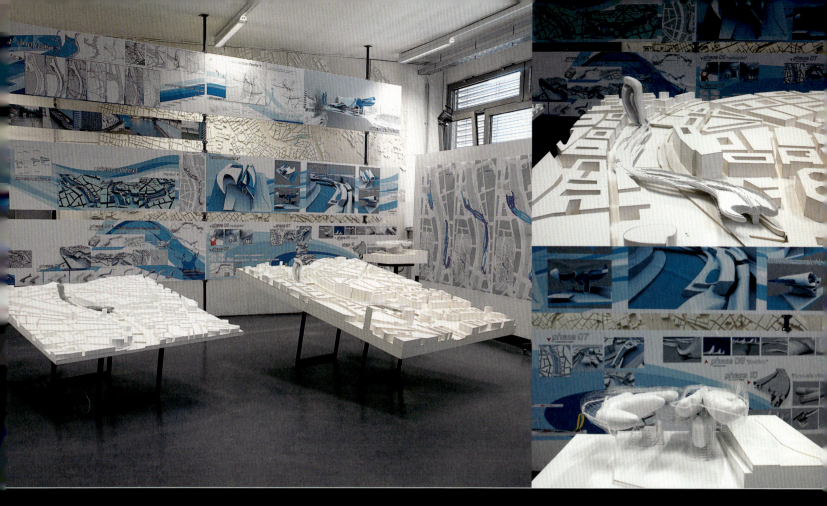

▲ **Urban Catwalk, Vienna** 2003
Martin Huber

▼ **BAM / Brooklyn Academy of Music, New York** 2002/03
Sandra Riess

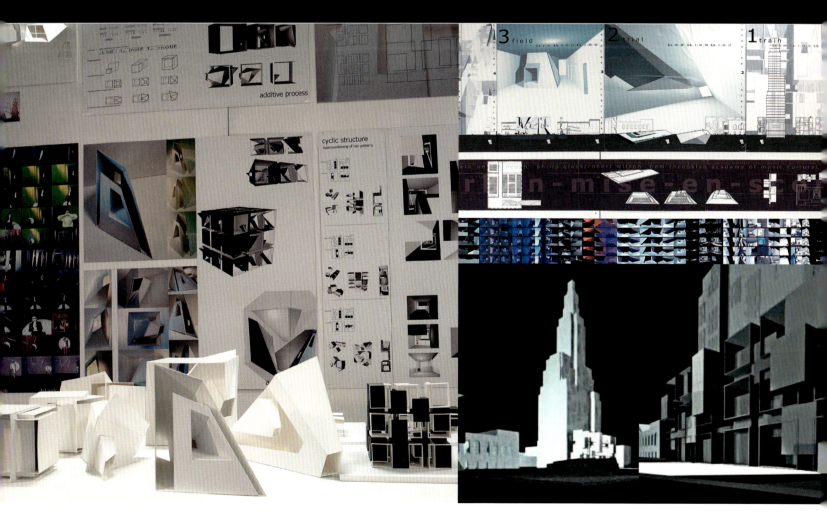

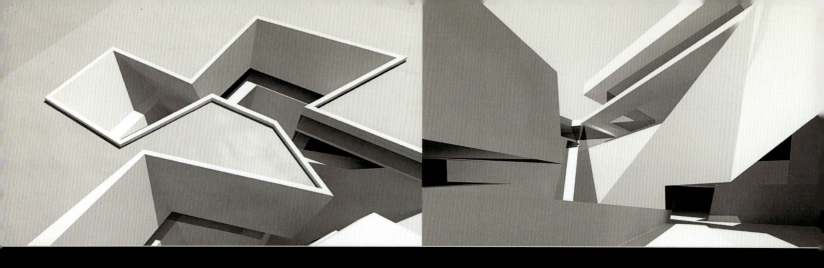

Abu Simbel -
Museum of Ancient Art 2002/03

Michael Gruber

The design strategy for this project refers to techniques and indexing used in archeological excavations. The museum is dug into the ground and organized as a 3-dimensional matrix. Similar to exploring archeological strata the visitor vertically traverses the historical periods while at the same level being able to experience different domains from one period. With multiple connections the curators' synopsis of relating matters is possible.

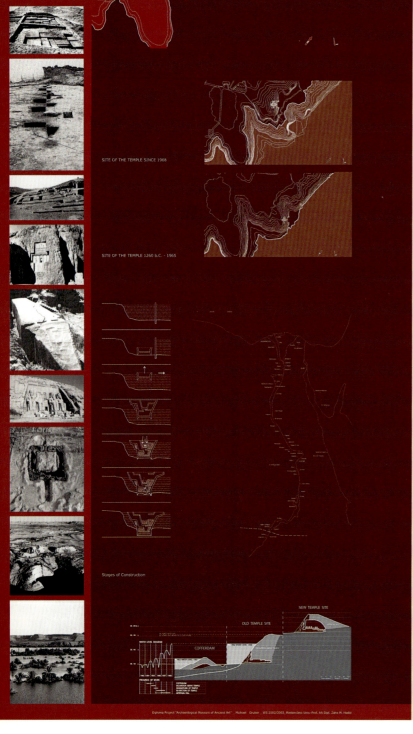

SITE OF THE TEMPLE SINCE 1968

SITE OF THE TEMPLE 1260 b.C. - 1965

Stages of Construction

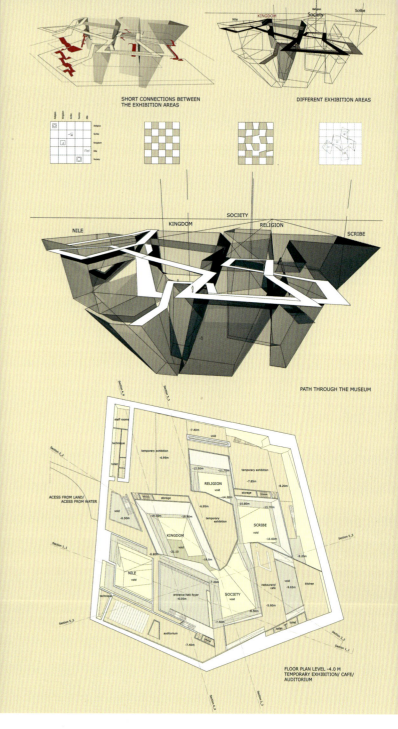

SHORT CONNECTIONS BETWEEN THE EXHIBITION AREAS

DIFFERENT EXHIBITION AREAS

PATH THROUGH THE MUSEUM

FLOOR PLAN LEVEL -4.0 M
TEMPORARY EXHIBITION/ CAFE/ AUDITORIUM

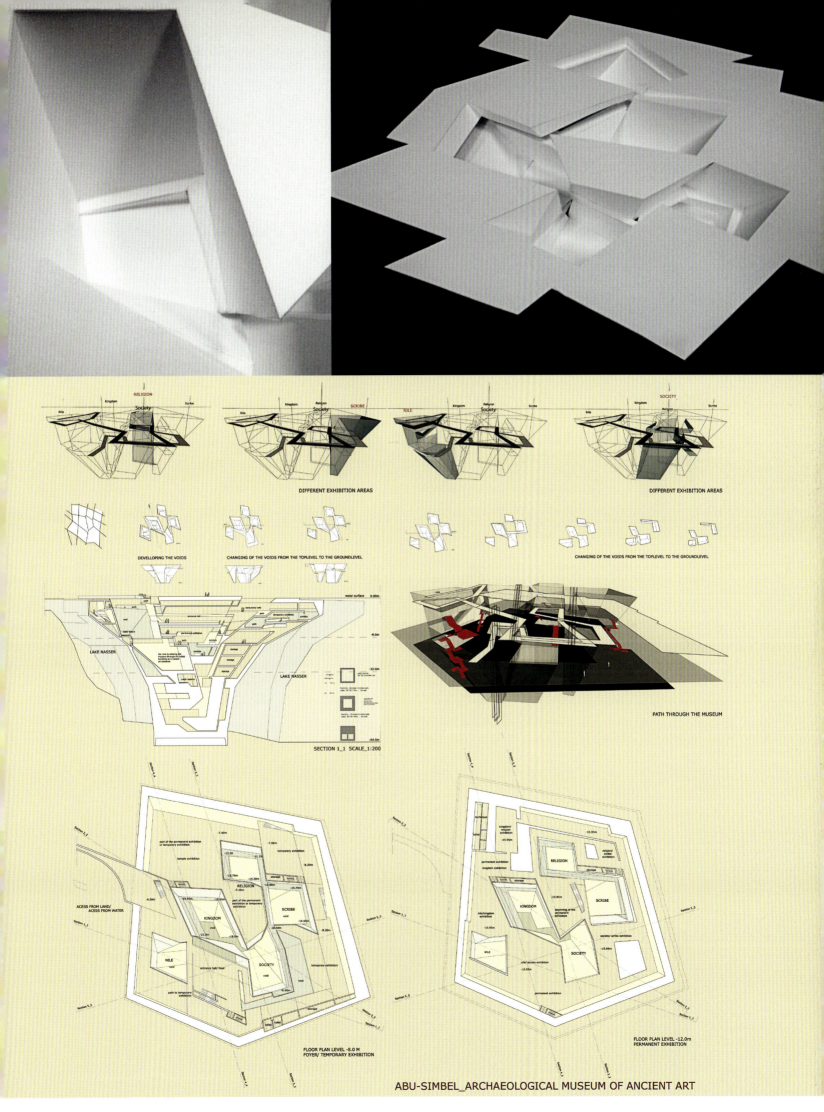

DIFFERENT EXHIBITION AREAS

DIFFERENT EXHIBITION AREAS

DEVELLOPING THE VOIDS

CHANGING OF THE VOIDS FROM THE TOPLEVEL TO THE GROUNDLEVEL

CHANGING OF THE VOIDS FROM THE TOPLEVEL TO THE GROUNDLEVEL

LAKE NASSER

LAKE NASSER

SECTION 1_1 SCALE_1:200

PATH THROUGH THE MUSEUM

ACESS FROM LAND/
ACESS FROM WATER

FLOOR PLAN LEVEL -8.0 M
FOYER/ TEMPORARY EXHIBITION

FLOOR PLAN LEVEL -12.0m
PERMANENT EXHIBITION

ABU-SIMBEL_ARCHAEOLOGICAL MUSEUM OF ANCIENT ART

Museum of Mathematics Alexandria 2002
Caren Ohrhallinger

This intricate building is generated using a mathematical concept based on fractal integer sequences and graph theory. The exhibition space consists of 48 irregular polyhedrons. Their shape, order and content are developed according to the above-mentioned theory. Corresponding to the sequence value, the complexity of the space emerges from ground floor to upper levels in all aspects.

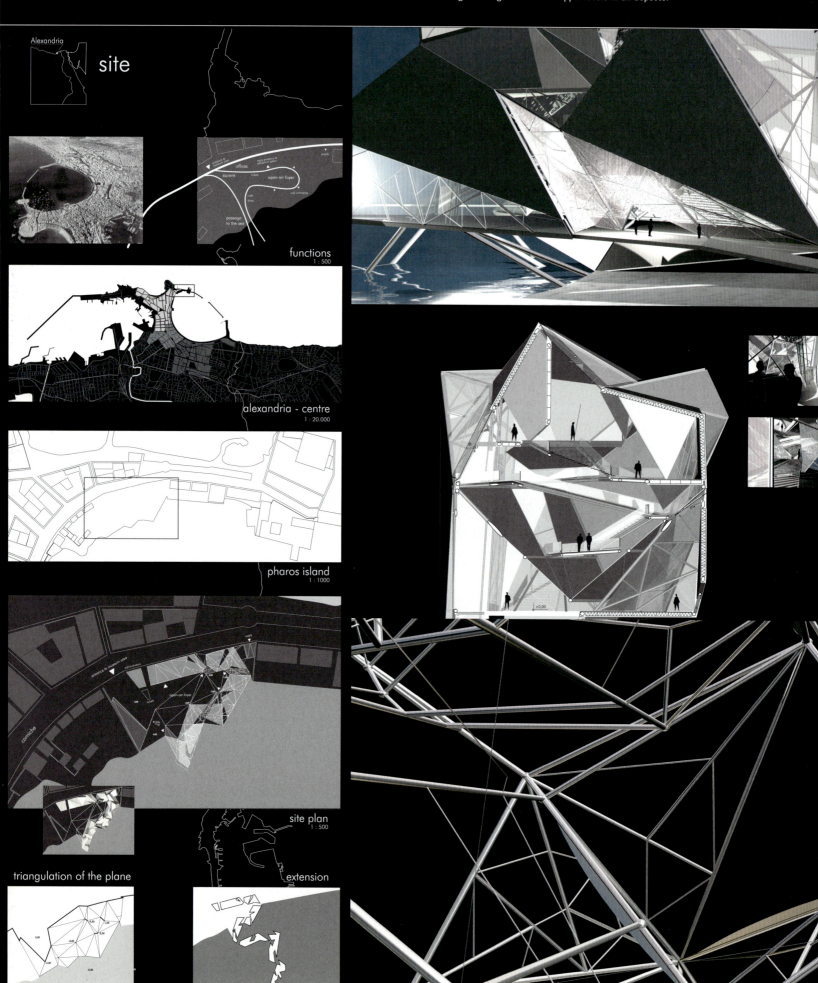

site

functions
1 : 500

alexandria - centre
1 : 20.000

pharos island
1 : 1000

site plan
1 : 500

triangulation of the plane

extension

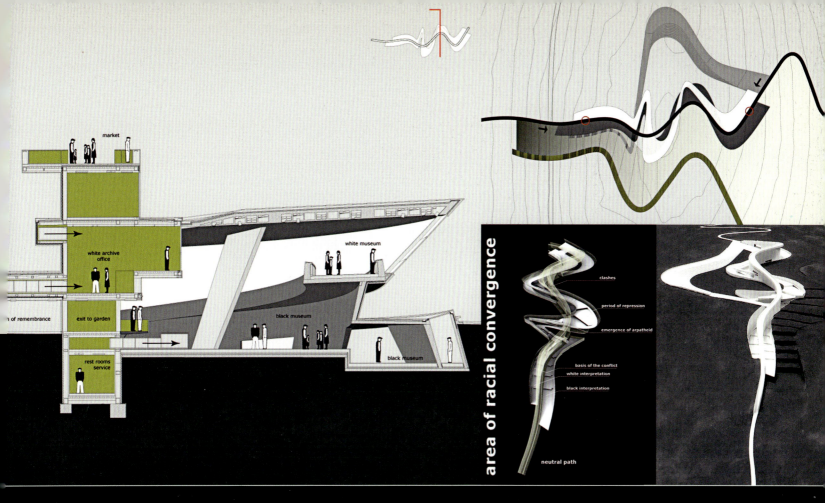

▲ **Bifocal Perspective**
Museum Pretoria 2003
Carola Stabauer

▼ **University for Landscape Development**
and Design Vienna 2002/03
Jörg Hilbich

area of racial convergence

clashes

period of repression

emergence of arpatheid

basis of the conflict
white interpretation
black interpretation

neutral path

market

white archive
office

exit to garden

rest rooms
service

white museum

black museum

black museum

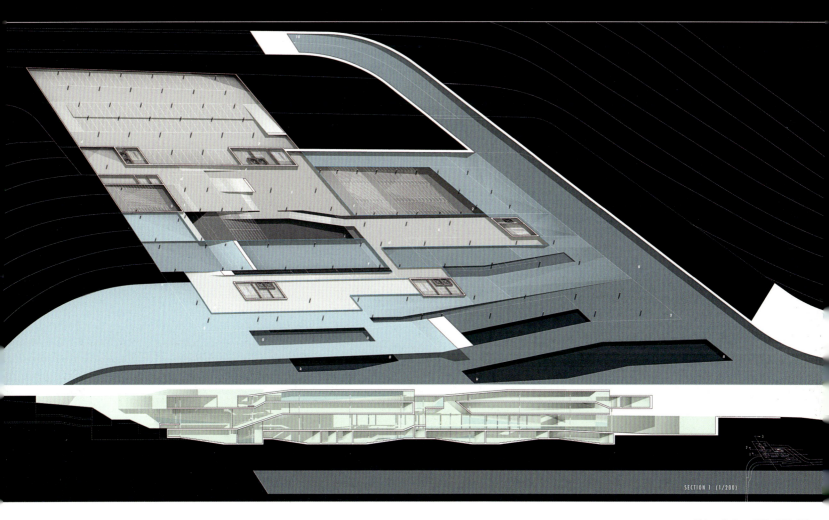

SECTION 1 (1/200)

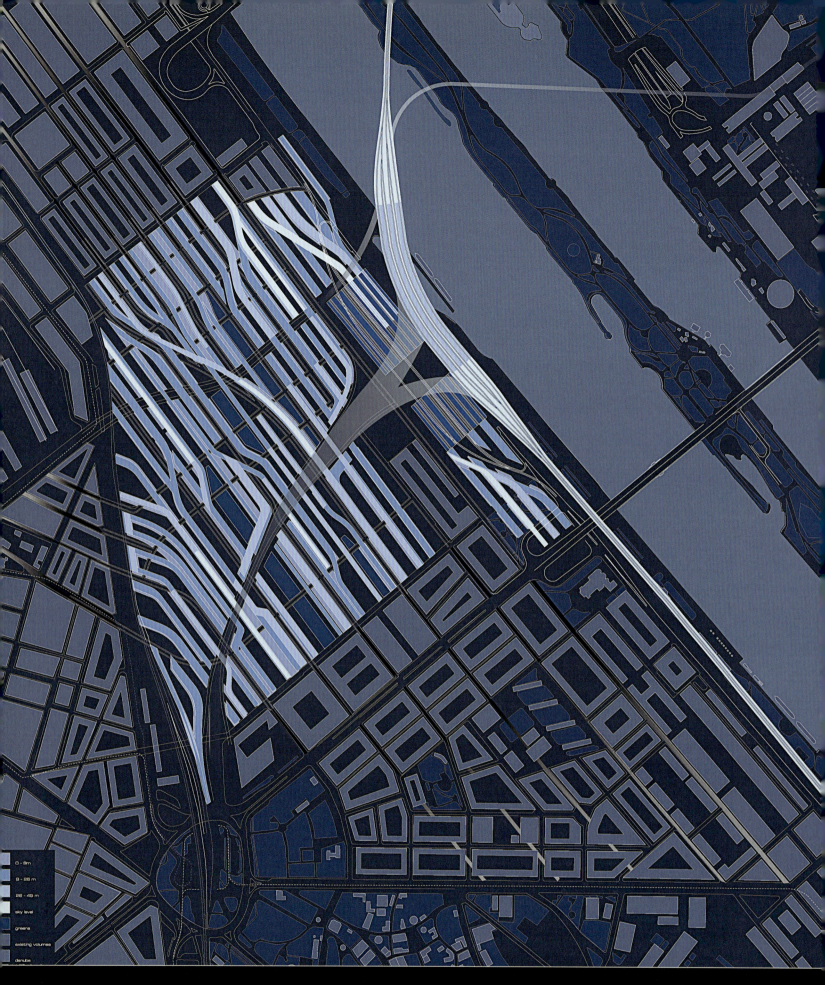

Legend (left side of image):

0 - 9m
9 - 28 m
28 - 45 m
sky level
greens
existing volumes
danube

Urban Link, Vienna 2001/02
Natalie Rosenberg, Thomas Vietzke

A central railway station as a bridge across the Danube river and the rail pattern at the Nordbahnhof site were the impulse for designing a rhizome-like linear imprint on this area as an urban proposal, creating a network of correlations in different types. The station itself – referring to trajectories of movement – is articulated as a system of blending tubes with protruding openings to generate a fluent spatial coherence.

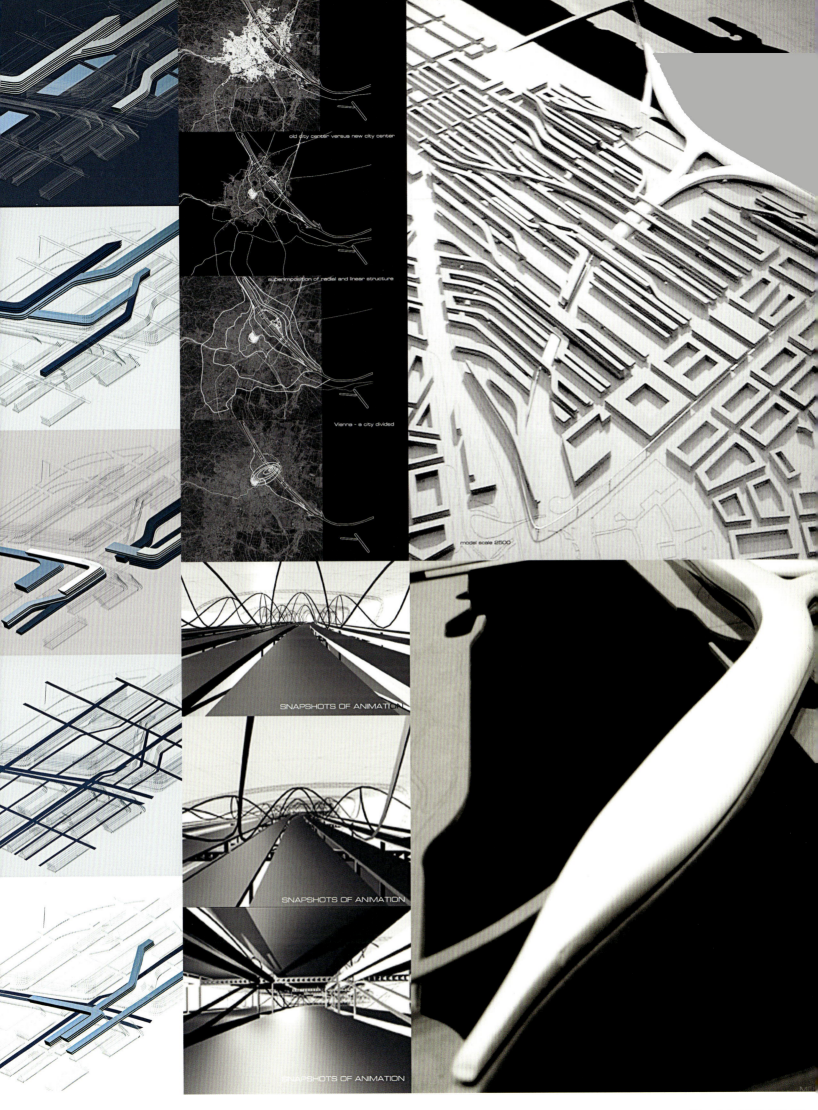

old city center versus new city center

superimposition of radial and linear structure

Vienna - a city divided

model scale 2500

SNAPSHOTS OF ANIMATION

SNAPSHOTS OF ANIMATION

SNAPSHOTS OF ANIMATION

▲ Thermal Bath Thingvellier Island 2002
Barbara Ziegerhofer

▼ FIX Center of Art and Mediatechnology Athens 2001/02
Thomas Ausweger

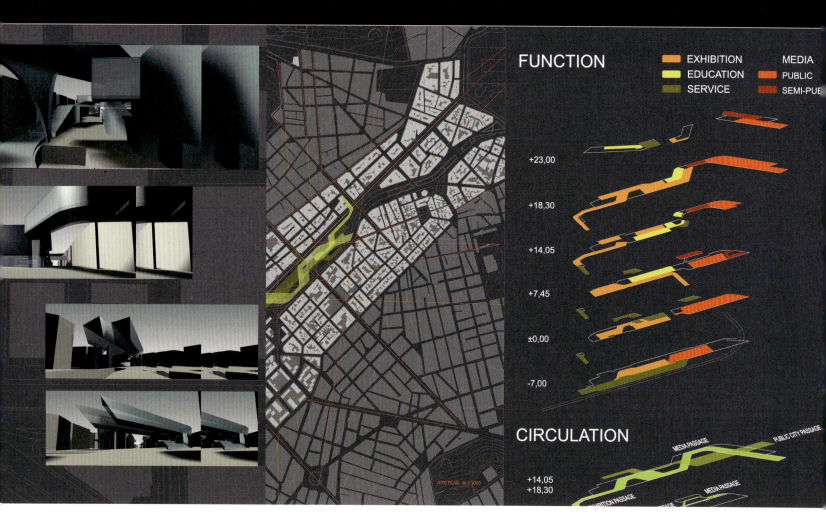

FUNCTION

EXHIBITION MEDIA
EDUCATION PUBLIC
SERVICE SEMI-PUB

+23,00
+18,30
+14,05
+7,45
±0,00
-7,00

CIRCULATION

+14,05
+18,30

City Fractal, Vienna 2001

Christian Neureiter, Bernhard Schratternecker

Through mapping lines and varying directions of the Gasometer site in Vienna a pattern is created, which is to be developed as a field condition of an urban proposal. Using the principles of fractal geometry the properties are scaled and multiplied. Thus the whole district, building types, floor plans and even the interior is derived from this unique encoded information to emerge in a great variety with a self-referential logic.

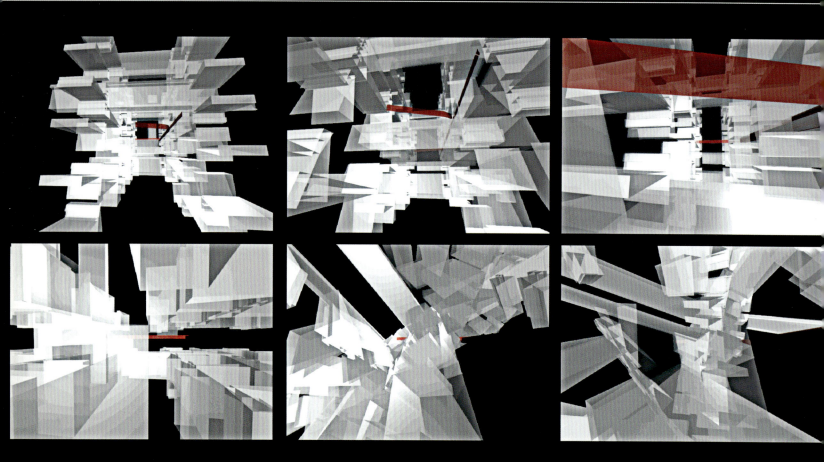

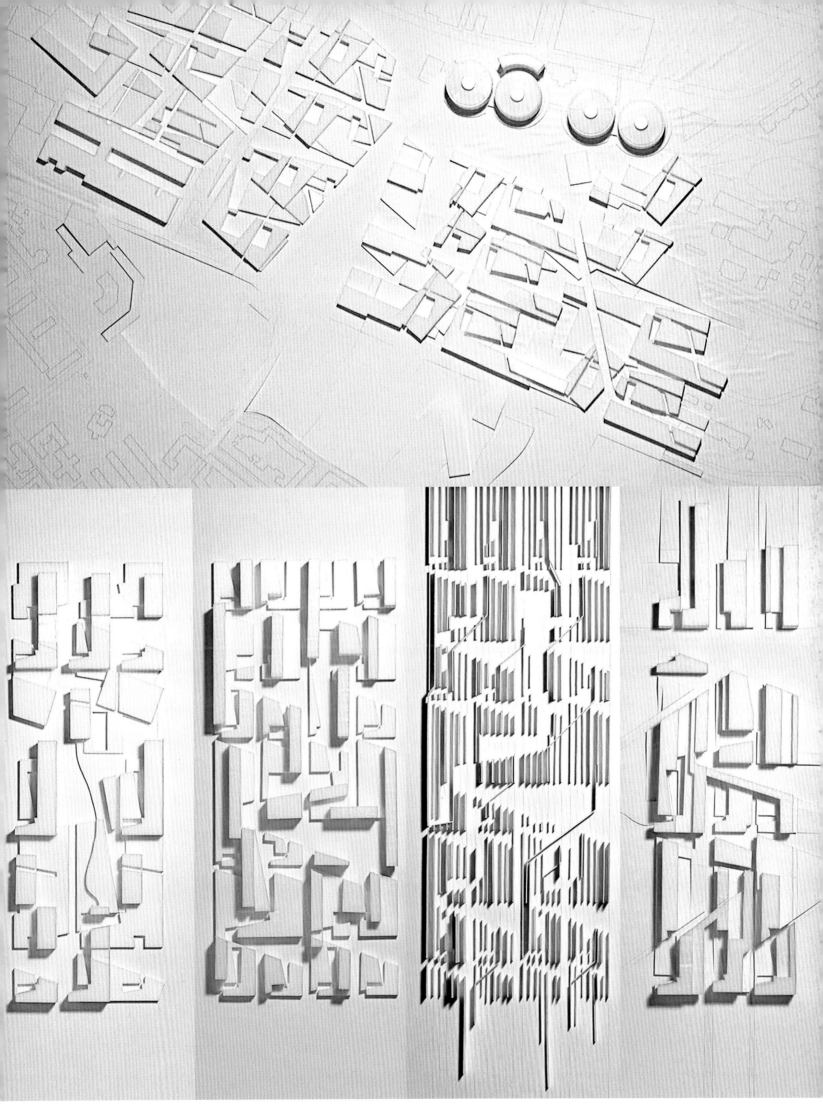

Stream City Vienna 2001

Anne Graupner, Nepomuk Wagner

In addition to the city center inside Ringstrasse and the Donau City, the project establishes a third focus for further development of Vienna towards Bratislava. By investigating manifest or latent imprints of river Danube the morphological substance of the urban body is elaborated as a transformed extension of the landscape. With regard to time-variable conditions, the basic outline of quarters is defined by a system of referential stream-lines.

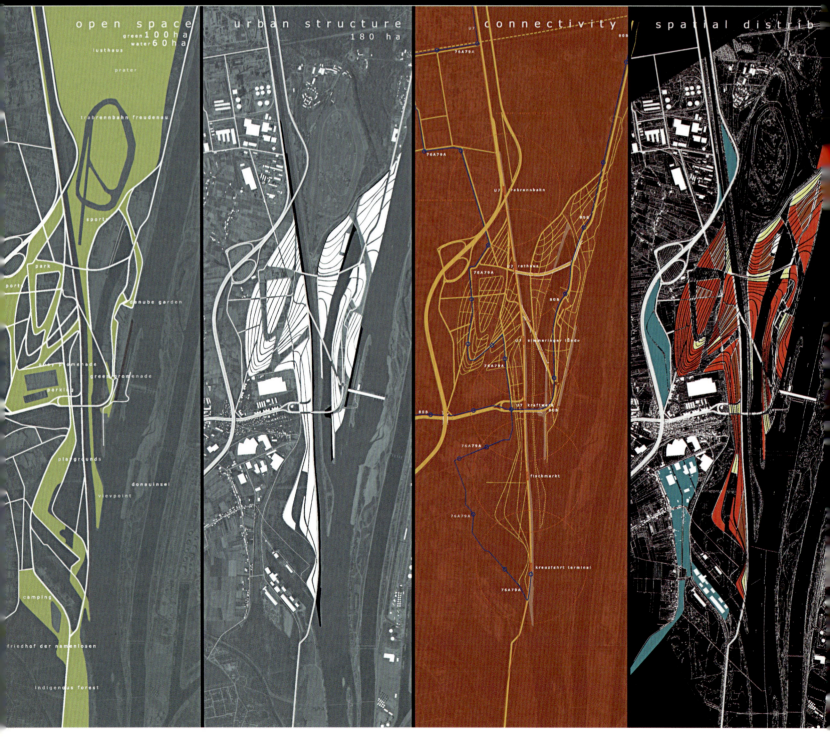

sunken
river courses

streamline

archipelago

streamgrid

BOOM AND BLOOM

Sulan Kolatan

The pleasure and privilege of being a frequent guest juror on the Studio Zaha Hadid reviews since its inception 10 years ago has given me a unique vantage point of both the evolution and constancy of the outstanding work produced throughout the years.

In fact, one of the most remarkable aspects of the studio has been the carefully constructed relationship between what evolves and what remains constant. Dedication to formal research, methodological and technological innovation as well as a 'problematization' of program – even, or especially, in its absence, as some of the most interesting discussions on program ensued in the instances of absence, are clearly the constants. The way these constants are addressed each term evolves the internal maturations of the studio and external cultural transformations in the world. This inside/out consciousness when coupled with the "exuberant excellence" of architectural production creates student work that *matters* beyond the limits of academia.

Studio Zaha Hadid operates on the premise that architecture involves the 'production of culture' and thus the projects are understood as speculative-creative responses to inquiries about current cultural conditions. Theories and techniques are explored as they pertain to current urban dynamics. In honor of this approach I would like to sketch out a few thoughts on theories and techniques of the booming and blooming urban now.

BOOM AND BLOOM_THE URBAN BIO-PHYSICAL

Over the last three decades there has been a growing ecological consciousness traceable through an ever-increasing body of (field) research on one hand, and the pursuit of a theorization of ecology, on the other. We are undergoing a significant phase of bio-physical transformation with the new speed and form of urbanization driving much of it.

This is a time when architecture should play a central role in shaping the public debate through speculative-creative responses coupling emerging research and theory, helping to project and realize productive future scenarios. But design is largely absent from these developments as current research is primarily metrics-based and pursued from a planning and management perspective or with only a narrow focus on building technology.

PARADIGM SHIFTS FAVORING BOOM AND BLOOM

Whether consciously or subliminally our discipline operates under the influence of the following widely accepted paradigms. An emerging shift is gaining increasing recognition. The selected theories, tools and techniques included in this course are linked to the following critical paradigm shifts:

Organic – Inorganic Divide
Old: The Organic World is alive and therefore active and open to change. In contrast, the Inorganic World is passive and fixed/stable.
New: Organic and Inorganic systems in nature transform based on their inherent behaviors and in response to external events, but transformation cycles have (radically) different speeds.
Systems
Old: Systems operate in layers of pure and discrete categories.
New: Systems are hybrid. They operate through means of networks, actants, machines, quasi-objects and assemblages.
Nature – Human Divide
Old: Humans affect the Natural World outside positively/negatively.
New: Humans constitute one system among many networks that together form the Natural World.
Nature – Culture Divide
Old: Culture is produced by humans and therefore is apart from or antithetical to Nature.
New: Since humans are part of Nature everything they produce is an extension of Nature.
Natural History – Social History Divide
Old: Natural and Social Systems are based on different rules (see paradigm shift 1) therefore they need to be examined separately.
New: Natural and Social Systems are both based on Networks. All networks exhibit similar behaviors and rules. Moreover, Social networks are embedded within Natural ones.

BOOM AND BLOOM THEORIES

"(…) Worse, Modernism has had the added consequence, even more dangerous at the present juncture, of identifying the taste for habitation with the past, with the innocent, with the natural, with the untrampled, so that, just at the moment when what is needed is a theory of the *artificial* construction, maintenance, and development of carefully *designed* space, we are being drawn back to another utopia – a reactionary one this time – of a mythical past in which nature and society lived happily together ("in equilibrium," as they say, in "small face-to-face communities" without any need for artificial design).

Even worse: Modernism has so intoxicated the very militants of ecology (those, you might have thought, who had the most interest in rethinking what it is to situate and to place) that they have proposed to reuse nature-and-society, this time to "save nature," promising us a future where we should be even "more natural"! Which means, if you have followed me, even less human, even less realistic, even more idealist, even more utopian. I am all for recycling, but if there is one thing not to recycle, it is the notion of "nature"!" - *Bruno Latour*

With ecology occupying a focal point of discourse present-day theorists are plowing historic philosophic texts for indices of ecologic thought – and finding it in the works of Schelling, Spinoza, Heidegger, Marx, Deleuze and Guattari, and others. This implies that ecological thought is not partial to a singular way of thinking but can and does exist within very different discursive frameworks.

Of the latter, it is modernist thought that continues to exert an unmatched influence over policy and planning, an influence dominant in the disciplines of architecture and urban design. So it is perhaps natural to find that much of architecture's academic and professional engagement with ecology follows a Modern track. And in doing so wittingly or unwittingly disregards the paradigmatic changes under way. In other words, it misses the point – not to mention critical opportunities – by operating on wrong premises. Theories of change such as Complex System Theory, Resilience Theory, Metabolic Eco-theory, and Speculative Realism are better-suited intellectual tools in developing ecologic strategies for (urban) design now.

BOOM AND BLOOM TECHNIQUES AND TOOLS
Since paradigm shifts occur across the board in all spheres of human activity, we can trace the emergence of a new understanding not only in theory but also in the recent trend towards tools and techniques based on complexity, adaptation and networking. If the referenced theories enable us to construct an eco-logic of/for the new metropolis, what kinds of tools can we avail ourselves of in order to measure and create this kind of metropolis?

The network effect between organic and inorganic systems, between humans and their natural and cultural environment produces an exponential increase in the speed and scale of change. Scale and speed, though quantitative values, generate changes in kind and quality *because* of the exponential nature of their increase. The city as we knew it is not just becoming bigger faster, it is becoming *something* else. Given the old paradigms and the accompanying sets of tools this transformation has the appearance of being "out of control" – not understandable, not manageable and certainly not designable. In addition to speed and scale, heterogeneity plays a substantial role in urban make-up and transformation. Ecology describes itself as

an integrated science focused on examining 'mutualistic' relations between many different elements. There is a convergence between theories and tools on the point of imbuing *everything* – whether organic or inorganic, natural or artificial – with intelligent agency or some kind of informational code that lends behavior, produces thing-specific responses to external conditions and allows for adaptation.

Architecture will benefit from availing itself of an emerging generation of tools from ecosystem studies including geo-simulation, remote sensing, multi-agent system (MAS), and automata-based modeling for their potential usefulness in a bio-physical approach to architectural design. While parametric software continues to play a critical role due to its capacity to create relational and relative values, a linkage with these tools is likely to enhance overall design resilience.

SULAN KOLATAN is the Principal of KOL/MAC LLC, an architecture and design firm she co-founded with William J. Mac Donald. She is currently Clinical Associate Professor at Rensselaer Polytechnic Institute and Adjunct Professor at the School of Architecture at Pratt Institute. Her firm has been internationally acknowledged as a leader in digital architecture and technologically innovative design. She holds a MS in Architecture and Building Design degree from Columbia University and a Dipl.Ing. Arch. degree from the RWTH Aachen, Germany. She has taught at the GSAP at Columbia University from 1989-2005 and served as Acting Chair of the Department of Architectural Design and Building Technology at the Technical University in Darmstadt in 2002-03. In addition to serving as a Visiting Chair and Critic at a number of distinguished universities, she frequently lectures and speaks at academic and professional conferences nationally and internationally. KOL/MAC LLC has collaborated with and/or received support from many leaders in their respective fields including Corian and Sentry Glass of DuPont (USA), AI Implant of Biotech Industries (Toronto), Alias (USA), Merck Chemicals (Germany), Autodesk (USA), C-TEK (USA), ARUP Advanced Geometry Unit (UK) and others. KOL/MAC LLC continues to be shown and published worldwide, notably, at MoMA New York, USA (multiple); the Cooper-Hewitt Smithsonian Museum New York, USA; the Centre Georges Pompidou Paris, France (multiple); the Barbican Art Gallery London, UK; the Art Institute of Chicago; the Mori Contemporary Art Museum Tokyo, Japan; the 1st International Architecture Biennial Beijing, China; VITRA Germany. Sulan Kolatan has received numerous academic and professional honors and awards, including the "40 under 40" award given every decade to the 40 best architects under 40 years. Most recently her Inversabrane project was nominated for the Zumtobel Environmental Award (Austria) and the INDEX Award (Denmark). In 2004 KOL/MAC LLC received the great honor to represent the United States at the International Architecture Biennale in Venice. KOL/MAC LLC projects are represented in the permanent collections of cultural institutions including the MoMA New York, the Centre Georges Pompidou Paris, the FRAC Orleans and the Architekturmuseum Frankfurt, Germany.

▲ **2001-2002** Studio trip to New York, participation in presentations at Yale University

▲ **2002-2003** Studio trip to Netherlands,excursion with Johann Traupmann and Jan Tabor

Studio trip to China / Maren Klasing, Felix Lohrmann

Final Jury / Zaha Hadid, Mark Goulthorpe, Sulan Kolatan, Bart Lootsma, Ross Lovegro
Aaron Betsky, Reiner Zettl, Hani Rashid, Johann Traupmann, Patrik Schumacher

Final presentation at Studio Hadid

Final Jury / Christian Seethaler, David Sarkisyan, Zaha Hadid, Christian Kronaus,
Brett Steele, Patrik Schumacher

Exploration of local traditions in Istanbul / Martine Nicolay, Sofia Hagen,
Ellen Przybyla, Uli Schifferdecker, Daniel Köhler, Christoph Hermann

Studio trip to Istanbul

Studio installation at the International
Architecture Biennale Rotterdam "Mobility"

▲ **2003-2004**   Studio trip to China with Zaha Hadid

▲ **2004-2005**   Studio trip to Moscow, installation at ARCH Moscow 2005   Studio trip to Moscow

▲ **2005-2006**   Studio trip to Istanbul, IMP Metropolitan Planning & Urban Design Center

Entrance examination / Baris Önal, Oskar Hanstein

Workshop with Yusuke Obuchi / AA DRL London, "Material Behaviour"

Workshop with Tom Barker / London
"What is now proved was once only imagined"

"New Urban Geometries", exhibition opening at the MUAR, Moscow / David Sarkisyan, Mascha Veech-Kosmatschof, Robert R. Neumayr

Studio trip to Dubai, exhibition at the Cityscape Dubai, Dubai International Exhibition Centre

▲ 2008-2009   Studio trip to New York, visit to the MOMA

Studio trip to New York, tutorials with Ali Rahim at the Austrian Culture Forum

Annual exhibition "The Essence 2010", Künstlerhaus, Vienna

Final Jury / Winka Dubbeldam, Johann Traupmann, Zaha Hadid, Ali Rahim, Mascha Veech-Kosmatschof, Evan Douglis

Final Review / Hani Rashid, Reiner Zettl

▲ 2006-2007   Studio trip to Dresden, Leipzig, Wolfsburg, Stuttgart

▲ 2007-2008   Studio trip to Nordpark Railway Station, Innsbruck

Exhibition in the Sliver Gallery, University of Applied Arts Vienna

▲ 2009-2010   Studio trip to Rome. opening of MAXXI

12th International Architecture Biennale, Venice, Austrian Pavilion

Final Jury / Zaha Hadid and Wolf D. Prix

Final Jury / Bernhard Sommer, Ali Rahim and Partik Schumacher

ACKNOWLEDGMENTS
Studio Zaha Hadid Projects 2000 – 2010
University of Applied Arts Vienna

STUDENTS
Aglas, Simon Emmanuel
Akin, Kerem (guest student SCI Arc)
Asgar-Irani, Kourosh
Attems, Huberta (Diploma WS 2000/01)
Ausweger, Thomas (Diploma WS 2001/02)
Bae, Mi Na
Bär, Matthias (Diploma WS 2004/05)
Baerlecken, Daniel (Diploma SS 2003 in cooperation with RWTH Aachen)
Bajcer, Josip
Bak, Johannes Michael (Erasmus student)
Beck, Nicola
Bilos, Mirta
Blum-Jansen, Martin (Erasmus student)
Breinersdorfer, Julian (Diploma SS 2007 in cooperation with TU Berlin)
Breuer, Bernhard (Diploma SS 2002)
Bryant, Andrew (guest student UCLA)
Büyükköz, Niran
Busurina, Irina
Bzduchova, Ivana
Carson, Will (guest student UCLA)
Cernica, Marius Stefan
Chyliková, Marcela
Csémy, Krisztián (Diploma SS 2010)
De Colle, Petra (Diploma WS 2006/07)
Dörstelmann, Moritz
Dragomanska, Yonka
Ebner, Klaus
Ehses, Lisa
Deters, Stephen (guest student UCLA)
Elias, Johannes (Diploma WS 2009/10)
Erevinov, Kaloyan (Diploma SS 2007)
Flemming, Svendsen
Friebel, Tamara (Diploma WS 2007/08)
Frincic, Jasmina
Fröschl, Manuel
Fürst, Paul (Diploma SS 2003)
Fuchs, Simone (Diploma WS 2005/06)
Gallnbrunner, Sebastian
Gasser, Mario (Diploma WS 2007/08)
Gellona, Pietro
Gorfer, Nina
Graupner, Anne (Diploma SS 2001)
Gregorowicz, Marcin (Diploma SS 2005)
Greis, Gilles
Grochowska, Agnieszka
Grössinger, Robert (Diploma WS 2004/05)
Gruber, Michael (Diploma WS 2002/03)
Grünkranz, Daniel (Diploma SS 2005)
Güllmeister, Roxelane-Rahel
Gypser, Florian (Diploma SS 2006)
Hafner, Romina
Hagen, Sofia Maria (Diploma WS 2007/08)
Hagmüller, Lois
Haller, Lukas
Hammerer, Carmen (Diploma WS 2001/02)
Hanstein, Oskar
Heep, Eldine (Diploma SS 2007)
Hermann, Christoph (Diploma SS 2010)
Hieger, Katharina
Hilbich, Jörg (Diploma WS 2002/03)
Hofmann, Konrad (Diploma SS 2008)
Hofstätter, Jörg (Diploma WS 2002/03)
Hornung, Philipp
Hoye, Siri Ulrikke (Erasmus student)
Huber, Martin (Diploma SS 2003)
Hugo, Jörg (Diploma SS 2004 in cooperation with RWTH Aachen)
Innauer, Markus (Diploma WS 2008/09)
Ivanov, Nikolay Hristov
Ivanov, Vladimir
Jacobi, Markus
Jug, Ivana
Kalatzi, Tatjana (Diploma WS 2001/02)
Karaivanov, Alexander

Karakurt, Nuray
Karimi, Monir
Kessler, Andrea (Diploma SS 2007 together with the Institute of Film and Media Arts / Digital Art)
Kim, Seogheon
Klasing, Maren (Diploma WS 2007/08)
Klaska, Jakub (Diploma WS 2009/10)
Kleindienst, Martin
Klien, Cornelia (Diploma WS 2009/10)
Köhler, Daniel (Diploma SS 2008)
König, Andrea (Diploma SS 2010)
Koljonen, Saara-Leena
Knize, Sarah (guest student UCLA)
Koren, Benjamin
Kovács-Dobak, Barnabas
Krcha, Martin (Diploma WS 2007/08)
Krisai, Lorenz
Kusztrich, Ulrike (Diploma WS 2000/01)
Linawaty, Hasmy (guest student SCI Arc)
Liu, Huan (guest student SCI Arc)
Löffler, Robert
Lohrmann, Felix (Diploma WS 2008/09)
Lopez, Manuel (guest student UCLA)
Lu, Bin (guest student SCI Arc)
Lubitz, Marion (Diploma WS 2004/05)
Luger, Sophie (Diploma SS 2006)
Masten, Tyan (guest student UCLA)
Mayr, Katharina (Diploma SS 2005)
Medicus, Florian
Mehlan, Jens (Diploma SS 2004 in cooperation with RWTH Aachen)
Miletich, Sabrina (Diploma SS 2010)
Milly, Thomas
Mitterer, Peter (Diploma WS 2008/09)
Mitsuhiro, Komatsu (guest student UCLA)
Moncayo-Asan, Galo
Monserrat, Antonio
Moroder, Matthias
Navasaityte, Rasa (Diploma SS 2010)
Negar, Niku (Erasmus student)
Neureiter, Christian (Diploma SS 2001)
Nicolay, Martine (Diploma SS 2008)
Nocker, Clemens (Diploma SS 2010)
Önal, Baris
Opperer, Christoph
Ohrhallinger, Caren (Diploma SS 2002)
Orthacker, Gerhild (Diploma SS 2007)
Ortner, Katharina
Ostermaier, Philipp (Diploma SS 2009)
Overbeck, Daniela (Diploma WS 2007/08)
Panatopoulou, Panajota
Papachristopulos, Constantin
Penev, Christo
Petrovic, Raffael
Peyrer-Heimstätt, Paul (Diploma SS 2005)
Pichler, Peter (Diploma SS 2008)
Pindeus, Maya
Prachensky, Andreas (Diploma WS 2000/01)
Plass, Madeleine (Erasmus student)
Preda, Irina-Elena
Przybyla, Ellen (guest student UCLA)
Pucher, Florian (Diploma SS 2004)
Puschmann, Florian
Reist, Daniel
Rettwender, Tom
Reitz, Judith (Diploma SS 2003 in cooperation with RWTH Aachen)
Revaj, Jan
Riess, Sandra (Diploma WS 2002/03)
Ritzer, Stephan
Rosenberg, Natalie (Diploma WS 2001/02)
Russell, Ryan (guest student UCLA)
Saffarian, Saman (Diploma SS 2009)
Schafelner, Johannes (Diploma WS 2005/06)
Schafelner, Judith (Diploma SS 2007)
Schamberger, Peter (Diploma SS 2007)

Schenker, Andrés (Diploma WS 2007/08)
Scheucher, Eva (Diploma SS 2005)
Schifferdecker, Uli
Schmidt, Birgit (Diploma SS 2008)
Schrattenecker, Bernhard (Diploma SS 2001)
Seits, Klaus
Sergiu-Radu, Pop
Shomrat, Hila
Smolinska, Magda
Sommerhuber, Lisa
Spiess, Martina
Stabauer, Carola (Diploma SS 2003)
Stage, Alexandra (Diploma WS 2000/01)
Stec, Peter
Steindl, Daniel (Diploma WS 2002/03)
Stewart, Phoebe
Stockhammer, Daniel
Stöcklmayr, Nicole (Diploma WS 2006/07)
Stracke, Ariane (Diploma WS 2006/07 in cooperation with RWTH Aachen)
Strasser, Felix (Diploma SS 2006)
Stiller, Bengt
Suchanek, Milan (Diploma WS 2008/09)
Tanzberger, Katharina (Diploma WS 2005/06)
Torres, Antonio (guest student UCLA)
Tsiakas, Dimitri
Tugushi, Nino
Unterberger, Florian
Van Almsick, Cornelis (Diploma WS 2006/07 in cooperation with TU Berlin)
Vassilara, Seva (Diploma SS 2001)
Vavrina, Mirek (Erasmus student)
Vietzke, Thomas (Diploma WS 2001/02)
Von Alvensleben, Albrecht
Wagner, Nepomuk (Diploma SS 2001)
Weilhartner, Anna (Diploma SS 2008)
Weisskirchner, Michaela (Diploma SS 2005)
Weisz, Philipp (Diploma SS 2009)
Wieneke, Marc
Wilhelmstätter, Jakob
Windt, Wolfgang
Wizany, Georg (Diploma WS 2009/10)
Wojtkowiak, Ewelina
Wu Shu, Yin
Wünschmann, Tom
Yin, Ming
Zeldovich, Pavel
Zhou, Jing Jing
Ziegerhofer, Barbara (Diploma SS 2002)
Zimmel, Christoph
Zirm, Gabriel

HEAD
Prof. Zaha Hadid since 2000 (2008/09 sabbatical year)
Prof. Patrik Schumacher 2008/09 as guest professor
Ali Rahim 2008/09 as guest professor

ASSISTANT PROFESSORS
Michael Budig since 2010
Mario Gasser since 2010
Christian Kronaus since 2001
Jens Mehlan since 2005
Robert R. Neumayr since 2007
Johann Traupmann since 1992
Mascha Veech-Kosmatschof since 2001

LECTURERS
Norbert Bauer until 2002
Ralph Mühlbacher until 2005
Patrik Schumacher until 2007/since 2009
Jan Tabor until 2009

ORGANIZATION
Susanne John since 2002
Claudia Türk until 2002

CURRENT TEAM
Studio Zaha Hadid
University of Applied Arts Vienna

ZAHA HADID

has been Head of Studio Zaha Hadid at the University of Applied Arts Vienna since 2000.
(Complete CV on page 6)

PATRIK SCHUMACHER

has been co-leading Studio Zaha Hadid at the University of Applied Arts Vienna since its inception in 2000.
(Complete CV on page 11)

MICHAEL BUDIG

studied architecture at Innsbruck University and the Bartlett School of Architecture, London. He is currently teaching and researching at Studio Zaha Hadid, University of Applied Arts Vienna, and the Department for Experimental Architecture Hochbau, Innsbruck University. He is co-director of moll budig architecture (www.mollbudig.com): his built and research projects include a metal recycling company in Innsbruck (AT), a parametrically driven shell structure for a factory in St. Georgen (AT), and studies on fiber reinforced and prefabricated concrete elements.

MARIO GASSER

studied architecture at the Technical University Vienna and the University of Applied Arts (Studio Zaha Hadid) where he received his diploma with distinction in 2008. He practiced architecture at Herzog & de Meuron in Basel and is currently working for Pichler & Traupmann Architekten in Vienna. He has been a member of the Institute of Architecture at the University of Applied Arts Vienna since 2010, currently Assistant Professor at Studio Zaha Hadid.

CHRISTIAN KRONAUS

is an architect and head of Christian Kronaus architects (www.kronaus.com). He studied architecture at the University of Applied Arts Vienna and at Columbia University, New York, receiving his diplomas in 1995 and 1998. In 2007 he received his doctorate degree at the Technical University of Vienna. Parallel to his professional practice, he has been a member of the Institute of Architecture at the University of Applied Arts Vienna since 2001, currently Assistant Professor at Studio Zaha Hadid.

JENS MEHLAN

is an architect, co-director and founding member of moh architects, Vienna (www.moh-architects.com). He studied architecture at the RWTH Aachen, the ETSU Sevilla and the University for Applied Arts Vienna, receiving his Diploma in 2004. Prior to the formation of moh architects he worked at CoopHimmelb(l)au. Jens has been teaching and lecturing internationally at various universities and is currently Assistant Professor at Studio Zaha Hadid at the Institute of Architecture at the University of Applied Arts Vienna.

ROBERT R. NEUMAYR

studied architecture in Vienna and Paris before completing his MArch with distinction at London's Architectural Association Graduate School Design Research Lab (AADRL). Co-founder of Vienna-based practice unsquare architects (www.unsquare.org). He is researching responsive environments, digital design strategies and parametric urbanism. He has been working, teaching and lecturing in Austria and internationally, currently teaching as an Assistant Professor in Studio Zaha Hadid at the Institute of Architecture at the University of Applied Arts Vienna.

JOHANN TRAUPMANN

is an architect, director and co-founding member of Pichler & Traupmann Architekten (www.pxt.at) – an award winning and internationally acknowledged architecture office. He studied Theology at the Faculty of Catholic Theology at the University of Vienna and subsequently architecture at the University of Applied Arts, Vienna. Lectured at the University of Catholic Theology Linz in 1993. Since 1992 member of the Institute of Architecture with various teaching obligations at the University of Applied Arts Vienna, currently Assistant Professor in the Studio Zaha Hadid. Member of Wiener Secession since 2001.

MASCHA VEECH-KOSMATSCHOF

is an architect, director and co-founder of Veech Media Architecture (www.veech-vma.com) – an internationally recognized design and architecture office commited to research, technological innovation and cutting-edge design. She studied architecture at the University of Applied Arts Vienna and subsequently at the Architectural Association, London, receiving an AA Diploma in 1991. Parallel to her professional practice, she has been a member of the Institute of Architecture at the University of Applied Arts Vienna since 2001, currently Assistant Professor at Studio Zaha Hadid.

SUSANNE JOHN

worked as secretary in the field of cultural events, was assistant in the organization team of international exhibitions: e.g. "Kunst und Diktatur" 1994, "Europa nach der Flut" 1995, both Künstlerhaus Wien and worked for the Gesellschaft bildender Künstler Österreichs, Künstlerhaus. In this function she was responsible for coordinating events and exhibitions of the members of this oldest association of Austrian artists. Since 2002 she has been staff member of Studio Zaha Hadid at the University of Applied Arts Vienna.